"In this beautifully illustrated, extensively do
nedy provides the most comprehensive arch
reliability of the Gospels and their account of
systematically through the different phases of the life of Jesus—from his birth to his ministry, trial, crucifixion, and resurrection—as recorded in the New Testament. As he does, he
shows that in each case, a surprising body of evidence supports the reliability of the Gospel
accounts of these events. Who knew that the actual site of the trial of Jesus before Pilate has
been identified by archaeologists? Or that each of the major figures in that trial—Caiaphas,
Herod Antipas, Pilate, Peter, and Jesus himself—have all been independently attested by
archaeological and documentary historical evidence in recent years?

"Kennedy skillfully shows his readers the evidence—photographic and otherwise—that
documents these important people, places, and events. A unique resource for anyone want-
ing to investigate the real historical Jesus."

Dr. Stephen C. Meyer, PhD, History and Philosophy of Science,
Cambridge University; author, *Return of the God Hypothesis*

"In *Excavating the Evidence for Jesus*, Titus Kennedy illuminates the world of late second-
temple Judaism. Kennedy's lucid prose simplifies complicated matters such as the nativity
census of Quirinius. He explores various theories and conspiracies and presciently shows
readers where the weight of evidence lies. I highly recommend this well-written and well-
researched book to my students and colleagues."

Scott Stripling, PhD, Provost and Professor of Biblical Archaeology
and History, The Bible Seminary, Katy, TX;
Director of Excavations at Shiloh and Khirbet el-Maqatir

"How credible are the Gospels, and how strong is the evidence for the historical Jesus? Kennedy's *Excavating the Evidence for Jesus* is an exceptional in-depth companion to the Gospel
accounts, summarizing the relevant archaeological finds and providing essential historical
background for New Testament times.

"Organized around specific events in the life and ministry of Jesus, one can take a bite-
sized deep dive into any particular question and come back with a satisfying archaeological
and historical evidence-based answer each time. Of course, one also can sit down and easily flow through the book from cover to cover: Sufficient details are provided so that one
feels the weight of the evidence yet is not bogged down or overwhelmed by technicalities.
In some details, Kennedy offers an evidence-based alternate to the traditional interpretation that is true to Scripture and worth considering.

"What I found especially effective is Kennedy's use of the historical evidence provided
by the early scoffers of Christianity and from the records detailing the early Roman efforts
to stamp out this radical cult: The descriptions provided by the ancient enemies of Jesus
confirm the highlights of his life. These details could not have been invented by the church
centuries later if they were common knowledge and mentioned by Christian critics in the
first and second centuries.

"Easily accessible and readable, the refreshing message again and again is that behind the Gospel accounts are real places, real people, and real events—in short, real history. The Gospel writers were telling us what they saw and heard, not what they (or followers centuries later) imagined or hoped. In an age where it seems that skeptics have the microphone in the popular media, Kennedy provides a detailed and convincing response: Even 2,000 years later, striking amounts of evidence survive to show why Jesus is the most important figure in human history and worth trusting. Every Christian and seeker will be strengthened by reading this book."

John A. Bloom, PhD, PhD, Professor of Physics; Director, MA of
Science and Religion Program, Biola University, La Mirada, CA

Excavating *the* Evidence *for* Jesus

TITUS KENNEDY

HARVEST HOUSE PUBLISHERS
EUGENE. OREGON

All Scripture quotations are from the (NASB®)New American Standard Bible®, Copyright © 1960, 1971, 1977, 1995 by The Lockman Foundation. Used by permisison. All rights reserved. www.lockman.org

Cover photo © Morphart Creation, michelangeloop, pixels outloud / Shutterstock

Cover design by Studio Gearbox

Interior design by KUHN Design Group

Photos on pages 19, 23, 42, 86, 253, and 275 are public domain

Photos of the James Ossuary on page 224 are © Paradiso and used with permission

All other photos are © Titus Kennedy

For bulk, special sales, or ministry purchases, please call 1-800-547-8979.
Email: Customerservice@hhpbooks.com

M is a federally registered trademark of the Hawkins Children's LLC. Harvest House Publishers, Inc., is the exclusive licensee of the trademark.

Excavating the Evidence for Jesus
Copyright © 2022 by Titus Kennedy
Published by Harvest House Publishers
Eugene, Oregon 97408
www.harvesthousepublishers.com

ISBN 978-0-7369-8468-3 (pbk)
ISBN 978-0-7369-8469-0 (eBook)

Library of Congress Control Number: 2021937787

Printed in the United States of America

22 23 24 25 26 27 28 29 30 / VP / 10 9 8 7 6 5 4 3 2 1

Acknowledgments

Acknowledgment and thanks should be given to all the archaeologists, explorers, historians, linguists, and biblical scholars who have come before, from ancient to modern times. Their incredible discoveries, detailed accounts, preservation of the past, and thoughtful research have enhanced the knowledge and understanding we have today and ultimately have made this book possible. Without their perseverance, dedication, curiosity, and intelligence, the world of Jesus would still be shrouded in mystery.

Also deserving of much gratitude and thanks are the archaeologists and scholars who taught and trained me, the friends who explored and worked with me, the individuals and institutions who supported and encouraged me in my research, the professors who polished my writing, and the staff and editors at Harvest House Publishers. All glory and honor to Jesus Christ.

Inasmuch as many have undertaken to compile an account of the things accomplished among us, just as they were handed down to us by those who from the beginning were eyewitnesses and servants of the word, it seemed fitting for me as well, having investigated everything carefully from the beginning, to write it out for you in consecutive order, most excellent Theophilus; so that you may know the exact truth about the things you have been taught (Luke 1:1-4).

—

Contents

Introduction

J esus of Nazareth is widely acknowledged as the most important and most famous figure in history, regardless of beliefs about God, religion, the Bible, Christianity, or the church. Even before researching, analyzing, and evaluating the prolific archaeological and historical material connected to Jesus and the Gospels, one must realize that the effect Jesus has had on history over the last 2000 years has been immense. Since the dawn of civilization until the present, no other person has had a more significant impact.

Looking only at the effect on history, beginning in the Roman Empire during the 1st century and going into the present age, indicates the existence of a historical person and events that happened in a defined time and place. Although Jesus was born in a small village called Bethlehem, in the client kingdom of Judea at the eastern fringes of the Roman Empire, the name of Jesus and the story of his life recorded in the four Gospels are known to some degree by billions of people around the world. It is clear that the life of Jesus and the message he brought has had global influence. Typing "Jesus" into internet search engines can yield approximately 665 billion results, which according to a study by Stony Brook University ranks "Jesus" in the number one position. Because of the influence of Jesus and his life, disciplines such as art, architecture, literature, medicine, politics, economics, society, religion, science, and history all changed.

The entire calendar year date system still used today throughout much of the world is even based around the birth and life of Jesus—BC as "before Christ" and AD as *anno Domini* "in the year of our Lord" (the BCE/CE designations are equivalent). This system of years was originally brought into use by a monk named Dionysius Exiguus (Dennis the Humble) who was asked by Pope John I in AD 525 to compile a new chronological table, primarily for calculating the dates for Easter Sunday. Prior to this, chronologies still revolved around the Roman emperors, although earlier church scholars such as Clement of Alexandria and Eusebius of Caesarea had also counted years from the birth of Jesus.

While AD 1 does not line up perfectly with year one of the life of Jesus, in part because Dennis did not or was not able to use chronological data from Josephus when composing the new system, the results were only off by a few years and the method of absolute year dates has proved to be an extremely useful invention. About 200 years later, the English monk Bede adopted this *anno Domini* calendar system, Charlemagne endorsed the system, it was in use throughout most of Europe by the 11th century, became the standard in Russia around 1700, and today it is the international norm for historical dates.

And yet, in modern times, Jesus of Nazareth is often regarded as either a mythological character or as an almost unknowable person whose legend accrued and increased over time. The ancient writings of the four Gospels and New Testament letters, which relay information about the life of Jesus, are often dismissed as unreliable religious books with little basis in fact. But archaeology and ancient historical texts, which contribute to our knowledge about the life of Jesus and the plausibility of the reliability of the Gospels, paint a different picture.

Archaeology over the last 150 years has not only contributed to our understanding of the historical context of Jesus, the Gospels, and the 1st-century world, but many discoveries have directly confirmed the accuracy of the Gospel accounts about his life and historical existence—and new discoveries continue to be uncovered and mysteries untangled.

Initially, the only followers of Jesus were a few disciples, but by the end of his time on earth this number seems to have been at least several thousand. By AD 100, there were church communities and Jesus followers in over 40 different regions. By the 4th century, Christianity had spread through much of the Middle East, Asia Minor, North Africa, and southern and western Europe. In the kingdom of Armenia, Christianity was adopted as the state religion in AD 301. Soon after, in 313, Emperor Constantine issued the Edict of Milan, legalizing Christianity in the Roman Empire. The story of Jesus and belief in him continued to spread, and in 380, Emperor Theodosius I issued the Edict of Thessalonica, making Christianity the official religion of the Roman Empire.

In just over 300 years, Jesus had gone from relative obscurity on the fringes of an empire built on polytheism that had even persecuted Christianity, to the figure that many in the empire, including the emperor, followed and worshipped. The effects of this transformation in thinking can be seen throughout the centuries that followed.

It seems uncanny that Jesus, who lived on the eastern edge of the Roman Empire and never left the area, who had only several thousand followers at his death, and who was shunned by both the religious and political establishment of the time is not simply remembered two millennia later but became the most famous and influential person in all of human history. While many may disregard the teachings of Jesus, or even make the outrageous claim that he never existed, no one can deny the tremendous and unparalleled impact Jesus has had on history.

It is noteworthy that the four Gospel accounts of Matthew, Mark, Luke, and John—which are the primary sources describing the life of Jesus—were composed during the 1st century AD using eyewitness testimony according to the claims of numerous ancient writings and supported by the historical and archaeological evaluations of many scholars throughout the centuries. Literacy in the Roman Empire has been estimated at up to 30 percent, and in the Christian community, particularly because of the importance placed on the written word of the Bible, literacy was high enough that the accounts about Jesus could be widely read and heard.

The Gospels, proliferated through meticulous hand copying and usually in the form of a codex, also have by far the highest representation of ancient manuscript copies in comparison to other writings of antiquity. Now, almost two thousand years removed, the autographs are no longer in existence. However, because of meticulous and careful copying over the centuries, the Gospel texts available today are essentially the same as those first written nearly two millennia ago.

Thanks to the preservation of ancient texts in libraries, monasteries, and churches, and the uncovering of additional ancient texts due to archaeology, there are presently hundreds of existing ancient manuscript copies of the Gospels. At least 43 papyri and 14 parchment Gospel manuscripts are known from the period covering only the first three centuries after the autographs were written. While the parchment manuscripts are fewer in number, they are also more complete, including two codices that contain nearly the entire four Gospels. If each Gospel is counted separately, then the number rises to 63 Gospel manuscripts from the first three centuries after the Gospels were first written.

The most numerous of these ancient Gospel manuscripts are of Matthew (26) and John (23). The earliest of these known manuscripts is usually considered to be P52, which contains a small section of John covering the trial of Jesus, and by the analysis of a few scholars it could date to as early as AD 90 or so. However, manuscripts of Matthew, Mark, and Luke from the 2nd century have also been preserved. Additionally, ancient translations of the Gospels into other languages exist in Syriac, Latin, Coptic, Slavic, Ethiopic, and Armenian.

At first glance, this may not seem particularly impressive. However, when compared to existing manuscript copies of other ancient works, such as the *Iliad* of Homer, *Gallic Wars* of Caesar, *Annals* of Tacitus, plays of Euripides, Flavius Josephus, and Philo of Alexandria, the four Gospels are much better attested than anything else from antiquity.

The specific literary genre of the Gospels has also been examined at length and debated, with opinions ranging from ancient biography to aretalogies (mighty deeds of a divine man) to historical narrative to theological documents. In the ancient world, however, all types of historical writings contained the worldview of the author or the culture, and at least a sprinkling of the supernatural or theological could be seen.

Undoubtably there is a uniqueness about the Gospel documents and a blend of various elements present in the texts, in addition to specific differences between the writings of Matthew, Mark, Luke, and John, which is why even the specific genre of the Gospels continues to be studied and debated. While archaeology alone cannot fully answer the question of genre, an archaeological analysis of these accounts about Jesus does allow one to assess their historical credibility regarding the information about the life, times, and person of Jesus. All of these factors are important when assessing the historical accuracy and transmission of the primary sources for the life of Jesus and evaluating the likelihood of egregious errors or the introduction of mythical elements for an audience that might have had access to an eyewitness, a second degree connection, or official records.

How could the story of Jesus spread so far and so rapidly, and those who followed him increase at such a rapid rate during the Roman period, if Jesus were merely a legendary character or only an obscure teacher whose actual life was shrouded in mystery and myth? What if Jesus was not simply a historical person, but one whose actions, words, and following caused such an intense wave in history that the world was forever changed?

A plethora of books have been written about Jesus, including volumes about the historical context of Jesus and books about the archaeology associated with Jesus. These writings range in perspective from Jesus being a fictitious character on one extreme, to the Gospels being absolutely accurate on the other side, and a wide spectrum in between. Books written for a general audience and books tailored for academic experts have appeared on the subject.

Excavating the Evidence for Jesus does not seek to replace all of those previous works, nor is it meant to be a comprehensive examination of the world in which Jesus lived. Rather, this book focuses on the archaeological and historical discoveries that directly and indirectly relate to the life of Jesus and the accounts of his life in the Gospels. While it cannot answer every question connected to the archaeology and history of Jesus, it seeks to offer an updated and supplemental source from the perspective of an archaeologist who has studied the archaeology, history, literature, geography, and Bible associated with Jesus, excavated at sites where Jesus was, researched and visited nearly all of the locations where Jesus walked, and examined the known artifacts connected with the life of Jesus.

It is my hope that with a thorough presentation and analysis of the archaeological remains associated with Jesus, arranged in an attempted chronological sequence, the reader will better understand the 1st-century world of Jesus, become familiar with the archaeological discoveries and historical arguments, and recognize the vast and varied evidence demonstrating the historical existence of Jesus and the reliability of the Gospel accounts about his life.

> At this time there was a wise man called Jesus, and his conduct was good, and he was known to be virtuous. Many people among the Jews and the other nations became his disciples. Pilate condemned him to be crucified and to die. But those who had become his disciples did not abandon his discipleship. They reported that he had appeared to them three days after his crucifixion, and that he was alive. Accordingly, he was perhaps the Messiah, concerning whom the prophets have reported wonders. And the tribe of the Christians, so named after him, has not disappeared to this day.—Josephus, *Antiquities* 18:63-64, ca. AD 93 (Agapius version).

THE ROMAN EMPIRE AT THE TIME OF JESUS

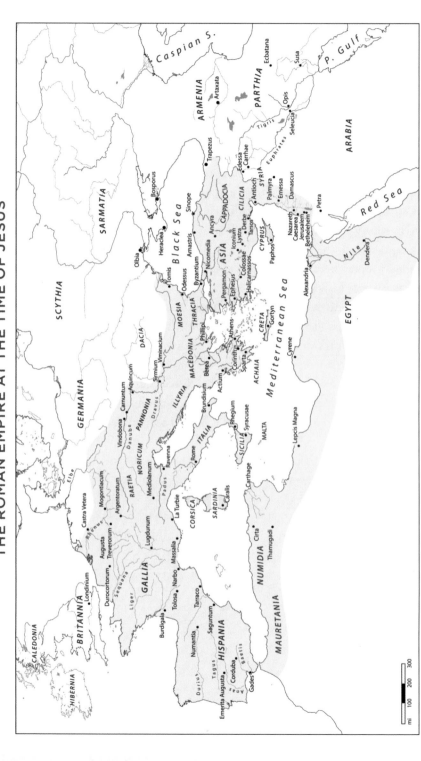

The Birth of Jesus, Bethlehem, and the Magi

The world of Roman-and-Herodian-dominated Judea and Galilee in which Jesus of Nazareth lived goes back to 63 BC when the Romans annexed the area and enlarged the Republic. Previously, the region had been a kingdom under the direct control of the Hasmonean Dynasty, but following the end of the Third Mithridatic War in 63 BC, the Roman general Pompey conquered the area and subdued Jerusalem. After initially being let into Jerusalem and occupying the city, Pompey besieged the temple complex to defeat those inside, breached the northern wall, defeated the Judeans who continued to resist, and then pulled down the walls of Jerusalem to prevent future rebellion.

After the defeat of the Hasmoneans, the Romans decreased the size of Hasmonean territory by giving back control of various conquered cities to their inhabitants. Most of those released areas are what came to be known as the Decapolis, and many of their coins show the institution of a new era once Pompey gave them relative independence. Once Herod the Great was dubbed king of the Judeans by the Roman Senate in 40 BC, and practically took power with the conquest of Jerusalem in 37 BC, his kingdom began to expand the lands under its control as a client state of Rome.

The Roman Empire itself officially began in 27 BC when Octavian was made *princeps*, or "first citizen," by the Senate, was given the power of imperium, and the title Augustus, or "venerated," was bestowed upon him. This occurred after Octavian avenged the assassination of Julius Caesar by 42 BC, then subsequently defeated the other two members of the Second Triumvirate, Marcus Lepidus and Mark Antony, by 31 BC. Although Julius Caesar had a short time as dictator (ca. 49–44 BC), this position was different than the later role of emperor, and his exercise of power and opposition within in the Senate eventually led to his assassination. Discovering that the will of Julius Caesar had named Octavian (Augustus) as heir, he also adopted the family name Caesar, which after the end of the Julio-Claudian dynasty and the year of the four emperors became a title indicating the office of emperor in AD 69.

Roman statue of Caesar Augustus

Augustus offered to return power to the Senate in 27 BC, but it refused, and cleverly, Augustus never took titles such as king or dictator, and even surrendered his position as consul in 23 BC. Yet, the Senate then granted him the power of a tribune and a censor, allowing him to effectively control the Senate and laws and enact censuses. Augustus also had the power to command the military forces in Rome, to impose his will on the governors of provinces, and to directly control the newly reclassified imperial provinces.

The extent of his power had never before been matched in the Roman Republic, and yet he was so trusted and beloved that his effectiveness as a ruler was unsurpassed by later Roman emperors. While legally the Roman Republic still existed during his reign, in practice it was now the Empire, as Augustus had essentially complete power and the love of the people, though a new constitution would eventually come into effect once Tiberius became emperor. Since Augustus had eliminated rival factions and consolidated power, Rome entered a time of internal peace called the Pax Romana or "Roman Peace."

During the period of the Gospels, life was relatively peaceful throughout the

Empire. While there were border wars, two of the most violent periods inside the Empire during the Pax Romana were rebellions in Judea Province after the time of Jesus in AD 66–73 and 132–136. Reflecting a time of peace, the number of Roman legions was reduced from 50 to 28, which required the expensive settlement of tens of thousands of military veterans in colonies around the Empire. This placed former Roman soldiers throughout the provinces and further Romanized many areas. The Praetorian Guard was kept in Rome to maintain order and assure that a rebellion against the emperor could not occur, although the Praetorian Guard eventually became a dangerous institution for many emperors.

Since Augustus controlled the finances and paid the legions, they were loyal to him. Augustus also personally owned the province of Aegyptus (Egypt), which was the largest grain producer and allowed him to distribute food to the masses and gain their gratitude and favor. Augustus also enacted many significant building projects in Rome, including aqueducts and the first permanent amphitheater in Rome. It was recorded that Augustus said he found Rome a city of brick and left it a city of marble (Suetonius, *Augustus* 29.149).

Ancient historical sources for the life and reign of Augustus are numerous, and in numerous cases these writings overlap with the context of the life of Jesus (*Res Gestae Divi Augustus*; Suetonius, *Augustus*; Livy, *History of Rome*; Velleius, *History*; Seneca, *Controversiae and Suasoriae*; Tacitus, *Annals*; Cassius Dio, *Roman History*; Josephus, *Antiquities*).

During the reign of Augustus, a brilliant general named Tiberius also rose to prominence, and in 39 BC, he became the stepson of Augustus. However, Augustus already had a son, Agrippa, and a nephew and son-in-law, Marcellus, who were expected to be his heirs. Tiberius was given certain privileges, but his personal success in politics, exploration, and especially military victories earned him the respect of many in the Empire. In 23 BC Marcellus died, in 12 BC Agrippa died, and in 9 BC his brother Drusus died, leaving Tiberius as the clear candidate for heir of Augustus.

It is around this time that the first events in the Gospels occur—the angel appearing to Zechariah, the pregnancy of Zacharias and Elizabeth, and the betrothal period of Joseph and Mary (Luke 1:5-38; Matthew 1:18). Meanwhile, Herod the Great (ca. 40–4 BC) was a client king of Rome ruling over the kingdom of Judea while Augustus (ca. 27 BC–AD 14) was at the height of his power and Tiberius was emerging to eventually succeed Augustus. Combined as a single historical narrative, the four Gospels would cover the period of

Herodian and Roman rule in Judea and Galilee beginning with the announcement to Zechariah and ending with the ascension of Jesus—perhaps a span of around only four decades in which history was drastically affected (Matthew 1:18–2:1; 27:45–28:20; Luke 1:5–2:1; 23:44–24:52).

Coin of Herod the Great reading "King Herod"

During the reign of Herod the Great and subsequently his sons and Roman prefects, Judea was a kingdom ultimately subject to Rome, including Augustus and Tiberius—the first two emperors of the new Roman Empire and among the most powerful political leaders in antiquity. The lands of these kings, tetrarchs, and prefects comprised the areas of Judea, Samaria, Idumea, Galilee, Perea, Gaulantis, Iturea, Batanea, Trachonitis, and Aurantis, which encompasses much of what today comprises modern Israel, the Palestinian Territories, northern Jordan, and southwestern Syria. It was this world into which Jesus of Nazareth was born.

THE ANNUNCIATION AT NAZARETH

The village of Nazareth in the region of Galilee where Jesus spent most of his life was so small and insignificant that there are no recovered written records mentioning Nazareth prior to the Gospels of Matthew, Mark, Luke, and John in the 1st century AD. Yet as the home of Jesus from childhood until his public ministry, and the village in which Mary and Joseph lived prior to the birth of Jesus, it is an essential site in an archaeological and historical investigation of Jesus (Luke 1:26–2:4; Matthew 2:23; 4:13; Mark 1:24; John 1:45).

Because Nazareth is located on a ridge approximately 1150 feet (350 meters) above sea level, the name has sometimes been connected to a Hebrew word for watch or guard. However, Nazareth may be derived from another Hebrew word using the same consonants that translates as branch, which is often connected to a prophetic passage in the Book of Isaiah about a "branch" from the root of Jesse, father of David (Isaiah 11:1). This Hebrew rendering of Nazareth is supported by a Hebrew inscription from the 3rd or 4th century AD found at the synagogue of Caesarea Maritima that refers to priests in Nazareth just after the Bar Kokhba Revolt in about AD 135. Several other references to Nazareth in the 2nd, 3rd, and 4th centuries are known, including by Tertullian, Origen, Julius Africanus, Eusebius, and Epiphanius.

Because of the lack of 1st-century documentation about Nazareth from sources outside of the Gospels and Acts, a few scholars have claimed Nazareth was not in existence during the time of Jesus, while a minority have accepted a 1st-century Nazareth but altered the story by proposing that Jesus was born in Nazareth rather than Bethlehem.

Old Nazareth and Mary's Well

Although for many years no definitive archaeological evidence had been recovered from ancient Nazareth that demonstrated the existence of the village during the time of Jesus, excavations and research eventually revealed both materials and structures dating to the 1st century in Nazareth. Archaeological remains have been found at Nazareth from the Bronze Age and Iron Age, then after an abandonment period of centuries, the village seems to have been resettled in the 2nd century BC during the Hasmonean period, and it had a primarily Jewish population through the time of Jesus and the early church.

Archaeological studies of Nazareth have clearly demonstrated that a village of approximately four hectares (about ten acres) existed in the 1st century BC and 1st century AD during the life of Jesus. The small size and agricultural character of Nazareth has led to population estimates of around 400 people, showing why the village was unlikely to appear in historical texts and how the question "Can anything good come out of Nazareth?" was probably indicative of the insignificance of the tiny agricultural village (John 1:46).

These excavations have specifically uncovered significant remains from approximately the 1st century such as houses, olive oil presses, wine presses, water cisterns, a vineyard tower, a mikvah (ritual bath), quarries, tombs, pottery, coins, and ritual stone vessels. A tomb inscription also demonstrates the use of

Aramaic in Nazareth. The site of the synagogue in Nazareth, however, remains unknown (Luke 4:16).

Nazareth was the location of one of the first events recorded about the life of Jesus—the annunciation of the birth of Jesus Christ set near the end of the 1st century BC. According to the Gospel of Luke, the angel Gabriel was sent from God to tell Mary that through the power of the Holy Spirit she would conceive and bear Jesus, the Son of God (Luke 1:26-38). To commemorate this momentous event, an ancient church was built at the site thought to be the house where Mary lived before her marriage to Joseph.

Ancient written sources and archaeology suggest that the Byzantine Church of the Annunciation was constructed in the 5th century AD after the reign of Constantine the Great, but that an earlier Christian building existed at the location in the 4th century AD or before. Underneath the modern Basilica of the Annunciation and the Crusader-period church of the 11th century, the remains of a 5th-century AD Byzantine church were found, measuring approximately 20 meters by 8 meters. A mosaic floor from this Byzantine-period church had a dedication reading "for Konon, deacon of Jerusalem" in Greek, and a decorative cross. Below the building, a baptismal font, mosaic floors including decorative crosses, plastered walls with various graffiti, and steps leading into a cave were discovered. The graffiti had phrases such as "Lord, Christ, help your servant

Archaeological ruins at the Church of the Annunciation in Nazareth

Valeria…and give the palm to pain…Amen" and "Lord Jesus Christ, Son of God, help Geno and Elpisius, Achille, Elpidius, Paul, Antonis…servants of Jesus."

The base of a column also has the name Mary carved into it in Greek, further linking the site with the tradition of Mary and the annunciation, although the inscription comes from after the church was already established. The pilgrim Egeria, writing in ca. AD 383, mentions the "cave in which Mary lived," and the altar placed near the entrance, which was apparently associated with an early church there (Egeria, *Itinerarium Egeriae*). However, she does not mention a formal church or basilica, which suggests that Constantine did not have a commemorative church, like those in Jerusalem and Bethlehem, built there during his reign.

A coin minted around the middle of the 4th century AD was found in the plaster, demonstrating that Christians used the site at least as early as the 4th century, and this building could be the church Joseph of Tiberias planned to build in Nazareth during the early 4th century (Epiphanius of Salamis, *Panarion* 30). There are suggestions from archaeological excavations that a building where Christians met may have even existed there as early as the 3rd century AD.

Archaeological excavations also revealed remains of various parts of the village of Nazareth from the 1st century AD underneath this church, nearby, and in scattered locations around the area, confirming that Nazareth was indeed occupied during the time of Jesus.

When Joseph and Mary were living in Nazareth before the birth of Jesus, the couple was betrothed and not yet formally married, which is why Joseph had been concerned about avoiding a scandal (Matthew 1:19). Similar to many ancient societies, Israelite parents were often involved in the selection of a husband or wife, but the son or daughter usually had significant say in who they would marry, and in many cases the decision was completely up to the potential bride and groom (Genesis 21:21; 24:1-9; 26:34-35; 28:1-5; 34:4; 38:6; Judges 14:1-3; Ruth 3:1-13; 1 Samuel 18:20-21). By the Roman period and the time of Jesus, men and women might arrange the marriage themselves, use an intermediary, or go through their parents.

Betrothal was the typical practice in the 1st century, which was similar to a legal contract and more binding than engagement (Matthew 1:18; 2 Corinthians 11:2). In the eyes of the community, the couple was legally or contractually married, although not practically married. During the time of the Roman Empire, the law required a couple to be married within two years after their betrothal, and therefore long and drawn out "engagements" were probably rare

(Cassius Dio, *Roman History*). Under the traditions of Judaism in the Hellenistic and Roman periods, which illuminate the typical customs for those living in Judea and Galilee during the time of Jesus, couples seem to have usually married one year after their betrothal. Once the potential match had been made, the future groom and the father of the bride would sign the betrothal agreement, which was an actual contract, and in some cases celebrate this occasion over wine or a meal (Tobit 7:11-14; Babylonian Talmud).

The ages of the bride and groom would usually be in the late teens for women and early twenties to early thirties for men, while the man was almost always older, often by several years. Generally, the average age of married couples in the Hellenistic and Roman periods seems to have been the late teens, although similarly the women would be slightly younger and the men slightly older. During the Roman period, a high percentage of girls were married in or by their late teens, and the laws of the Empire even permitted girls to be betrothed at age ten and married at age twelve, although this seems to have happened very rarely. In the literature of Judaism, marrying early was advocated in order to propagate the family and to protect from temptation, and eighteen to twenty was a recommended age for men (Pseudo-Phocylides, *Sentences*, 175-76; Rule of the Congregation 1QSa). Therefore, it is probable that Mary was in her late teens while she and Joseph were betrothed and awaiting their marriage.

Then, in about 8 BC, Augustus issued a decree for a census of the Empire, eventually reaching the client kingdom of Herod and the regions of Galilee and Judea, which were connected administratively to Syria Province (*Res Gestae Divi Augustus* 8; Luke 2:1-3).

THE CENSUS OF QUIRINIUS AND THE BIRTH OF JESUS

According to the Gospel of Luke, just before the birth of Jesus, a census throughout the Roman Empire was enacted (Luke 2:1). This empire-wide census recorded in Luke uses a word meaning "the inhabited earth," or in the context of ancient Rome, the Roman Empire. This census also seems to be recorded in official Roman records, specifically in *The Deeds of the Divine Augustus*, which mentioned censuses of between approximately four and five million citizens, indicating that the scope of these censuses were indeed empire-wide and not merely localized (*Res Gestae Divi Augustus* 8). Specifically, these three censuses recorded the number of male Roman citizens as 4.063 million in 28

BC, 4.233 million in 8 BC, and 4.937 million in AD 14, demonstrating over-all population growth in the empire. The census taking place just prior to the death of Herod the Great in 4 BC could only have been the census of Augustus initiated in 8 BC. Because Luke stated that the census covered the Roman Empire, only a massive census such as those recorded by Augustus would fit the requirements; a localized and pos-sibly unpreserved census record cannot be the census mentioned in the Gos-pel of Luke.

If a census was also imposed on Judea as part of the larger Empire, Joseph could have been required to participate. After learning of the cen-sus, Joseph traveled back to Bethlehem because apparently his family home was located in Bethlehem—not Naz-areth where he was currently living (Luke 2:4). While none of the Gospels indicate that Joseph was originally from Nazareth, it is possible that Mary may

Res Gestae Divi Augustus inscription

have been from or at least lived in Nazareth, and the three eventually returned to Nazareth in Galilee rather than live in Judea during the brutal reign of the ethnarch Archelaus (Matthew 2:19-23).

This transition of control from Herod the Great presiding over the entire region to his sons Archelaus, Antipas, and Philip acting as ethnarchs and tetrarchs also places the census and the birth of Jesus just prior to the death of Herod the Great. Records from the Roman Empire relating to censuses demonstrate that they involved all those residing away from their own districts, not only Roman citizens, and summoning people to their homes for the registration of the cen-sus was the normal protocol. For example, a census edict from Egypt Province ca. AD 104 (British Museum papyrus 904) provides insight into this practice:

> Gaius Vibius Maximus, Prefect of Egypt: Seeing that the time has come for the house to house census, it is necessary to com-pel all those who for any cause whatsoever are residing out of their

provinces to return to their own homes, that they may both carry out the regular order of the census and may also attend diligently to the cultivation of their allotments.

Another Roman census document from about AD 48 (Oxyrhynchus papyrus 255), relating to a census during the time of Emperor Claudius, records the testimony of a man named Thermoutharion and states that people living with him, probably a reference to specific family members previously mentioned in the document, have returned to his house for the census. Many other similar census papyri are known, including those which indicate that the census responses occasionally came in the year following the original census order from the emperor (cf. P. Mich. 176-180). Thus, not only is an empire-wide census consistent with historical data, but the census being imposed in Judea and Joseph and Mary going to Bethlehem to register are also actions consistent with Roman records from the period. Further, registration records suggest that at times people did not or were unable to respond to the census until the year following the initial issue date, meaning Joseph may not have arrived in Bethlehem for the census until the year after it was ordered by Augustus.

The Roman official administering the census near the birth of Jesus was recorded as Quirinius, designated as a ruler in Syria Province at the time (Luke 2:2). Publius Sulpicius Quirinius was a Roman aristocrat who lived from ca. 51 BC to AD 21, attaining the rank of consul in 12 BC by the appointment of Caesar Augustus (Tacitus, *Annals*; Cassius Dio, *Roman History*).

However, Caius Sentius Saturninus, a consular, served as imperial legate of Syria Province from ca. 9–6 BC when the aforementioned 8 BC census of Augustus would have taken place. Tertullian around AD 200 noted that Sentius Saturninus did hold a census according to the orders of Augustus, that it also took place in Judea, and it was relevant to the birth of Jesus (Tertullian, *Adversus Marcionem* 4.19).

Yet, matters are often further confused because in the late 1st century AD, Josephus mentioned Quirinius along with Coponius in Judea around AD 6 taking account of the substance of the province, taxing, and spending the money left by Archelaus after his exile, and this is often incorrectly assumed to be the census that Luke mentions (Josephus, *Antiquities* 18.1-3). Not only was this event recorded in Josephus, a localized assessment type of census connected to transition of government in Judea, but the Quirinius census of Luke and the Quirinius assessment of Josephus seem to be separated by several years.

Although it is often assumed that Luke claims Quirinius was the Roman legate of Syria at this time, the term used can have a general meaning of ruling, commanding, or leading. The word used could refer to the legate of a province, such as an imperial province like Syria, but it is also the term used in Luke 3:1 to describe the position of Pontius Pilate, who obviously was not a legate, as a prefect of Judea. Therefore, the Gospel account notes only that Quirinius was a ruler in Syria Province who administered a Roman census around the time of the birth of Jesus.

The Quirinius census inscription "Lapis Venetus"

While Quirinius was the legate of Syria Province in AD 6, he was also in the area earlier functioning as a military commander. According to Roman records, Quirinius held a military command that placed him in the province of and around Cilicia, including the area of Syria Province, and he was the leader of several legions in the area before eventually being appointed *legatus propraetor* of Syria Province as a former consul (Tacitus, *Annals* 3.22-48; cf. Florus, *Epitome of Roman History* 2.31; Suetonius, *Tiberius* 49). While commanding legions in Galatia, Cilicia, and Syria, Quirinius would have held a position of high authority in the Roman Empire. His presence in these regions occurred sometime between 12 BC and AD 1, but we are unsure of specifics in time and position because of the lack of detailed chronological information.

However, this does place Quirinius in the area of Syria around the time that Jesus of Nazareth was born, and it may also be significant that when Saturninus was legate of Syria Province, there were multiple governors—suggesting that Quirinius, as Luke states, could have been a ruler of Syria ca. 8 BC or 7 BC (Josephus, *Antiquities* 16.280, 285, 357, 361). Therefore, a possible scenario is that Saturninus was the legate and Quirinius the highest ranking military commander in Syria (Josephus, *Antiquities* 17.89). Why the Gospel of Luke mentions Quirinius in connection with the census rather than Saturninus is due to the function of Roman government. Roman records demonstrate that military officials oversaw and administered censuses, and Quirinius is even mentioned as a legate in the context of a census in Syria Province during the reign of Augustus.

The Lapis Venetus is a Latin funerary inscription dedicated to the Roman officer Q. Aemilius Secundus and found in Beirut, which in Roman times was part of Syria Province (Lapis Venetus, Corpus Inscriptionum Latinarum vol. III, no. 6687). It states that by order of P. Sulpicius Quirinius, who is called a legate of Caesar in Syria, Secundus conducted a census of the city-state of Apamea, Syria. This inscription also notes that Quirinius ordered Secundus to fight the Ituraeans on Mount Lebanon, an area north of the Sea of Galilee, which was part of the kingdom of Herod the Great and later in the tetrarchy of Philip.

Occasionally, the inscription is erroneously connected to a regional tax assessment and acquisition of the money of the deposed Herod Archelaus in Syria and Judea, carried out by Quirinius and Coponius (Josephus, *Antiquities* 17.354, 18.1-102). However, the census in this inscription, which was not a localized tax assessment, more logically connects to the census of the Empire documented in the Deeds of the Divine Augustus and initiated in about 8 BC. The inscription demonstrates that the census was a military affair, ordered by a legate and carried out by officers at the local level. Quirinius may have held the position of *legatus legionis* in Syria Province, commanding at least three legions in the area at this time, which agrees with his portrayal as legate and military commander in the epitaph. Because it was Roman practice for a military official, such as Quirinius, to administer the census, it is logical that the Gospel of Luke would associate Quirinius the military commander with the census rather than Saturninus the governor.

Thus, the census mentioned in this inscription may have been conducted around 8 BC and following as part of the census of the Empire that Augustus commanded and Luke recorded in relation to the birth of Jesus. Because Quirinius held a military command in the province of and around Cilicia and was the leader of several legions in the area before eventually being appointed *legatus propraetor* of Syria as a former consul, it is plausible that Augustus may have appointed Quirinius to another position of high authority while fighting the Homanadensian War in Cilicia, which was a province bordering Syria (Tacitus, *Annals*; Florus, *Epitome of Roman History*).

Another inscription that occasionally has been connected to Quirinius is the Lapis Tiburtinus, found near the ancient villa of Quintilius Varus at Tivoli, east of Rome. The inscription records the career of a distinguished Roman, but unfortunately the inscription is damaged and the name is unreadable. The text states that this person became proconsul of the province of Asia; it also appears to mention being the proconsul of Syria, and that he had been honored with two victory celebrations. An explanation has been suggested that the inscription implies this unknown person was the proconsul of Syria twice, and combining that with an assumption that Quirinius twice was the governor of Syria during both the birth of Jesus in Luke and the time of Coponius in Josephus. However, the inscription states that this official was once proconsul of Asia and then of Syria, which does not match what is known of Quirinius.

Because the wording is ambiguous and the fragmentary condition of the inscription makes it even more difficult, the Lapis Tiburtinus should only be attributed to a Roman consul based on a comparison of career and the archaeological context in which it was found. Since the inscription was found very near the villa of Quintilius Varus, but it also may describe a career similar to that of L. Calpurnius Piso, it might be attributed to either.

Combining the sources of Luke, Josephus, Justin Martyr, Tertullian, and the Lapis Venetus, the census order may have been relayed by Saturninus, the legate of Syria from ca. 9 to 6 BC, while Quirinius as a military leader may have administered the census. If Quirinius was a military leader in Syria at this time, Roman protocol demonstrates why Luke would mention Quirinius the military leader administering the census instead of Saturninus the legate.

This scenario could also be supplemented by two inscriptions found in Pisidian Antioch that mention Publius Sulpicius Quirinius as a *duumvir*, a title that describes a pair of joint magistrates. Perhaps Quirinius was a temporary procurator of the sub-province of Judea, or Quirinius could have been the military legate while conducting the census, sharing powers with Saturninus.

The Roman census data from the writings of Augustus and contemporary papyri demonstrates that there was a census ordered in 8 BC for the Empire, and that people were called to their hometowns to register for the census. The funerary inscription of Secundus mentions a census administered by a military official in Syria Province, the legate Quirinius, and the Emperor Augustus. Documents describing the life of Quirinius demonstrate that he was a Roman official holding positions of both high military and civil authority before, during, and after the birth of Jesus of Nazareth, and information places him in Syria sometime around that time.

An analysis of the available information suggests that Quirinius was not the governor of Syria Province at the time of the birth of Jesus of Nazareth, but that as the military commander he would have administered the census ordered by

Emperor Augustus, possibly in conjunction with Saturninus. In this scenario, after the census of Augustus was initially ordered in 8 BC and Joseph and Mary eventually received word in Galilee, they traveled to Bethlehem, settled into their makeshift accommodations, and eventually Jesus was born, placing the birth around 8 BC or perhaps more likely in 7 BC.

BETHLEHEM

The town of Bethlehem in Judah, only a few miles south of ancient Jerusalem, has existed for thousands of years. Until the time of Jesus, however, it was relatively obscure. Bethlehem ("house of bread"), also called Ephrath, was occupied from at least the time of Jacob, then into the times of Joshua, the judges, the Israelite monarchy, and Jesus (Genesis 35:19; Joshua 15:59 LXX; Judges 17:7; Ruth 1:1-2; 1 Samuel 17:12; Micah 5:2; Matthew 2:1; Luke 2:4).

Archaeological discoveries have also demonstrated that Bethlehem was a town during these times, with materials found at the site from the time of the patriarchs in the Middle Bronze Age, a possible mention in the Amarna Letters of the Late Bronze Age, the time of David in the Iron Age II, and the time of Jesus in the Roman period. In ancient times, farming and shepherding were

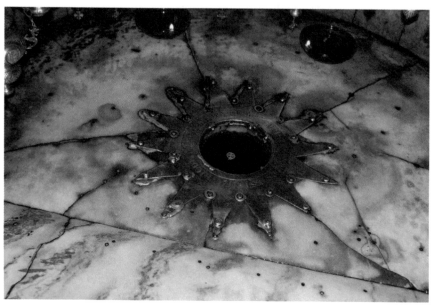

Traditional birth location of Jesus in a cave underneath the Church of the Nativity

common economic activities around Bethlehem. For centuries it was a small village of little importance, but due to the Gospels and the story of Jesus, Bethlehem has become a town known all over the world.

Matthew and Luke record the birth of Jesus in Bethlehem, while unnamed people in the Gospel of John refer to this idea (Matthew 2:1-6; Luke 2:4-7; John 7:41-42). Because Joseph was from the line of David and his family home was in Bethlehem, he was required to go there for the registration of the census (Luke 2:4-5). Because of the prophecy found in the Book of Micah, the link to King David, and the birth of Jesus there, Bethlehem quickly became a crucial location in the gospel story (1 Samuel 17:12; Micah 5:2). Due to its importance, the location of the birth of Jesus was remembered, and soon after the time of Jesus, Christians seem to have visited the place regularly.

According to early church writers of the 2nd and 3rd centuries, Jesus was born in a cave in Bethlehem that was apparently known in antiquity, and Origen reported that the pagans spread the word about Jesus being born in a specific cave of Bethlehem (Justin Martyr, *Dialogue with Trypho* 78; Origen, *Contra Celsus* 1.51). Based on the presence of the manger, the cave was perhaps an animal shelter connected to a house. During the time of Hadrian, when he was rebuilding Jerusalem as Aelia Capitolina and covering major sites associated with Jesus, he had a shrine to Adonis placed over the location of the birth of Jesus in Bethlehem in about AD 135 (Jerome, *Letter 58 to Paulinus*). Therefore, even the pagan Roman authorities recognized the significance and importance of Bethlehem as the place where Jesus Christ was born. Finally, Emperor Constantine ordered the Church of the Nativity constructed to commemorate the site in AD 327.

THE BIRTH OF JESUS AND
THE CHURCH OF THE NATIVITY

The story of the birth of Jesus in Bethlehem stretches back 2,000 years to the time of the Pax Romana, when Caesar Augustus ruled the extensive and powerful Roman Empire. The Gospels of Matthew and Luke, which both state that Jesus was born in Bethlehem, are the primary sources for this account. Because manuscript and textual evidence indicates that Matthew and Luke were composed in the middle of the 1st century AD, several writings from the 2nd century AD support the existence and acceptance of these Gospel accounts, and early copies and fragments are still in existence, these narratives must not be far removed from the life of Jesus.

In addition to the birth stories found in Matthew and Luke, secondary sources from antiquity also reference the birth of Jesus and corroborate details within the biblical narratives, and archaeological investigation has uncovered remains from the 1st century-village of Bethlehem and a 4th-century church that was supposedly built over the cave where Jesus was born.

The Gospel birth accounts begin by noting the betrothal of Mary and Joseph and the conception of Jesus by the Holy Spirit (Matthew 1:18-21; Luke 1:26-45). All of this occurred late in the reign of Herod the Great (ca. 40–4 BC), a prolific builder but paranoid king who seems to have died around March of 4 BC (Josephus, *Antiquities* 17.167-191; Matthew 2:1; Luke 1:5). During the pregnancy of Mary, a decree for a census of the entire Roman Empire was issued by Caesar Augustus. Since the Herodian Kingdom was a client state of Rome and administrators of Syria Province were responsible for official Roman matters there, the census was directed by a military commander named Quirinius according to Roman protocol (Luke 2:1-2). Emperor Augustus (reigned ca. 27 BC–AD 14) ordered his second known census of the Roman Empire in ca. 8 BC, which appears to be the census associated with the birth of Jesus (Augustus, *Res Gestae Divi Augusti*). Meanwhile, Quirinius was a commander of legions in Cilicia and Syria to the north, apparently as one of two rulers in Syria Province at the time (Tertullian, *Adversus Marcionem*; Tacitus, *Annals*; Josephus, *Antiquities*).

Ancient stone manger found at Nazareth

Joseph and Mary traveled to Bethlehem to register for the census because that was the family hometown of Joseph who was in the line of David (Luke 2:3-5). By the time Joseph and Mary arrived in Bethlehem, there was no place for them in the guestroom (*kataluma*) of the house, perhaps because other relatives were occupying the available space during the census. While this word is often translated "inn," Luke uses it elsewhere clearly as a guestroom or extra room in a house, while a separate word (*pandoxeion*) is used for an actual inn (Luke 22:11; Luke 10:34). It is also unlikely that Bethlehem even had an inn, since it was only a small Judean village at that time and inns were more common in Hellenistic areas, major highways, and larger cities.

So, they instead went to where the animals were kept at night, which was probably a cave under or adjacent to the house according to early sources. Jesus was then born and placed in a manger in Bethlehem (Luke 2:6-7). The manger would have been stone, which was the typical type of manger used in the area of Bethlehem in ancient times. Stone is abundant and found almost everywhere, while wood that can be used in construction is relatively scarce.

Caves next to, under, or integrated into the house were often used as storage areas for homes in the 1st century. Animals could have been kept in a cave or in a stone pen near the house, while the courtyard of the house would typically not be used for animals. Records that state Jesus was born in a cave rather than in an animal pen, outside, or in a courtyard go back to writings of the 2nd century AD. Excavations in the caves under the Church of the Nativity in Bethlehem found evidence that they were used during the Roman period in the 1st century, demonstrating that people in Bethlehem around the time of Jesus did indeed use the caves.

As might be expected of such a significant event for Christianity, over the generations many people remembered and passed on the knowledge of the

Section of the original mosaic floor from the 4th-century Church of the Nativity

birthplace, and specifically the cave, in which Jesus was born, although initially no public building or memorial structure existed there. Prior to the 2nd century AD, many were aware that the birth of Jesus occurred in Bethlehem, and Emperor Hadrian (reigned ca. AD 117–138) even attempted to erase, defile, and syncretize the memory of the birth of Jesus by constructing a shrine to the god Adonis over the cave (Justin Martyr, *Dialogue with Trypho*; Origen, *Contra Celsum*; Jerome, *Letter 58 to Paulinus*; Anonymous, *Protoevangelium of James*).

However, the memory of the birthplace of Jesus persisted despite the attempts by Hadrian, which may have actually helped preserve the location. After the conversion of Constantine, the emperor ordered a church to be erected over the cave in about 327 AD, which his mother, Helena, oversaw (Eusebius, *Life of Constantine*; Sulpicius Severus, *Sacred History*; Sozomen, *Ecclesiastical History*). The Church of the Nativity, mostly completed by AD 333 but totally finished in 339, was one of four major commemorative churches that Constantine had constructed in the Holy Land.

This church had an elaborate mosaic floor, Corinthian columns, five aisles, a nave on the east end, and stairs by the nave that went down into the cave where it was thought that Jesus was born. Although this original version of the church was burned down in the 6th century during the Samaritan revolt, it was rebuilt soon after by Emperor Justinian. Remnants of the original church have survived, including sections of the mosaic floor, foundations, columns, and the cave.

As with many sites and events associated with Jesus, claims have been made that this particular cave was originally a cult site to Adonis, and Christians merely took this site over and built a church there. Yet, multiple writers in the 2nd century AD attested to the birth of Jesus having occurred at this cave, and slightly later sources from antiquity relate that Emperor Hadrian built a shrine to Adonis at the location as part of his wider campaign to obscure the historical memory of Jesus in the hope that Christianity could be eliminated from the Empire (e.g., the Roman temple built over the tomb of Jesus in Jerusalem). Astonishingly, details such as Jesus being born in a village of Judea (Bethlehem) were acknowledged and recounted in the 2nd century AD by a pagan Roman philosopher named Celsus who wrote a polemic against Christianity (Celsus, *The True Word* in Origen, *Contra Celsum*).

Celsus also wrote about Mary and even mentioned the story of the virgin birth of Jesus. The record of the virgin conception and birth of Jesus is found in both the Gospels of Matthew and Luke (Matthew 1:16-25; Luke 1:26-38). A few other New Testament writings suggest knowledge of the virgin birth in early

Christianity (John 8:39-41; Galatians 4:4-5; Romans 1:1-4; Philippians 2:6-8; Hebrews 7:3). According to early church writers, such as Tertullian, Irenaeus, Justin Martyr, Ignatius, and Aristides, the belief in the virgin birth of Jesus was widely accepted in the early 2nd century, rather than invented around that time or later.

In the writings of Celsus, which are partially preserved by quotations referenced by Origen and were probably composed around AD 175, acknowledgment of the belief in the virgin birth of Jesus by Christians is shown to be known even in pagan circles of the 2nd century. Celsus, however, claimed that this was simply a fabricated story and instead offered his own version—that Jesus, who was born in a village of Judea of a poor woman of the country, invented his birth from a virgin because his mother was sent away by her carpenter husband after she was convicted of adultery, and that the biological father was actually a Roman soldier named Pantera (Origen quoting Celsus, *The True Word*, in *Contra Celsus*, 1.28).

Pantera (sometimes rendered Panthera or Pandera, Latin meaning "panther") was a common male name in use during the Roman period, and representative of a typical Roman legionnaire. The discovery of a 1st-century AD tombstone of a Roman soldier named Tiberius Julius Abdes Pantera, who served around the time of Jesus and was probably about ten years old when Jesus was born, demonstrates usage of the name but would have no connection to the allegation (CIL XIII 7514). This tombstone was discovered in the Roman cemetery at Bingerbruck, and the soldier was from Sidon, but he was only slightly older than Jesus and would not yet have been a soldier. Rather than refuting the story of the virgin birth of Jesus, Celsus demonstrated that the belief was known throughout the Roman world by the 2nd century AD, even by those outside the Christian community. Jesus as the son of Pantera or Pandera is also related by the Jerusalem Talmud around AD 200 and the Tosefta in the 2nd century AD, with the implication that Jesus was conceived out of wedlock. Both Celsus and the Talmud probably received their information from a common story that was circulating in the Roman Empire by the 2nd century.

However, the fact that both Celsus and sources such as the Tosefta recount and retell the unique circumstances surrounding the birth of Jesus demonstrates that knowledge of the nativity story was widespread. It is also important to note that the pagan and Jewish sources do not dispute the birth of Jesus in a village of Judea under what could have been typically regarded as a scandalous situation, with Mary pregnant before the wedding occurred.

Clearly, the ancient accounts, including those outside of the Gospels, state that Jesus was born in either Bethlehem specifically or in a village of Judea. Yet, a few scholars have even claimed that Jesus was not born in Bethlehem of Judea. These hypotheses are merely unwarranted speculation completely contrary to all the evidence.

Many have also asserted that there is no archaeological evidence that Bethlehem was occupied in the 1st century BC and 1st century AD, and therefore the birth story must be unhistorical. However, recent archaeological excavations in and around the Church of the Nativity have confirmed that the village was indeed occupied during the Roman period and the time of Jesus. Rather than the accounts in Matthew and Luke being historically inaccurate or the only sources relating to the birth of Jesus, the birth itself and various details are both illuminated and corroborated by archaeological discoveries and various writings from antiquity. A thorough examination of the evidence demonstrates that Jesus of Nazareth was born at the end of the 1st century BC in Bethlehem, probably in a cave that was part of a house, and now underneath the Church of the Nativity.

THE DATE OF THE BIRTH

Traditionally the birth of Jesus Christ is celebrated on December 25, although objections have been made that this date is an inaccurate result of religious syncretism (combining beliefs and practices) or speculation. The most common criticisms of December 25 being a plausible date for the birth of Jesus include allegations that the day was originally a pagan festival day, eventually chosen as a replacement sometime after Christianity was legalized in the Roman Empire, or that the weather during December in Bethlehem does not agree with details in the birth narrative of the Gospel of Luke.

The Roman festival of Saturnalia, honoring the god Saturn, is often cited as the inspiration behind the church-sanctioned date for Christmas, but Saturnalia was celebrated from December 17–23, not on December 25, and therefore it was not a replacement festival or holy day. According to the Gospel of Luke, when Jesus was born, shepherds were watching over their sheep at night in the area outside of Bethlehem (Luke 2:8). Some suggest that if Jesus were born in December, shepherds would not be out in the fields at night because it would be too cold, and thus Jesus must have been born during a warmer month.

However, this claim has two major problems. First, according to weather data, Bethlehem in December is not cold enough to prohibit shepherding or staying with the flock at night. The average high in Bethlehem in December is 57° F (14° C), the average low is 45° F (7° C), and there is typically about one snow day in the month. Ancient pastoralists in other regions routinely carried out their duties in much colder temperatures, such as the Eurasian steppe, Mongolia, the Himalayan region, and many other areas. Although changes in modern times have been drastic, nearly eliminating the ancient ways of the nomadic pastoralist, one can even today witness shepherding in the Levant during the month of December. These current shepherds, however, usually have some type of permanent structure or location that they live in, rather than setting up temporary structures as they move their herds around the region.

Second, staying with the flock at night by sleeping at the gate of the sheepfold was a common practice of shepherds in pre-industrialized society, and survives today in some areas. The birth narrative in the Gospel of Luke mentioning the shepherds is plausible with what would have been taking place during antiquity around Bethlehem in December.

According to information in the Gospel narratives, synced with dates of festivals from the Law of Moses, another argument can be made for the birth of Jesus in late December. In the Gospel of Luke, Zechariah was carrying out his priestly duties, possibly in connection with the Day of Atonement (Yom Kippur), which takes place on the tenth day in the month of Tishri (September–October), when he was told that his wife Elizabeth was going to have a child (Luke 1:8-13; Leviticus 23:26-28). Just after the period of Zechariah's priestly service in connection with the holy day, Elizabeth became pregnant during the second half of the month of September (Luke 1:23-24). Six months later, in approximately late March of the following year, Mary became pregnant (Luke 1:26-45). After a nine-month pregnancy, Jesus would have been born around late December.

For those who may object to the idea that Zechariah was participating in duties related to the Day of Atonement or one of the other festivals or holy days in the month of Tishri, evidence from early Christian writings suggests that Jesus was born on the 25th of December. Some of these accounts specifically place the conception of Jesus in late March, as the Gospel of Luke appears to indicate. The church father Irenaeus, writing in the late 2nd century, placed the conception of Jesus on March 25 and the birth of Jesus nine months later on December 25 (Irenaeus, *Adversus Haereses*). The historian Sextus Julius Africanus of the late 2nd century and early 3rd century, recorded that March 25 was the day of the conception of Jesus Christ, which extrapolates to an approximate

December 25 birth (Sextus Julius Africanus, *Chronographiai*). A commentary
from the early 3rd century may also attest to the idea that Jesus was born on
December 25 (Hippolytus of Rome, *Commentary on Daniel*).

Another church father writing about the same time, ca. AD 200, recounts
that some calculated the birth of Jesus to be the 25th of the Egyptian month
of Pachon (Clement of Alexandria, *Stromata*). Although it has been proposed
that this would equate to May 20 in our current calendar, the ancient Egyptian
calendar was originally a wandering calendar prior to the reform of the Coptic
calendar. This means that ancient Egyptian months would not consistently correlate to any of our current calendar dates, and the exact year must be known.

Further, Clement only mentions that he had heard of sources making this
calculation, and not that it was the accepted date. Finally, in the 4th century, a
chronological work states December 25 as the day that Jesus Christ was born
in Bethlehem, and another sermon on December 25 commemorated the day
as the birth of Christ (Valentinus, *The Chronography of 354*; Gregory of Nazian-
zus, *Oration*).

Interestingly, these accounts are not concerned with the celebration of
Christmas, but merely with recording the dates of the conception and birth of
Jesus Christ. Therefore, evidence is strong at least for a very early tradition that
Jesus was born on the 25th of December. These writings also demonstrate that
the date was established prior to Emperor Constantine becoming a Christian
and legalizing Christianity throughout the Roman Empire.

Thus, the December 25 date had nothing to do with religious syncretism
or attempting to replace pagan holidays with Christian holidays after the legal-
ization of Christianity. In fact, there is not one suggestion in any of the early
writings that the date for Christmas was chosen to supplant a pagan celebration, and this idea only appeared in the 12th century and finally became pop-
ularized in comparative religion studies of the 19th century. On the contrary,
early Christians were not only societal outcasts but also sought to clearly separate their beliefs and practices from those of the imperial cult or other pagan
systems. Numerous early manuscripts suggest that the birth of Jesus probably
occurred on or around December 25, and it remains a possibility.

THE MAGI

After the birth in Bethlehem and once the 40 days of purification were completed, Joseph and Mary took Jesus to Jerusalem to offer a sacrifice according to

the Mosaic Law (Luke 2:22-24; Leviticus 12:1-4). There at the temple, the couple offered two birds because they did not have the financial means to purchase a lamb (Luke 2:23-24; Leviticus 12:8).

Excavations from ruins adjacent to the southwest corner of the Temple Mount in Jerusalem found a stone vessel fragment with the Aramaic inscription *QRBN* ("sacrificial offering") along with a drawing of two upside-down birds dating to the 1st century, illustrating this practice of offering two doves or pigeons as a sacrifice during the time of Jesus. Following an undefined but short time in Jerusalem keeping the requirements of the Law, the three returned to the tiny village of Nazareth, where Joseph and Mary had lived prior to the census (Luke 2:39). It was there in Nazareth that the magi seem to have encountered Jesus when he was a child about two years old or younger, while Bethlehem remains a less probable location due to chronological and narrative issues (Matthew 2:16).

Near the end of the 1st century BC, Joseph, Mary, and Jesus were eventually visited by the enigmatic and misunderstood "magi" from the east (Matthew 2:1-16). Popularly, these magi are often referred to as "three kings," but very little is known about who these men were, how many there were, or precisely where they came from. The Gospel of Matthew is the earliest surviving record of these mysterious magi who visited Jesus as a young child—the other three Gospels do not mention this occurrence, and no reference is made to their visit in any other New Testament book.

The idea that there were three magi is connected to the three gifts presented to Jesus as recorded by Matthew—gold, frankincense, and myrrh. Although coinage was standard in the 1st century, gold was still used to trade and make purchases, but its wide circulation gives no clue as to the origin or route of the magi. Myrrh, a spice used in anointing and embalming, and frankincense, a valuable resin used in perfume, medicine, embalming, and incense, were both acquired and traded by the Nabateans whose kingdom was based at Petra and stretched east towards the Euphrates River, with trade routes going all the way to the Persian Gulf (Diodorus Siculus, *Bibliotheca Historica*).

These three gifts of gold, frankincense, and myrrh were also given by Seleucus II Callinicus Pogon in 243 BC as part of an offering to Apollo at Miletus. The offerings and their sources indicate that the magi did come from the east, and that their gifts were appropriate during that period for an offering to divinity.

That Joseph and Mary had to offer two birds at the temple in Jerusalem because they could not afford to buy a lamb for sacrifice is another indicator that the magi did not visit them and give them the gifts in Bethlehem, including the gold, before they departed for Jerusalem to make the sacrifice (Luke 2:23-24).

At least two apocryphal sources probably composed in the 2nd century AD also discuss the visit of the magi, and multiple early church fathers also include this visit in writings about the birth and early life of Jesus. The *Protoevangelium of James* and its discussion of the magi has been known for centuries, and a 3rd- or 4th-century AD manuscript of this work is still in existence (Papyrus Bodmer 5).

Another ancient manuscript, however, was rediscovered in the Vatican Library and claims to be a first person account of those magi who visited Jesus. Called the *Revelation of the Magi*, the existing copy is an 8th-century AD Syriac manuscript, but the original account may have been composed as early as the 2nd century AD. This document, unfortunately, does not give us all the answers about the magi, nor is it completely consistent with the birth narratives of Matthew and Luke or the visit of the magi in Matthew. It is also considered pseudepigraphal as it was not written by the actual magi who visited Jesus, although it reflects 2nd-century AD knowledge of those magi.

The story claims that the magi who visited Jesus were a large group—at least twelve men rather than three—of monk-like mystics from a distant land called Shir at the shore of the Great Ocean, and descendants of Seth who had been awaiting a centuries-old prophecy that a brilliant star would one day appear to herald the birth of God in human form. This prophecy has been suggested as a possible reference to the star mentioned by Balaam and there may be a veiled reference to it in Isaiah (Numbers 24:17; Isaiah 60:3). While the exact location of Shir is unknown, there are locations in Persia named or containing the component "shir," and the "Great Ocean" could refer to bodies of water such as the

Magi visiting the infant of Jesus, from the tomb of Severa ca. AD 250

Persian Gulf or Arabian Sea connecting to the Indian Ocean, indicating that Persia was thought to be the region from which they came.

This "star in the east," star of Jesus, or star of Bethlehem as it is sometimes incorrectly referred to, is only recorded in the Matthew account—the only Gospel that also cites the Old Testament prophecy about Bethlehem from the Book of Micah and the only book in the New Testament that mentions the magi. Because this star, as it is described in Matthew, does not fit the properties of a common star, it has led to much inquiry and speculation, and its identification has often been debated.

The Greek word for "star" (*aster*) used in the New Testament had a variety of meanings in ancient literature, including planet, comet, angel, or light, including a divine light (cf. Matthew 2:1-10; Revelation 1:20). The Hebrew word *kokav*, which is commonly rendered as "star," is also often used to refer to angels and equated with "the sons of God," or angelic beings (cf. Job 38:7; Daniel 8:10). Divine lights were also used to guide the Israelites, and one appeared before Paul on the road to Damascus (Exodus 13:21; Acts 9:3). Thus, it is linguistically possible that the "star" could mean an angel or a divinely sent light, and not just a star, comet, or planet.

If the "star" was a planet or a comet, only certain dates for the appearance of the star are possible. A conjunction with Jupiter and Saturn dating from 7 BC has been proposed, or alternatively with Jupiter and Venus in the Leo conjunction in 2 BC. Conjunctions, however, are regular astronomical occurrences and not unique events. Comets have also been suggested, but the closest known comet dates to 11 BC, years before the birth of Jesus, they were often interpreted as bad omens, and they move rapidly across the sky rather than linger and reappear over a long period of time.

In addition to the chronological restrictions—two of which from 11 BC and 2 BC do not agree with known historical information associated with the birth of Jesus found in the Gospels of Matthew and Luke—the language used in the Matthew narrative does not accommodate planets, comets, or even stars. The account of Matthew states that it was the "star" of Jesus and that this "star" moved and went directly over the specific house where Jesus and his family were residing. "The star, which they had seen in the east, went on ahead of them until it came to a stop over the place where the Child was to be found" (Matthew 2:9).

The "star" was described in anthropomorphic terms, as if it were an angelic being or being controlled by an intelligent agent. Matthew states only that a star appeared, as if it had not existed or was not visible before. The star then disappeared by the time the magi arrived in Jerusalem and saw Herod, which was approximately three weeks of travel from the Babylon area. Finally, once the magi were told of the prophecy about Bethlehem and left their audience with Herod in Jerusalem, the star reappeared with perfect timing, leading them to the exact house and standing over where the child Jesus was with his family in Nazareth (Matthew 2:9; cf. Luke 2:21-39).

The way in which this "star" and its actions are described makes a star, comet, or planet interpretation impossible. Stars, comets, and planets cannot pinpoint an exact location such as a house in the small village of Nazareth. Stars do not disappear and reappear, do not move through the atmosphere of the earth, and do not come to rest over a house. That the star was "leading" the magi is language pointing to a sentient agent, such as an angel or divinely controlled light.

Significantly, the earliest sources outside of the Gospels and the description in Matthew all agree on a single understanding for the star, increasing the probability of a correct interpretation. The *Protoevangelium of James*, composed about AD 140–170, with an existing manuscript from the 3rd century AD, describes the "star of Bethlehem" as an angel that guided the magi. This is the earliest known manuscript that describes the star associated with Jesus.

The recently rediscovered *Revelation of the Magi* relates a similar understanding of the star the magi followed. The story records that the star was a luminous child directing them to Judea, which seems to be the author's depiction of an angel. This general interpretation is found in various writings, as angels are often associated with bright lights and with guides in ancient literature (Enoch 18:13-16; Diodorus Siculus, *Bibliotheca Historica* 16). Therefore, the usage of "star" in the context of the nativity of Jesus was probably referring to an angel, perhaps projecting a light that guided the Magi from the east to meet and worship Jesus.

Although the *Revelation of the Magi* and the *Protoevangelium of James* contain historical memory and relevant information from antiquity, these stories were written more than a hundred years after the time of Jesus and may not have used eyewitness testimony. While consistency is found in certain details, such as mention of the cave in Bethlehem associated with the birth of Jesus, the visit of the magi, or the identification of the star, other components appear to conflict between sources, such as Joseph and Mary living in a house in Bethlehem or the magi visiting Jesus immediately after his birth (Anonymous, *Revelation of the Magi*). Several particulars may have been fabricated or based on speculation, so caution and comparative analysis should be used when evaluating these sources.

A variety of ancient documents give a more comprehensive and accurate picture of who these magi were. The word *magi* (plural) originally seems to derive from Old Persian *magush*, transmitted through Greek as *magos* (singular) and *magoi* (plural). This Persian word is the origin of the word *mage*, which typically refers to a practitioner of magic. The earliest reference to magi comes from the Old Persian Behistun Inscription of Darius (ca. 520 BC), but it does not give any specific meaning or description. A Greek text of Heraclitus (ca. 6th century BC) claims the magi participated in impious rituals—likely rituals that were contrary to Greek practice.

Later texts are clearer about who magi are and what they do. Herodotus recorded two meanings for magi—one as a tribe of the Medes, and the other as a special caste whose duties included interpretation of omens and dreams (Herodotus, *Histories*). Pliny the Elder wrote that magi practiced some type of magic and wrote magical texts (Pliny the Elder, *Natural History*). Strabo placed them in Media and remarked that they lived a sedentary life, which would accord with their status as scholars, advisors, and astrologers (Strabo, *Geography*). Other Hellenistic period authors additionally associate magi with astrology, magic, and dream interpretation. This association seems to have been generally understood during antiquity, as the Greek term for magi is used in the Septuagint (LXX) version of the Book of Daniel in reference to advisors of Nebuchadnezzar who were consulted for making decisions and interpreting dreams (Daniel 1:20; 2:2; 4:7; 5:7).

In the New Testament, two additional people described as magi are recorded in the Book of Acts—Simon and Elymas (Acts 8:9; 13:8). Details about what specifically these two men did are not included in the text, but Simon is said to perform amazing "magical" acts and Elymas appears to be a trusted advisor of Sergius Paulus the proconsul.

Josephus mentioned magi who were advisors and dream interpreters of Nebuchadnezzar, and he also recounted a later story about a man who pretended to be a magi and seemed to have powerful skills of persuasion working in the court of Felix (Josephus, *Antiquities* 20.142). Texts from the Hellenistic and Roman periods convey the same meanings for magi. All of these texts about magi suggest that the magi who visited Jesus were generally similar in their training and abilities—educated, intelligent men who were experts in astrology, interpreted dreams, and served as advisors to rulers. The magi in Matthew followed a "star" to find Jesus, they were apparently a class of men revered as knowledgeable and wise since they were requested to advise Herod and his experts about the birth of the Messiah, they were "warned in a dream" to avoid Herod, and they originally came from "the east" (Matthew 2:1-12).

The place in "the east" that the magi traveled from appears to have been either Persia, which encompassed Media after the 6th century BC, or farther south in Chaldea, where the magi class originated and where astrological advisors and dream interpreters called magi had been active for centuries. The reference to "Shir" in the *Revelation of the Magi* suggests the area of Persia. Regardless, both Persia and Chaldea were part of the Parthian Empire in the 1st century BC, and at the time that the magi left to visit Jesus, Phraates IV was king (ca. 37–2 BC). Ancient artwork illustrating the magi who visited Jesus also shows their origin in the Parthian Empire through their distinctive clothing and hats. The way in which these magi are depicted on a visitation of Jesus scene from the tomb of Severa from about AD 250 in Rome matches with images

P52 manuscript fragment of the Gospel of John from ca. AD 90–175

of Parthian men around the time of the birth of Jesus, including a denarius of Augustus struck in 19 BC showing a Parthian man kneeling in submission and returning the Roman standards captured from the Battle of Carrhae.

It should come as no surprise that masters of astronomical observation, dream interpretation, advisement, and probably divination came from the area of ancient Mesopotamia, since many of these activities had been in practice there for thousands of years prior to the magi mentioned by Matthew. The general information about the magi in the Gospel of Matthew matches what is known from other ancient texts about magi spanning the 6th century BC through the 1st century AD. Although we may never know exactly how many magi visited Jesus, their names, or the specific city they traveled from, the existing ancient texts give a moderate understanding of who they were and demonstrate that the details about them recorded in the Gospel of Matthew are historically consistent.

Manuscript copies of the Gospels of Matthew and Luke, containing the accounts of the birth of Jesus, have survived for nearly 2000 years. Probable 2nd-century AD manuscripts of both Matthew and Luke, including P4, P67, P75, P103, and P104 have preserved sections of the two Gospels that include the nativity narrative in copies that were made only several decades to a little over a century from the original writings.

In addition to Matthew and Luke, secondary sources from antiquity, including even those hostile to Christianity, reference the birth of Jesus and corroborate details found within the narratives. An archaeological and historical analysis of the birth narratives from the Gospels also demonstrates that these accounts are reliable in details such as geographic locations, names and positions of officials, political situations of the era, procedures of the Roman Empire, cultural norms in Galilee and Judea, and that knowledge of specific events around the birth of Jesus was widespread in antiquity.

SELECTED BIBLIOGRAPHY
(CHAPTER 1)

Anderson, J.G.C. "The Position Held by Quirinius for the Homanadensian War" in *The Cambridge Ancient History*, vol. X, ed. S.A. Cook et al. Cambridge: Cambridge University, 1989.

Arndt, W., F.W. Gingrich, F.W. Danker, and W. Bauer. *A Greek-English Lexicon of the New Testament and Other Early Christian Literature*. Chicago: University of Chicago Press, 1996.

Augustus, *Res Gestae Divi Augusti.*

Bagatti, Bellarmino. *The Church from the Circumcision.* Jerusalem: Franciscan, 1971.

———. *Excavations in Nazareth.* Jerusalem: Franciscan, 1969.

———. *Gli Antichi Edifici Sacri Di Betlemme in Seguito Agli Scave E Restauri Praticati Dalla Custodia Di Terra Santa* (1948-51). PSBF 9. Jerusalem: Franciscan, 1952.

Birley, Anthony, ed., "The Titulus Tiburtinus." *Roman Papers*, vol. 3. (1984).

Blaiklock, E.M. *The Archaeology of the New Testament.* Grand Rapids: Zondervan, 1974.

Blomberg, Craig. *Jesus and the Gospels.* Nashville: B&H Publishing, 2009.

Brown, Francis et al., *Enhanced Brown-Driver-Briggs Hebrew and English Lexicon.* Oak Harbor, WA: Logos, 2000.

Cassius Dio, *Roman History.*

Chancey, Mark, and Adam Porter. "The Archaeology of Roman Palestine." *Near Eastern Archaeology* 64.4 (2001).

Cheesman, G.L. "The Family of the Caristanii at Antioch in Pisidia." *Journal of Roman Studies* 3 (1913).

Dark, Ken. *Roman-Period and Byzantine Nazareth and Its Hinterland.* London: Routledge, 2020.

———. "Early Roman-period Nazareth and the Sisters of Nazareth Convent." *Antiquaries Journal* (2012).

Dessau, H. ed., *Inscriptiones Latinae Selectae.* Berlin: Weidmann, 1962.

DeVries, LaMoine. *Cities of the Biblical World*. Peabody, MA: Hendrickson, 1997.

Ehrenberg, Victor, and Arnold Jones. *Documents Illustrating the Reigns of Augustus and Tiberius*. Oxford: Oxford University Press, 1976.

Evans, Craig, and Stanley Porter, eds. *Dictionary of New Testament Background*. Downers Grove, IL: IVP Academic, 2000.

Finegan, Jack. *Archaeology of the New Testament*. London: Routledge, 1981.

Florus, *Epitome of Roman History.*

Grenfell, B.P., A.S. Hunt et al. *Oxyrhynchus Papyri*. London: Egypt Exploration Fund, 1898.

Josephus, *Antiquities.*

Justin Martyr, *Apology.*

Kenyon, Frederick, and Idris Bell. *Greek Papyri in the British Museum*. London: British Museum, 1917.

Kramer, Joel. *Where God Came Down: The Archaeological Evidence*. Brigham City, UT: Expedition Bible, 2020.

Landau, Brent. *Revelation of the Magi*. New York: HarperCollins, 2010.

Lewis, Naphtali, and Meyer Reinhold. *Roman Civilization. Sourcebook II: The Empire*. New York: Harper and Row, 1966.

Liddell et al., *A Greek-English Lexicon*. Oxford: Clarendon, 1996.

Livy, *History of Rome.*

Maier, Paul. *The Genuine Jesus*. Grand Rapids: Kregel, 2021.

Mazar, Benjamin. "The Royal Stoa in the Southern Part of the Temple Mount." Proceedings of the American Academy for Jewish Research 46-47 (1979-80).

Moulton, James, and George Milligan. *The Vocabulary of the Greek Testament*. London: Hodder and Stoughton, 1952.

Pearson, B.W.R. "The Lucan Censuses, Revisited." *Catholic Biblical Quarterly* 61 (1999).

Pixner, Bargil. *Paths of the Messiah: And Sites of the Early Church from Galilee to Jerusalem*. San Francisco: Ignatius, 2010.

Reed, Jonathan. *Archaeology and the Galilean Jesus*. Harrisburg: Trinity Press, 2000.

Rist, John. "Luke 2:2: Making Sense of the Date of Jesus Birth." *Journal of Theological Studies* 56.2 (2005).

Rosenfeld, Ben-Zion. "Innkeeping in Jewish Society in Roman Palestine." *Journal of the Economic and Social History of the Orient* 41.2 (1998).

Salway, Benet. "What's in a Name? A Survey of Roman Onomastic Practice from c. 700 B.C. to A.D. 700." *Journal of Roman Studies* 84 (1994).

Schürer, Emil. *The History of the Jewish People in the Age of Jesus Christ.* Edinburgh: Clark, 1987.

Seneca, *Controversiae and Suasoriae.*

Sherwin-White, A.N. *Roman Society and Roman Law in the New Testament.* Grand Rapids: Baker, 1978.

Smith, Mark D. "Of Jesus and Quirinius." *Catholic Biblical Quarterly* 62.2 (2000).

Spijkerman, Augustus. *The Coins of the Decapolis and Provincia Arabia.* Jerusalem: Franciscan, 1978.

Suetonius, *Augustus.*

Tacitus, *Annals.*

Taylor, Lily Ross. "Quirinius and the Census of Judaea." *American Journal of Philology* 54 (1933).

Tertullian, *Adversus Marcionem.*

Thomas, Robert and Stanley Gundry. *A Harmony of the Gospels.* Chicago: Moody Press, 1978.

Velleius, *History.*

Flight to Egypt, Herod, and Return to Nazareth

After the magi visited and worshipped the infant Jesus in Nazareth, Joseph took Mary and Jesus to Egypt so they could escape the wrath of Herod, who was seeking to kill Jesus (Matthew 2:13-15; cf. Hosea 11:1). To the north of Judea was Syria Province, which had been annexed to the Roman Republic by General Pompey in 64 BC during the Third Mithridatic War when the Romans defeated King Tigranes the Great of Armenia. It was a republican province, which meant that by the time of the Empire, the Senate appointed a magistrate to rule the province rather than the emperor. Since Syria was on the eastern border of the Empire, its magistrates were usually patrician-class Romans with military experience who were commanding legions to defend or expand the Empire or to quell rebellion. To the east and the south was the region of Arabia, encompassing most of the Sinai Peninsula and Saudi Arabia. During the 1st century, this region was under the control of the Nabatean Kingdom, which had familial ties to the Herodians. In AD 106, the area of the Sinai and far northwest Arabia was annexed by the Roman Empire, becoming the province of Arabia Petraea.

To the south was the province of Aegyptus, or Egypt, which was slightly smaller than modern Egypt. Egypt was a Roman province and therefore part of the same empire as the client kingdom of Judea, which meant safer access on Roman roads, no problems crossing national borders, the same currency, and people all spoke the same international language of Koine Greek.

ESCAPE TO EGYPT

The family of Jesus probably used a major road that ran along the shore of the Mediterranean, now often referred to as Via Maris or Way of the Sea, to access Egypt. While the name Via Maris, which is a Latin translation of Way of the Sea, is not known from any documents of the Roman period, the road it refers to existed long before the time of Jesus (Exodus 13:17; Matthew 4:15). The other primary road in the region ran just east of Judea and was known as the King's Highway, which would have allowed Joseph to bring the family back to Nazareth in Galilee while also avoiding Judea and Archelaus (Matthew 2:19-23). These two road systems helped connect the continents of Europe, Asia, and Africa through the Middle East.

A third major road connected the King's Highway with the Way of the Sea, and this ran from Damascus through the Galilee region and to the Mediterranean coast. By the time of Jesus in the 1st century, the Roman road system had as many as 29 major highways converging in Rome, running through about 30 provinces besides additional client kingdoms and territories, which were all interconnected by hundreds of roads.

A description of Roman roads from the time of the Empire says, "There is hardly a district to which we might expect a Roman official to be sent, on service either civil or military, where we do not find roads. They reach the Wall in

Roman-period paved city road in Galilee

Britain, run along the Rhine, the Danube, and the Euphrates, and cover, as with a network, the interior provinces of the Empire" (*Itinerarium Antonini Augusti*).

Although roads are often mentioned in accounts about Jesus, it seems that there were no major paved Roman highways in Judea and Galilee during the time of Jesus, with the first being constructed under Claudius around AD 56, and others built during the First Judean Revolt between AD 66–73 to allow rapid movement of the Roman army, according to the writings of Josephus and various Roman milestones discovered along the routes (Josephus, *Wars*). Rather, most of the roads that Jesus traveled on would have been *via terrena* (road of leveled earth) or perhaps *via glareata* (road with gravel surface).

Egypt was also outside the jurisdiction of Herod the Great, and therefore Jesus would have been safe from Herod's assassination decree. At the time of this flight to Egypt, it was an Imperial Province ruled by the emperor Augustus, who had annexed it for Rome in 30 BC after defeating the coalition of Cleopatra VII and Mark Antony at the Battle of Actium. Like Judea, Egypt was under the control of the emperor by way of a prefect. Egypt was extremely important for the emperor since it was one of the wealthiest provinces in the Empire due to its massive grain production and developed economy. The province of Egypt was administered locally by a governor who usually held the office for three to

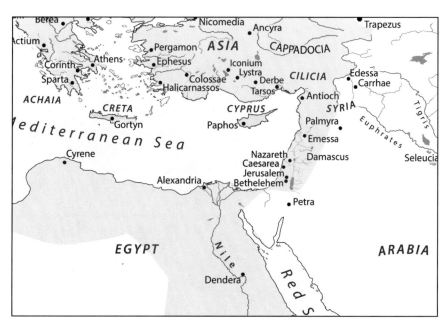

Judea and the adjacent Roman province of Egypt

four years and governed from Alexandria, one of the largest cities in the Roman Empire at the time.

When Jesus and his family fled to Egypt, the prefect of the province would have been Gaius Turranius, who held the position from 7–4 BC and was in charge of the important grain supply. Egypt was not only near Judea, but there was also a substantial population of Jews there, particularly in Alexandria. Many of the Jews living in Egypt may have traced back to before the Babylonian exile, and the family might have sought help from relatives or friends (Jeremiah 43:7; 44:1; Acts 2:10). Of all the areas adjacent to Judea and Galilee, Egypt was the most disconnected from the influence of Herod the Great while still part of the Roman Empire and easily accessible, since Herod was related to the nearby Nabateans and was politically involved with the rulers of Syria Province.

The Gospels do not specify which city in Egypt nor the duration of the stay, but Athanasius of Alexandria in the 4th century claimed that Jesus was four years old when he left Egypt, suggesting a stay of about two years. Celsus, the 2nd-century philosopher and critic of Christianity, also acknowledged and noted that Jesus was in Egypt during his childhood (Celsus, *On the True Word*, quoted by Origen, *Contra Celsus* 1.38). The city of Alexandria had a thriving community of Jews, including the famous philosopher Philo of Alexandria, but

Dair al-Adhra, one of many traditional locations of Jesus and his family in Egypt

according to ancient tradition the family of Jesus lived in Cairo during their stay in Egypt. Abu Serga, or the Saints Sergius and Bacchus Church in Cairo, was constructed in the 4th century AD and allegedly preserves the location where Jesus and his family lived in Egypt. While this church is ancient, and it is possible that Jesus and his family stayed in Cairo, there is no evidence to pinpoint the exact location or even the correct city, and numerous legends and traditions exist about locations of Jesus and his family in Egypt. However, it is logical and historically consistent that Joseph would have fled with his family to Egypt when Herod was attempting to kill the baby Jesus (Matthew 2:13-15).

THE "MASSACRE OF THE INNOCENTS" IN THE GOSPEL OF MATTHEW

Meanwhile, back in Judea, the tragic and infamous event known as the "Massacre of the Innocents" was occurring. Herod was "troubled" with the news that the future king and Messiah had apparently been born in Bethlehem, just as the prophecies foretold (Matthew 2:1-6). Apparently afraid that he may lose his kingship, Herod secretly consulted the magi to find out approximately when this child would have been born (Matthew 2:7). Herod also requested that the magi report the child's location to him so that he could worship him—a ploy to destroy the child (Matthew 2:8).

However, the magi were warned in a dream not to return to King Herod, so he had no idea where Jesus was living (Matthew 2:12). Eventually realizing that he had been tricked and believing that this child posed a threat to his power, Herod flew into a rage and ordered all the male children two years old and under in Bethlehem and its outskirts to be killed (Matthew 2:16). Since Herod talked secretly with the magi, perhaps the killings were carried out in a covert manner and not widely known until many years later.

Although the number of children slain is unknown, Bethlehem was described as a village (John 7:42) and was quite small and insignificant in comparison to nearby Jerusalem. Due to its size, the number of children killed in the massacre might be estimated anywhere between 10 and 100. While Matthew never uses the term *massacre* or an equivalent, any of those figures could fit the term *massacre* in the sense of multiple tragic deaths, although not on the numerical scale of a few of Herod's other recorded violent outbursts.

Because the details of the massacre are related only in the Matthew account, many critical scholars and skeptics maintain that this event never really happened, but that it was either propaganda against King Herod by the Gospel writer and falsified fulfillment of prophecy (cf. Matthew 2:17-18 and Jeremiah 31:15) or misconstrued history based on Herod executing his own sons.

The main objection is the silence of Josephus, not any contradiction or implausibility. However, Josephus is by no means exhaustive in his description of Herod's actions or other events of the 1st century in Judea, and his emphasis is on major cities and political leaders rather than the deaths of children in a small village. Even the high-profile story of the votive golden shields in Jerusalem involving Pontius Pilate was not recorded by Josephus (Philo of Alexandria, *Embassy to Gaius*). While no other currently known 1st-century AD source clearly reports the event, there are early records mentioning or alluding to the slaughter, and the act is perfectly consistent with the character of Herod the Great.

Biographical information indicates that not only would Herod be capable of ordering the execution of babies and infants, but that this type of action fits his psychological profile. The most comprehensive existing material for the life of Herod the Great is found in the writings of Josephus. While Josephus does not include the massacre of the children of Bethlehem, he does include several political executions, assassinations, and even mass slaughters ordered by Herod throughout his reign (cf. Josephus, *Wars* 2.84-88; *Antiquities* 17.173-178). The list of people Herod had killed includes Mattathias Antigonus and 45 of his men, John Hyrcanus II, the high priest Aristobulus III, his mother-in-law Alexandra, his wife Miriamne, various people suspected of revolt, 300 military leaders, many Pharisees, and his sons Alexander, Aristobulus IV, and Antipater II.

It is particularly relevant that Herod ordered the executions of three of his own sons during the period of 7–4 BC, which was the approximate time Herod would have also ordered the killing of the male children in the Bethlehem area (Josephus, *Antiquites* 16.392-404). During this tumultuous period near the end of his reign, Herod also burned to death several Judeans for removing a golden eagle from the temple and ordered the mass killing of perhaps hundreds of influential citizens in the event of his death. The executions of Herod's sons, who were apparently seen as threatening his throne, are similar in motive and measure to the massacre of the children to attempt to prevent a prophesied king from rising to power.

Although Herod displayed paranoia and violence throughout his reign, these problems seem to have been exacerbated in the final years of his life when he suffered from chronic and painful sickness. Further, Herod may have seen a precedent in what Suetonius recorded concerning the time of the birth of Augustus. According to this Roman historian of the early 2nd century AD, an omen was observed at Rome a few months prior to the birth of Augustus that a king for the Romans would be born, prompting the Senate to attempt a decree prohibiting the rearing of any male child born that year. However, senators who had pregnant wives apparently prevented the decree from being enacted so that they might be the father of the prophesied king (Suetonius, *Augustus*).

Therefore, the order to execute all two-year-old-and-younger male children in Bethlehem in order to prevent a prophesied king from taking the throne is to be expected from what is known about Herod in similar situations, policies of the period, and especially his violent, paranoid psyche near the end of his life.

In addition to precedents and consistent behavior, there are ancient sources that refer to or perhaps allude to the "Massacre of the Innocents" or the slaughter of babies in Bethlehem ordered by Herod the Great. The most ambiguous source comes from a document typically considered an apocryphal Jewish text, often referred to as the Assumption of Moses, that may have been written in the 1st century AD. Although the earliest known copy of this text exists in a 6th-century Latin manuscript, based on its mention by earlier authors Athanasius and Origen, and certain linguistic features, it is likely that it was originally composed in Greek in the 1st century and then translated. While not explicitly referring to the event in the Gospel of Matthew, the author wrote about Herod in a prophetic style, recording that an insolent king would succeed the Hasmoneans, and that he would slay the old and the young (Anonymous, *Assumption of Moses*).

Because the immediate context of this statement compares Herod to the pharaoh who ordered the execution of the male Hebrew babies in Egypt about the time of the birth of Moses, it is plausible that the author is referring directly to an instance in which Herod ordered the execution of male children two years old and younger in Bethlehem (Exodus 1:15-16; Matthew 2:16). A 2nd-century apocryphal gospel also mentions that Herod sent agents to murder the male children two years old and under in the vicinity of where Jesus was born after realizing he had been tricked by the magi (Anonymous, *Protoevangelium of James*).

Finally, a pagan Roman author, writing about AD 400, also refers back to the "Massacre of the Innocents" by Herod. He famously recorded the saying of Augustus, "I would rather be Herod's pig than his son" (Macrobius, *Saturnalia* 2.4). More importantly, just before this quote, Ambrosius related that Caesar

Augustus heard about how King Herod had ordered boys in Syria under the age of two years to be put to death, including the king's son—which could have been a conflation with the execution of Herod's adult sons about the same time, or simply a reference to Herod also killing his own sons.

While the "Massacre of the Innocents" is not recorded in major Roman historical works of the 1st century AD, the event is attested from a variety of ancient Roman sources outside of the Gospel of Matthew and through authors of differing religious beliefs. Therefore, the evidence from ancient written sources indicates that rather than an allegory, mistake, or conflation of events, the "Massacre of the Innocents" recorded by Matthew was an actual historical event.

THE DEATH OF HEROD THE GREAT

Herod I, or Herod the Great, was a Roman client king of Judea who reigned for approximately 37 years (ca. 40–4 BC), following a term as governor of Galilee, but only ruling from Jerusalem beginning in 37 BC. Herod, who was probably born ca. 74 BC, lived to about the age of 70. After a reign filled with assassinations, execution, and political intrigue, Herod died in 4 BC. Josephus described Herod's symptoms as extremely painful and with inflamed entrails, an intense appetite, and edema of the feet and belly (Josephus, *Antiquities*). These pains were apparently so unbearable that Herod tried to commit suicide but was stopped by his cousin, Achiabus. However, at his magnificent palace complex in Jericho, soon after an eclipse of the moon typically dated by astronomers to March of 4 BC, Herod the Great died after a prolonged sickness of what is thought to be kidney disease.

Herod had also left instructions that upon his death, many influential Judeans who had been recently rounded up and imprisoned in the hippodrome in Jericho were to be executed. This seems to have been both an act of vengeance and a way to force mourning in the land, appearing as if the people could be mourning Herod even though they would be instead mourning the results of his orders. Fortunately for a great many people, the command to execute the prisoners was disobeyed, and this wish was not enforced by the heirs of Herod the Great.

Although in many ways a tyrant, Herod also kept order in his kingdom and made it a prosperous place. After Herod died, though, the situation in Judea unraveled. Due to confusion over his will, his failed policies, paranoia, and violence, riots broke out after his death, and the kingdom was thrown into anarchy for a period. Out of this emerged the brutality of Archaelaus, one of his sons and the short-lived Ethnarch of Judea.

Josephus wrote extensively about the life of Herod the Great, including the period and circumstances surrounding his death. He gained much of his knowledge of Herod by utilizing the *Histories* of Nicolaus of Damascus, a close friend of Herod and an eyewitness to many events who also relied on autobiographical knowledge from Herod's own writings (Josephus, *Antiquities* 14-17). Josephus is also known to have consulted Herod's memoir. Because of the use of autobiographical sources, witnesses, and other primary sources from the 1st century, the material about Herod the Great found within the writings of Josephus should be considered extremely accurate. It is highly unlikely that Josephus miscalculated major events in the life of Herod by two or three years, or contradicted himself when writing about Roman-period Judea in which he lived only decades after Herod the Great. Herod's reign is also anchored chronologically by events attested outside of the writings of Josephus, such as an important visit of Augustus in 20 BC (Cassius Dio, *Roman History*).

The standard lunar-eclipse date associated with the death of Herod is attached to a lunar eclipse of March 13, 4 BC. This eclipse may not be the most reliable event to base the entire chronology of his death upon, but with other chronological anchors the eclipse can give a probable date of death. While it is unclear whether it was full or partial, or if it was recorded primarily as an omen, it is the only eclipse mentioned in Josephus.

However, the chronology of Herod's death can be determined by other means. All three regnal dates of his successors match a coronation date of 4 BC, since their reign lengths are recorded and their ending years are synchronized with Roman chronology. The ten-year reign of Archelaus was recorded as spanning from the death of Herod and the time he was declared king to his exile in AD 6, meaning the rule of Archelaus was dated from 4 BC when his father died (Josephus, *Antiquities*; Josephus, *Wars*). The reign, exile, and chronology for Archelaus were also noted by Strabo in the 1st century and Cassius Dio in the 2nd century (Strabo, *Geography*; Cassius Dio, *Roman History*).

It is also relevant to note that Archelaus would not have exercised royal authority before the death of Herod the Great because Herod was extremely paranoid and possessive about his kingship, demonstrated by many political murders, including his own sons, and multiple versions of his will. Josephus also mentions that Philip the Tetrarch died after a 37-year reign in the twentieth year of Tiberius or AD 33, equaling 4 BC for the beginning of Philip's reign.

Finally, there is Antipas, whose reign dates are confirmed by numismatic data from the coins he minted, along with the records of Josephus. The latest coins of Antipas are "year 43," then he was removed from power and exiled by Caligula in AD 39, with his territory given to Agrippa I by Caligula, not by Claudius who became emperor in AD 41. This means the reign of Antipas started in 4 BC from the death of Herod the Great (Josephus, *Antiquities* 18.240-252 and *War* 2.181-183). There is also no evidence whatsoever of a Herodian coregency with any of Herod's sons from 4 BC to 1 BC.

Thus, standard chronology dates the death of Herod to 4 BC and places the birth of Jesus before this time, as Luke relates that Herod the Great was still king just before the birth of Jesus. Matthew specifies that Herod died a significant amount of time after the birth, while Jesus and his family were in Egypt (Matthew 2:14-16). Alternative theories place Herod's death as late as 1 BC, but these conflict with historical and numismatic evidence.

The crux of the recalibration of King Herod's chronology, which would affect the chronology of Jesus significantly, rests upon a redating of Philip the Tetrarch and recalibrating Antipas, Archelaus, and Herod to fit the revision. This theory relies upon an obscure textual variant in a manuscript copy of Josephus that substitutes the twenty-second year of Tiberius for the twentieth year of Tiberius, so that Philip's 37-year reign would have begun in 2 BC or 1 BC instead of 4 BC (Beyer, *Chronos, Kairos, Christos II*).

Josephus may confuse the exact timing of a few Parthian events around Philip's death, but if so, he does in general and not exact terms. While the textual variant certainly exists, it is found only in a single 12th-century Latin manuscript copy of Josephus—no others contain this variant. The best manuscripts of Josephus are considered to be Codex Ambrosianae F 128 and Vaticanus Graecus 984, dating to the 11th and 14th centuries and in the original Greek language.

Finally, the only empire-wide census that took place near the birth of Jesus was announced in 8 BC, and perhaps took a year or two to be conducted. So, unless one relies on an obscure textual variant that contradicts all other data, or unless one can demonstrate a reason to shift the entire Roman chronology three years, there is no need to move the death of Herod to a later year. Thus, Herod the Great died in 4 BC, probably in March, after a bout with a painful disease that may have contributed to his increase in paranoia and violence during his final years. Once Herod was dead and it was safe for Jesus, Joseph led his family back to the land of Israel, but he was careful to avoid Judea where Archelaus was now ruling, and settled the family in Nazareth (Matthew 2:19-23).

Remains of the mausoleum of Herod at Herodium

After King Herod the Great died in 4 BC, his corpse was transported from his palace at Jericho to his fortress palace of Herodium, near Bethlehem, to be buried. Prior to his death, Herod had made arrangements that his final resting place would be a mausoleum constructed at Herodium around 10 BC. However, Herod had chosen and built Herodium long before in memory of his great victory over the Parthians there (Josephus, *Wars*).

When the funeral procession from Jericho arrived at Herodium to bury Herod, he was clothed in purple, wore a diadem and golden crown, and had a scepter in his right hand (Josephus, *Wars*). Herod was then interred in a sarcophagus that was placed in his mausoleum. Before the possible discovery of Herod's tomb, archaeologists and historians agreed that it was built at Herodium, but scholars were and continue to be divided on whether the mausoleum was located in lower or upper Herodium.

When remains of a mausoleum were finally discovered on the hill of Herodium, including the sarcophagus shattered into hundreds of red limestone fragments, some with rosette designs common on tombs, ossuaries, and sarcophagi of the period, the search for the tomb of Herod seemed to be over.

Reconstruction of the fragments revealed an original sarcophagus measuring about 2.5 meters (over 8 feet) long, topped with a triangular cover. The craftsmanship of the sarcophagus was elaborate, but not on the level of famous monumental sarcophagi such as the one made for Alexander the Great. Further, no inscription was discovered on the fragments that could identify the deceased. However, the intentional and intense destruction of the sarcophagus is consistent with what many residents of Judea would have done to the burial place of Herod in retaliation for his tyrannical and violent acts, his friendship with the Romans, and his syncretism with Hellenistic and Roman culture and religion.

Materials discovered in the area of the mausoleum and sarcophagus, such as pottery and coins, along with the writings of Josephus, demonstrate that the site was occupied during the first Judean revolt against Rome from ca. AD 66–73 (Josephus, *Wars*). However, it is far more likely that the tomb of Herod was desecrated soon after he died rather than 70 years later when the generations that knew his rule were no longer alive. Rather, this probably happened decades earlier—perhaps as soon as the Herodian ethnarch Archelaus was exiled and the Roman prefect Coponius took over Judea in about AD 6 (Josephus, *Antiquities*).

The mausoleum itself, while partially destroyed, was obviously made with precision and in the style of monumental Hellenistic tombs of the period. Built against the side of the mountain, the base of the mausoleum was about 30 feet by 30 feet and has been estimated at approximately 80 feet high. It was built of the shining white limestone seen throughout Jerusalem and typical of monumental structures built by Herod. In design and stone, the mausoleum is similar to the 1st-century BC "Tomb of Absalom" in Jerusalem.

The elaborate sarcophagus probably belonging to Herod the Great

To reach the mausoleum, a ramp and staircase beginning in the lower palace complex and winding around the mountain was constructed. In addition to the red sarcophagus tentatively identified as that of Herod, the remains of two white limestone sarcophagi were found around the tomb. These have been suggested as belonging to Malthace, Herod's fourth wife and mother of Archelaus, and Glaphyra, the second wife of Archelaus. Since Archelaus took over the rule of Judea following his father's death, it is plausible that the others buried at Herodium were closely related to him (Matthew

2:22). Bone fragments were also found around the tomb, demonstrating that people had indeed been interred there rather than it being only an intended burial place.

While it is certain that Herod the Great was buried at Herodium and the currently known evidence is convincing, many scholars have also challenged the identification of the mausoleum on the mountainside as the tomb of Herod. Criticisms include the lack of an inscription to substantiate the claim, the supposed modesty of the tomb, and the location of the mausoleum.

It seems obvious that this tomb belonged to one of the Herodians, but alternate suggestions place the tomb of Herod at the top of the mountain or in another area of lower Herodium. However, since no other structure clearly identified as a tomb has yet to be discovered at the site, and no sarcophagi have been found in any other building at Herodium, it is probable that the desecrated tomb of King Herod the Great has been discovered.

JUDEA AND GALILEE AFTER HEROD

Following the death and burial of Herod the Great in about March of 4 BC, the kingdom of Herod was eventually divided among three of his sons and his sister. But due to confusion about the will and a power struggle, legal intervention by Rome was necessary and months elapsed. Herod had changed his will many times due to his paranoia and the execution of some of his sons, so the final form of his will had not been approved by Caesar Augustus prior to his death. This predictably led to a dispute between two of his sons, Antipas and Archelaus, who each thought he should become the next king.

These two sons traveled to Rome, and while most supported Antipas because of the cruel character and acts of Archelaus, Augustus followed the final form of Herod's will and split the kingdom among four family members. The journey to Rome by Archelaus to secure what he believed to be his kingdom, and the negative attitude the people of Judea had toward Archelaus, may have been alluded to by Jesus in the parable of the minas (cf. Luke 19:12-27).

The end result of the dispute and appeal to Augustus was that none of Herod's heirs received the title *king*. Instead, three of his sons and his sister were allotted territories to rule with lesser titles. Archelaus received Judea, which also included the areas of Idumea to the south and Samaria to the north. Archelaus was called *ethnarch*, or ruler of a people, and fittingly his portion was largest. Antipas received Galilee and Peraea and was called *tetrarch*, or ruler over a

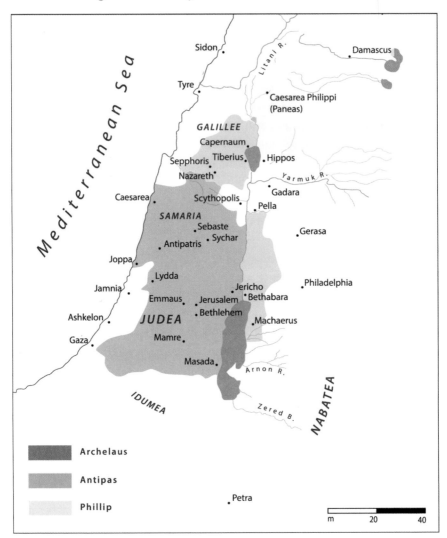

Regions ruled by Archelaus, Antipas, and Philip after the death of Herod the Great and division of his former kingdom

fourth. Philip was also called *tetrarch* and ruled the regions of Gaulanitis, Trachonitis, Batanaea, and Panias in the northeast. Salome I, the sister of Herod, was referred to as *toparch*, or ruler of a place, as she was given cities and their surrounding areas in the Gaza region and just north of Jericho, including Jabneh, Ashdod and Phasaelis. This "Herodian Tetrarchy" as it is often called due to the splitting into fourths only lasted until AD 6 when Rome took direct rule over the Judea region and made it a province of the Empire. Coins and the records of Josephus attest to these titles, some of which are also found in the Gospels (cf. Matthew 2:22; Luke 3:1).

In Judea, Archelaus, honored on the coins he issued as Herod the Ethnarch, ruled only from 4 BC to AD 6 due to his cruel, violent, and self-serving nature. Archelaus replaced several high priests in Jerusalem (Josephus, *Antiquities* 17.339); diverted water from Neara to his new palace at Jericho (Josephus, *Antiquities* 17.340); married his brother's wife, Glaphyra (Josephus, *Antiquities* 17.341); and retaliated against an angry crowd of Pharisees during Passover, attempting to thwart a possible rebellion by executing about 3000 of them (Josephus, *Antiquities* 17.213-218).

Bronze prutah coin issued by Herod Archelaus with his family name "Herod"

Archelaus is mentioned by name only once in the Gospels, but based on information from other ancient sources, the reason Joseph decided to avoid Judea and the rule of Archelaus in favor of Galilee and Antipas is obvious (Matthew 2:19-23). After experiencing the tyranny of Archelaus, a delegation of Judeans and Samaritans traveled to Rome in order to complain and hopefully convince Rome to depose him (Josephus, *Antiquities* 17.342-344). Even Philip and Antipas apparently brought accusations against Archelaus to Caesar Augustus (Dio, *Historia*, LV 27.6).

Finally, in AD 6 he was banished to Gaul and his territory became the province of Judea (Iudaea) directly under the control of the Romans. Thus, Herodian rule of Judea ended. The first prefect of this new province was a Roman named Coponius, who ruled primarily from Caesarea Maritima. Meanwhile, the adjacent areas, ruled by Antipas, Salome I, and Philip, and the Decapolis cities, were not part of the province and only under indirect Roman rule. The Roman prefects continued to govern Judea Province until AD 41, when Agrippa I was temporarily given authority there until AD 44, after which Roman procurators governed the province.

In Galilee, Herod Antipas ruled from ca. 4 BC to AD 39. While typically referred to as Antipas in order to distinguish him from others bearing the name "Herod," the Gospels refer to him as Herod or Herod the tetrarch—a name he adopted in ca. AD 6 (Matthew 14:1; Mark 6:14; Luke 3:1). Philo, although not mentioning him by name, alludes to Herod Antipas in passing as one of the tetrarch sons of King Herod who were in power over various regions of Judea Province during the time of Pontius Pilate (Philo of Alexandria, *Embassy to Gaius* 300).

Early in Antipas's reign as tetrarch, John the Baptizer rebuked him for marrying Herodias, because she had been married to a brother of Antipas (Mark 6:14-18). This eventually resulted in the execution of John after the birthday party of Antipas. As a result, his popularity with certain segments of the population was abysmal, and even Josephus states that public opinion generally regarded his defeat in the war with Nabatea as punishment from God for the unjust execution of John (Josephus, *Antiquities* 18).

However, historical sources suggest that Antipas otherwise lived marginally in line with Judaism and never attempted to do anything drastically offensive, such as building Roman temples, putting his face or the emperor's face on a coin, or erecting statues and other images in the area of the temple—all things done by other Herodian rulers.

As tetrarch of Galilee from 4 BC to AD 39, Antipas was in power during both of the ministries of John and Jesus, and he was even involved in the trial of Jesus. After an initial encounter with Pilate, Jesus was taken to Herod Antipas, the local ruler of Galilee where Jesus had lived most of his life (Luke 23:8-12). Although extremely curious about Jesus, once they met, Antipas apparently had no interest in Jesus being executed.

In the Gospels, Jesus makes reference to Antipas at least twice in less than flattering terms. Once Jesus compares him to a reed shaking in the wind and

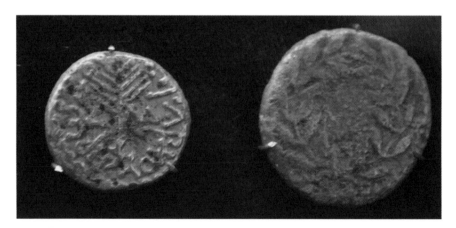

Coin of Herod Antipas issued AD 30 reading "Herod tetrarch"

one who wears soft clothing and lives in a luxurious royal palace, which appears to be a reference to one of the coins of Antipas featuring a reed, as if he is swayed to whatever direction the political wind is blowing (Luke 7:24-25).

Another time, when a group of Pharisees told Jesus that Antipas was seeking to kill him, Jesus refers to Antipas as a fox (Luke 13:31-35). A survey of ancient Roman, Greek, and Hebrew sources on the metaphorical use of fox suggests that this was intended to convey that the person was crafty, deceitful, cowardly, and lacked true power. Later, Jesus may even reference the epic military failure of Antipas against Nabatea, although most scholars date that battle to AD 34 or later rather than AD 33 (Luke 14:31; Josephus, *Antiquities* 18.111-113).

Antipas fortified and established his capital first at Sepphoris, and then decided to build his new capital city of Tiberias on the west side of the Sea of Galilee in about AD 19 (John 6:23). Overall, Antipas was a stable and relatively fair ruler who lasted much longer than his brothers, although he was eventually banished to Gaul in AD 39 when Agrippa accused him of treason during the tumultuous reign of Emperor Caligula.

Salome I, sister of Herod the Great, was given a section in the region of Gaza and another small territory north of Jericho when the kingdom was divided among the heirs. As these were all cities or small places, she was a *toparch*, or ruler of a place. While Salome was nominally the queen of this region and lived in a palace at Ashkelon, she likely exercised little authority and merely followed the instructions of Rome. When Salome died in AD 10, according to her will her lands were designated to pass to Julia, wife of Augustus, and essentially became part of the Roman province of Judea.

Philip, or Philip the Tetrarch, ruled the region to the east of the Sea of Galilee, including Caesarea Philippi from 4 BC to AD 34. He was a son of Herod the Great and the half brother of Antipas and Archelaus. Some scholars do not consider Philip the Tetrarch part of the Herodian Dynasty because there is currently no evidence that he used the name "Herod." However, he was an heir of Herod the Great and received a piece of the kingdom (Luke 3:1).

Jesus performed several miracles in this region but never appeared to have any problems with the local authorities. Perhaps because this was a Hellenistic area, and very few Judeans who practiced the Law would have lived there, the majority of the people had no issue with Jesus as God—or in the Hellenistic mindset, a god—teaching new ideas and performing miracles.

Philip had a peaceful reign of approximately 37 years during which he erected temples, named places after the emperor and his family, and remained on good terms with the Romans. Of the immediate heirs of Herod the Great, Philip appears to have had the most tranquil time in power, and unlike his brothers Archelaus and then Antipas, was never deposed or exiled.

AT HOME IN NAZARETH

Although several famous and significant events in the life of Jesus occurred in the city of Jerusalem, Jesus spent most of his years in the village of Nazareth. The discovery and excavation of an ancient house in Nazareth near the Church of the Annunciation not only provides additional evidence that Nazareth was a town occupied during the 1st century and the time of Jesus, but analysis of the find also shows that a family observing the Law of Moses lived there during that time. Interestingly, this house had another church built around it during the Byzantine period, and it was revered as the childhood home of Jesus. The Church of the Nutrition, as it is called, and its accompanying 1st-century house designated "Structure 1," are located in Nazareth beneath the convent of the Sisters of Nazareth, which is up the street from the Church of the Annunciation.

When constructed, the house was cut into the rocky hillside, and the rest of the structure was built with stone and mortar. It is a courtyard-style house, and

The "Church of the Nutrition" and 1st-century ruins in Nazareth

one of the doorways stands intact. The ground floor was chalk and a staircase led to an upper floor. Stone, being prevalent in this area, was the most obvious and economical material for construction.

Inside the house, remnants of cooking pots, a spindle whorl for textile manufacture, and ritual limestone vessels were discovered. These limestone vessels are important for identifying the residents as people who observed the Law of Moses, since earthenware vessels can become ritually impure and are then intentionally destroyed, but stone vessels and other materials such as metal do not, therefore serving as a useful indicator of the traditions of the people (Leviticus 6:28; 11:33; 15:12). Various stone vessels are found throughout ancient Israel and Judea of the Roman period, typically indicating where populations of Judeans observing the Law resided, in contrast to people who followed Hellenistic culture.

The house was then abandoned later in the 1st century AD, suggesting that the residents had moved elsewhere. When a church was constructed around the house in approximately the 5th century AD during the Byzantine period, decorative mosaic floors, marble column capitals, four apses, and possibly an altar in the Byzantine style were used. An inscription carved into marble appearing to read "Christo" was also discovered.

Coins from the 4th century discovered in the cave church structure imply that a community of Christians in Nazareth met in the cave church at least as early as the 4th century AD at the beginning of the Byzantine period, when many of the most important churches associated with the life of Jesus were built. This intricately decorated Byzantine church, itself built over an older cave church, shows an even earlier tradition of reverence around the original house.

A Latin text called *De Locis Sanctis* from ca. AD 670, based on a pilgrimage by Bishop Arculf, describes Nazareth as having two churches, one of which is beside a house. It goes on to describe the house as the one in which the Lord was nourished in his infancy. The *Itinerarium Egeriae*, written by the pilgrim Egeria about the 4th century AD, mentions a large and splendid cave in Nazareth, apparently made into a church or shrine, where Mary the mother of Jesus had lived. While it is possible that Jesus could have resided in this house in Nazareth, more importantly the archaeological discoveries conclusively demonstrate that Nazareth was a Judean village during the 1st century and the life of Jesus, reflective of the title "Jesus of Nazareth," and not a location later added into the story.

During the majority of his life, Jesus lived in Nazareth, where he and his family presumably resided in a house similar to that of other common people living in ancient Judea, Samaria, or Galilee during the 1st century. Throughout the Gospel narratives, various houses are often mentioned in the context of the life of Jesus, the disciples, and events in his ministry. Knowledge of domestic life during this time is helpful in better understanding the historical, cultural, and social context of the Gospels. While reference to a standard house plan for the Roman period in the region of Judea is impossible due to personalization of each house, general characteristics can be derived from archaeological sources.

Just as houses in the region from earlier periods were typically built on stone foundations with mud brick, the houses of the common people in the 1st centuries BC and AD also employed this construction method, although it seems many houses were also constructed primarily of stone (Botha, "Houses in the World of Jesus" 41; Matthew 7:24-25). Mud brick, however, is not resistant to water, so coating the house with plaster at regular intervals was often required.

Since stone is easily available in the region while wood is not, stone was a primary building material. In the region of Galilee, basalt is the most abundant type of stone, while throughout Judea a white limestone is found almost everywhere. For a person of the lower or middle classes, uncut or roughly hewn fieldstones would usually be used, rather than carefully shaped ashlar blocks, which required much more work and skill.

The house was usually constructed as a series of rooms built around or adjacent to a courtyard, and the house was typically square or rectangular rather than round. Houses had few doors and windows, and both the doors and windows were quite small, with an emphasis on structural integrity of the house, weather, and security. Because of this, door lintels and frames were sturdy and windows were usually placed high.

Houses often had an upper floor, although these may have covered only part of the house and sometimes were simply a rooftop balcony (Mark 14:13-16; Luke 12:3). The upper floor was reached by a ladder or sometimes a staircase, depending on the need for space and the wealth of the owner.

Inside, the walls may be coated with plaster, or in the homes of the wealthy may even have painted frescoes in colors such as red, black, and blue. A typical floor was just dirt, probably overlaid with grass or rugs, but many houses had floors made of stones or a layer of plaster.

Most roofs were constructed over wood beams using branches and grass covered with mud or clay, and often coated with pitch or plaster to seal the roof, which would have to be redone periodically (Mark 2:4). The homes of the wealthy used roof tiles, or at times employed a vaulted stone structure.

Houses also varied widely in size due to family size and wealth. Houses the equivalent of a small studio apartment have been found, while houses accurately described as mansions have also been discovered. Courtyards were a typical feature of many but not all houses, ranging from a peasant farmer to a wealthy aristocrat (Beebe, "Domestic Architecture and the New Testament" 91; Mark 14:54).

Houses of the common classes apparently had guest rooms at least some of the time, and people were not always restricted to tiny spaces in their houses (Mark 14:13-15; Luke 2:7). Depending on the location of the home and the economic status of the owner, a house may have been a private residence surrounded by streets or land, or it may have been attached to other residences as part of an *insula* or apartment complex type of construction. These *insulae* were found all over cities in the Roman world—including Judea Province and Galilee—due to their preservation of space and building materials. In villages and in the country, however, houses in Judea and Galilee would have generally been stand-alone buildings.

Both domestic and commercial activities usually took place within the house, such as pottery making, sewing, tool making, carpentry, and tanning hides. Houses were lit by natural light during the day, and by oil lamps set on stands, hung from the ceiling, or placed in alcoves built into the walls (Matthew 5:15). The ground floor seems to have been primarily the public area and work areas, while the upper rooms were the private living quarters. A table may have been present in the main roofed room of the house (Luke 14:10).

Houses often had a cistern or a water storage area carved into the bedrock below or adjacent to the house. Round ovens, placed in the ground and constructed of clay, were typically found in courtyard areas of houses. In wealthier homes or those with more space, ritual baths or even plastered bathtubs are sometimes found (Luke 11:38). Toilets have been found only in a small percentage of houses.

Using caves adjacent to, under, or integrated into part of the house was also a construction technique which made the cave a room, such as a cellar (Luke 11:33). These caves cut into the hillside or underground were often transformed into storage areas, a section of the house, or as a place to keep animals, where a stone manger would also have been placed or carved (Luke 2:16). Alternatively, animals may have been kept adjacent to the house in a pen made of field stones. People had windows, doors, rugs or stone floors, plastered walls, a roof, private rooms, a water source, light sources, an oven, furniture, and sometimes even bathtubs and toilets.

Village life in Judea and Galilee during the time of Jesus was similar in many ways to that of villages and towns throughout antiquity in various parts of the world. The main economy was based on agriculture, people lived in small and simple houses, the general population earned very little money, most were employed in a trade while very few were scholars, and the government of the nation usually seemed far removed. Although probably over half of the population of Judea lived in villages or towns, these people had almost no influence on the politics of the region, as nearly all the power and wealth was held by a few people in the cities of Jerusalem and Caesarea.

The elite of the cities, not just wealthier but more Hellenized, often looked down upon the villagers as ignorant, poor, and uncivilized, so a clear rift existed between rural and urban. However, the cities were dependent upon the villages for survival, since the food supply came from the rural areas, and villagers often paid taxes or rents to the owners or government in the cities.

The individual village settlements were small, with most having a population of less than 2000 people, but due to their close proximity to each other, especially around the Sea of Galilee, village life was not so isolated. On the surface, villages throughout the Roman Empire in the 1st century were not substantially different from a technological and economic standpoint. In fact, due to the spread of Hellenism and the Roman way of life, there was probably much more uniformity across much of the world than earlier in history.

However, village life in the time of Jesus was also unique in aspects related to religion due to monotheism, the Law of Moses, and the dedication of much of the population to retain their beliefs and practices passed down from ancient Israel. Therefore, the most obvious differences between Judean villages and other settlements throughout the Roman Empire include the worship of one God, food laws, ritual washing, and the synagogue. Since nearly every other culture in the Empire at this time was polytheistic, the monotheism of Israel was an exception—and a uniqueness that most Romans not only disagreed with but often could not even understand.

In the archaeological record, differences in the religious practices of Judean villages are manifested in the presence of ritual baths (*mikveh*), stone vessels, synagogues rather than temples or shrines, the absence of pig bones, and the lack of human or animal images in artwork. Even small villages such as Nazareth had a synagogue—which would have served not only as a house of prayer, teaching, and worship commonly used on the Sabbath, but also as a community and educational center (Matthew 13:54; Mark 6:1-2).

Stone vessels were common in Judea for ritual purposes, since according to the Law of Moses stone would not become impure, unlike pottery (John 2:6). The Gospel of Mark even includes an explanatory note on Judean purity customs, since the Roman reader would be totally unfamiliar with this cultural practice (Mark 7:3-4). The parchments and papyri have not survived the centuries, but each village would have had at least one copy of the Bible, and probably various commentaries and apocryphal literature also.

The common village resident was employed in some form of agriculture or a trade directly relevant to daily life, such as making pottery, construction, weaving, baking, tool making, and medicine. Working in the fields, processing the crops, and tending to the animals were the most typical jobs, while physicians, scholars, soldiers, and government workers were rare. Typical agricultural jobs included planting, harvesting, and threshing grain, pressing olives and grapes for oil and wine, and herding sheep and goats (Matthew 21:33-34; 25:32; Mark 4:26-29; Luke 2:8; 16:4-7; John 10:1-5). Those that lived on a lake or the ocean were often employed in fishing, since it was an efficient form of food production that required little technology (Luke 5:1-10). The agricultural and pastoral lifestyle so prevalent in Roman-period Judea is the reason that Jesus uses so many references to agriculture, fishing, and herding in his teaching.

Soldiers were stationed in key locations, such as Capernaum, but in a typical rural village there would rarely be any military or official Roman presence (Luke 7:1-10). Some villages had an inn that travelers could use, but this was uncommon in rural Judean settlements as most travelers would stay with family or close friends. The inn during this period was more common in Hellenistic culture or those towns that had adopted Hellenistic practices (Luke 10:33-35).

Jesus and Joseph are often called carpenters, although the word used in the Gospels (*tekton*) can refer to any craftsman, and examination of ancient and current Nazareth suggests stone masonry to be a craft that might have occupied much of their time (Matthew 13:54-56; Mark 6:1-3; cf. Justin Martyr, *Dialogue with Trypho* 88). Besides food producers, craftsmen were probably the second most common profession.

While professional scholars and teachers were uncommon, Judean villages usually had a much higher rate of literacy than villages of other areas in the Roman Empire due to the centrality of learning and studying the Bible in the culture. Physicians were scarce, but probably at least one person in a nearby group of villages or towns was a skilled doctor (Mark 5:25-27).

Tax collectors, though unpopular and a profession reserved for only a small percentage of the population, lived or worked in many villages (Matthew 9:9-11). According to the Gospels and the Mishnah, tax collectors were among the professions that were thought of derisively, although many of the professions listed in the Mishnah, such as shepherds, were considered contemptuous only by the religious elite.

Clothing was very standardized, utilizing simple tunics, cloaks, and sandals or shoes, and a particular trade or profession could not usually be distinguished based on clothing.

The synagogue, situated in a central location, often additionally functioned as a school, and boys especially in 1st-century Judea were educated in the Bible in addition to their trade or profession. However, this education was not the equivalent of the professional scribes and religious scholars, who considered the typical literate villager to be uneducated since they did not study under one of the masters to become a scholar (John 7:14-15; Acts 22:3).

Since in the Judean villages the entire population usually held the same beliefs and practiced the same customs, ideological conflict rarely surfaced and the community typically had close ties. For example, the whole village normally participated in weddings and funerals. Burials would take place outside of the village, while weddings were normally hosted at a house. Village entertainment

The 1st-century synagogue at Magdala

in Judea and Galilee involved singing, storytelling, and games, in contrast to a Hellenistic town, which would perform plays and host sporting events. While the first language of these villagers was Aramaic, with knowledge of Hebrew for reading the Bible, most of them probably had at least a basic knowledge of Koine Greek and perhaps even a little Latin.

Synagogues in the time of Jesus functioned as a place of study, worship, and community gathering. The Greek word *sunagoge* means "a bringing together or assembly," and in the context of a building in ancient Judea, it was a place of assembly or a meeting house. The origin of the synagogue building is debated among scholars, with differing views as to the time in which the synagogue was first established and used by the exiles who returned to Judah after the Babylonian captivity. Generally, the earliest date that synagogues are believed to have come into use is the 6th century BC during the Babylonian exile, while the majority of scholars prefer a date in the 3rd century BC due to the available evidence.

The need for an assembly building probably came about as a way for Judaism to survive in the Diaspora away from the temple in Jerusalem and the priestly system. While this appears to have arisen in the 3rd century BC, the rationale for establishing a system or place of gathering would be sensible in the context of the Babylonian captivity in the 6th century BC, when the temple was destroyed for 70 years and many of the people were living outside of Judah.

However, in the time of Ezra and Nehemiah in the 5th century BC, even though public assembly and reading of the Bible took place, there are no indications that a synagogue building or system was in use (Nehemiah 8:1-6). While the practices of communal prayer and study obviously preceded this time, the earliest evidence for an actual synagogue building is found on a dedication inscription from the 3rd century BC in Egypt. The stone inscription from Schedia in northern Egypt mentions Judeans dedicating the synagogue during the reign of Ptolemy III Euergetes around 246–221 BC (CIJ 2.1440). Numerous other synagogue dedication inscriptions in Egypt have been found that date to the 2nd century BC and later. What appears to be a Samaritan synagogue from the middle of the 2nd century BC was excavated on the island of Delos in the Aegean Sea, while a possible synagogue from the 3rd century BC in Stobi, Macedonia, was also discovered.

There are a variety of ideas about why the synagogue came into use. Because the earliest evidence for synagogues comes from the Diaspora, the institution may have developed out of a need for a place of religious community for practitioners of Judaism since the temple was far away in Jerusalem and most of the people around them were pagans. In ancient Judea, a synagogue from the early 1st century BC was discovered at the Hasmonean palace in Jericho, and remains of other synagogue buildings from the late 1st century BC and 1st century AD have now been uncovered in places like Capernaum, Magdala, Gamla, Masada, Herodium, Modi'in (Khirbet Umm el-'Umdan), and probably Caesarea Maritima, Qumran, Qiryat Sefer, Khirbet Qana, Beth-Shemesh, et-Tuwani, and Chorazin. First-century AD remains were finally discovered at Chorazin recently, including the remains of a stone "platform" underneath the ruins of the 3rd-century synagogue, indicating that the synagogue rebuild at Chorazin was similar to the situation at Capernaum. The Caesarea Maritima 1st-century synagogue was even mentioned by Josephus as a building adjacent to a plot of ground owned by a Greek (Josephus, *Wars* 2.285). Although the Herodium and Masada synagogues date to about AD 66 or later, after the time of Jesus, and the Jericho synagogue of the 1st century BC was probably not rebuilt, these three synagogues still attest to the presence and use of synagogue buildings in Judea during the Roman period. Minus those three exceptions, it is likely that the other synagogues were in existence during the time of Jesus, and when combined with the Theodotos inscription from Jerusalem, archaeological remains of as many as 12 synagogues from the time of Jesus have been discovered.

In the city of David area of ancient Jerusalem, an important and unique 1st-century AD inscription written in Greek and commemorating the construction of a synagogue was discovered. Found during excavations of a cistern, the limestone slab had either fallen in as a result of the AD 70 destruction of the city, or it was intentionally dumped in the cistern as a result of subsequent clearing and rebuilding activities during the Roman period. The stone measures 75 cm long and 43 cm high and 22 cm thick, features a carved border, and contains ten lines of Greek text (CIJ 2.1404).

The inscription, dating to before AD 70 and possibly as early as the time of Herod based on paleography and provenance, translates as "Theodotos, son of Vettenus, priest and *archisynagogos* (synagogue ruler), son of an *archisynagogos* and grandson of an *archisynagogos*, built the synagogue for the reading of the Law and for the teaching of the Commandments, and the hospice, the chambers, and the water fittings as a guesthouse for those in need from foreign places, which his fathers founded with the elders and Simonides."

This text makes it clear that a new synagogue in Jerusalem had been built

The Theodotos synagogue inscription from Jerusalem

on the same location as an earlier synagogue, matching a trend noticed from excavations of other ancient synagogues. The Theodotos dedication indicates synagogue buildings at that location went back multiple generations, indicating that a synagogue had been in use in Jerusalem from at least the 1st century BC. Perhaps not merely coincidence, this synagogue inscription was found in the same neighborhood as the Pool of Siloam, where a threat of being cast out of the synagogue is referenced in the John narrative about Jesus healing a blind man (John 9:1-22). Regardless, the Theodotos inscription demonstrates that at least one synagogue existed in Jerusalem around the time of Jesus.

Although this particular Jerusalem synagogue was funded and built by Judeans, that was not always the case in antiquity. Funding of synagogue construction by a foreign benefactor is known from ancient synagogue inscriptions, and the Gospel of Luke also relates that a Roman centurion in Capernaum paid for the synagogue to be built there (Luke 7:1-5). Therefore, according to the current archaeological evidence, known and probable synagogues existed in a total of ten cities of Judea and Galilee during the 1st century and approximate time of Jesus. The narratives in the Gospel accounts of Jesus visiting synagogues in various locations appear to be consistent with what archaeology has uncovered, and this is also a feature of society that written sources from the Roman period portray for Judea and Galilee.

By the 1st century AD and the time of Jesus, the synagogue was a major part of Judaism and synagogues were in use in cities and towns of Judea Province as well as other parts of the Roman Empire. First-century sources such as the Gospels, Acts, Josephus, and Philo mention synagogues in numerous locations, demonstrating that it was a common practice to establish a building for the worship of God, study of the Bible, and community gatherings not only in Judea, but also throughout many other areas of the Roman Empire (Josephus, *Wars* 2.285-291; Josephus, *Life* 280; Philo, *On Dreams* 2.127; Philo, *Flaccus* 45; Matthew 9:35; Mark 1:21; Luke 4:16; John 9:22; Acts 9:1-2).

The synagogue building was often designed to face toward Jerusalem, and while most appear to have been constructed in a rectangular fashion, analysis of ancient synagogues reveals that there was no standard architectural plan. Inside the synagogue were benches for seating, a platform or podium from which the scrolls would be read, and decoration such as mosaic floors, vine leaves, the menorah, and a manna jar (cf. Mark 12:38-40).

During the 1st century, the books of Moses were usually read in the synagogue every Sabbath (Acts 15:21). The Pharisees typically had control of the synagogue and could "cast out" anyone who did not agree with their theology (John 12:42-43; 16:2). According to ancient inscriptions and texts, the authority structure included officials or leaders and staff, while various qualified individuals were allowed to speak or teach (Luke 4:16-20; 13:10-17; John 18:19-20; Acts 13:13-15). Judgments and discipline were also often conducted in the synagogue, since it was the main place of religious authority and assembly besides the temple in Jerusalem (Matthew 10:17; Acts 22:17-21). Evidence from archaeology and ancient texts suggests that men and women worshipped together in the synagogue during antiquity. However, much of what is known about the particular liturgy that took place in the synagogue comes from the Mishnah and is reflective of the 2nd and 3rd centuries AD (Megilla 3:4–4:10).

Generally, the residents of the villages were much poorer than the average city dwellers, who were often part of the economic elite and connected to the wealth and power of the Roman government or the temple in Jerusalem. The average pay for a laborer in the villages was only one denarius or even less per day (Matthew 20:1-2). A Roman legionary was paid an annual salary of 225 denarii in the 1st century, although he also received other benefits and bonuses. About 300 denarii would buy an expensive bottle of perfume, but about 200 denarii might feed 5000 people and only 2 denarii could pay for lodging, food, and medical care for a short period of time (Mark 14:3-5; Luke 10:33-35; John

6:5-7). Since a denarius was 3.9 grams of silver at the time of Jesus, at modern prices this would equate to approximately $3.45 USD.

While an annual income of around $1240 might seem miniscule to many readers, not only is this figure similar to the average wage of many countries around the modern world, but the buying power in Roman-period Judea was magnitudes higher, and for basic food costs might be a difference of a factor of around 100. Bartering was used, but bronze and even silver coins were normal currency. Therefore, essential purchases such as food, lodging, and clothing were well within the means of a common laborer, but any luxury items were almost certainly out of the budget for an average person.

This division of wealth is apparent in examination of the pottery vessels, architecture, jewelry, and coins discovered in archaeological excavations. The exception to this trend is the presence of manor houses in rural Judea, which were owned by the wealthy who probably also had an urban residence. The wealthy in the cities ate more often and consumed more meat than the villagers, who normally ate two meals a day with bread as the main staple. However, the village population of Judea prospered enough that they were able to go up to Jerusalem for the major festivals (Luke 2:41-42).

Wine was the normal beverage, although often used in a much more diluted state than today. Its value was not so much in the taste but because the alcohol killed bacteria in the water and provided extra calories.

Streets were narrow and were either dirt or covered with small stones, although wealthier villages or towns had their main street paved with square stone slabs typical of Roman roads. Houses were small, and open space inside the village was very limited. Torches may have been placed around the main street at times, but once it was dark most villagers would be in their homes.

Because no sewer systems existed, villages probably had an unpleasant odor since sewage and garbage would be dumped in or adjacent to the village, and animals roaming the villages added to the variety of smells.

Daily life in a village of Judea or Galilee in the time of Jesus normally involved many hours of work, little pay, and perhaps only two meals. The conveniences and comforts of urban and modern life were usually absent, but the Sabbath and various holy days offered a time of rest, relaxation, and celebration.

SELECTED BIBLIOGRAPHY
(CHAPTER 2)

Beebe, H. Keith. "Domestic Architecture and the New Testament." *Biblical Archaeologist* 38, no. 3/4 (1975).

Blomberg, Craig. *Jesus and the Gospels*. Nashville: B&H Publishing, 2009.

Botha, Pieter. "Houses in the World of Jesus." *Neotestamentica* 32, no. 1 (1998).

Cohen-Tavor, Achia. Interview at Chorazin Excavations, 2020.

Evans, Craig. *Jesus and His World: The Archaeological Evidence*. Louisville: Westminster, 2012.

Filson, Floyd. "Ancient Greek Synagogue Inscriptions." *Biblical Archaeologist* 32, no. 2 (1969).

Galor, Katharina. "Domestic Architecture in Roman and Byzantine Galilee and Golan." *Near Eastern Archaeology* 66 (2003).

Gutman, J. *Ancient Synagogues: The State of Research*. Chico: Scholars, 1981.

Hirschfeld, Yizhar. "Early Roman Manor Houses in Judea." *Journal of Near Eastern Studies*. vol. 57, no. 3 (1998).

Hoehner, Harold. *Herod Antipas: A Contemporary of Jesus Christ*. Grand Rapids: Zondervan, 1980.

Kloppenborg, John. "The Theodotos Synagogue Inscription and the Problem of First-Century Synagogue Buildings." *Jesus and Archaeology*, ed. James Charlesworth. Grand Rapids: Eerdmans, 2006.

Kokkinos, Nikos. *The Herodian Dynasty*. London: Spink Books, 2010.

Levine, Lee. *The Ancient Synagogue*. New Haven: Yale University, 2005.

———. *Ancient Synagogues Revealed*. Jerusalem: Israel Exploration Society, 1981.

Liddell et al., *A Greek-English Lexicon*. Oxford: Clarendon, 1996.

Magness, Jodi. *Stone and Dung, Oil and Spit: Jewish Daily Life in the Time of Jesus*. Grand Rapids: Eerdmans, 2011.

Magness, Jodi. "Where Is Herod's Tomb at Herodium?" *Bulletin of the American Schools of Oriental Research* 322 (2001).

Maier, Paul. "Herod and the Infants of Bethlehem." *Chronos, Kairos, Christos II.* Macon: Mercer University Press, 1998.

Netzer, Ehud. "In Search of Herod's Tomb." *Biblical Archaeology Review* 37:1 (2011).

———. "A Synagogue from the Hasmonean Period Recently Exposed in the Western Plain of Jericho." *Israel Exploration Journal* 49, no. 3/4 (1999).

Reed, Jonathan. *Archaeology and the Galilean Jesus.* Harrisburg, PA: Trinity, 2000.

Richardson, Peter, and Amy Marie Fisher. *Herod: King of the Jews and Friend of the Romans.* New York: Routledge, 2017.

Shanks, Hershel. "Was Herod's Tomb Really Found?" *Biblical Archaeology Review* 40:3 (2014).

Stripling, Scott. "The Rise of the Synagogue in Biblical Times." *Bible and Spade* 33.3 (2020).

Vermes, Geza. *The Nativity: History and Legend.* New York: Doubleday, 2007.

Political Context, Baptism, and Galilee

I n the fifteenth year of Tiberius Caesar, Jesus of Nazareth was baptized and began his short but significant ministry, sending ripples across history and forever changing the world. According to the Gospel of Luke, in this same year, Pontius Pilatus was prefect of Judea Province, Herod Antipas was the tetrarch of Galilee, Philip was the tetrarch of Ituraea and Trachonitis, Lysanias was tetrarch of Abila, Caiaphas and Annas were high priests, and John the Baptizer was roaming the wilderness (Luke 3:1-2).

This information gives the political context for the life of Jesus in his final years and allows a specific chronological placement in conjunction with another passage from the Gospel of John about the number of years since Herod the Great had started rebuilding the temple in Jerusalem (John 2:20). According to Roman records, the fifteenth year of Tiberius would have started in September of AD 28 when counting from the death of Augustus, although arguments have also been made suggesting that the years mentioned by Luke could be counted from AD 12 or perhaps AD 13, after Tiberius returned from Germania and was given equal authority with Augustus (Suetonius, *The Lives of Twelve Caesars*).

Tiberius's sole rule as emperor was from AD 14–37, ending when he was assassinated at age 77 (Tacitus, *Annals*). He is mentioned by name only once in the Gospels, yet he is referred to by his adopted family name of Caesar multiple times, including the famous "render to Caesar" quotation about a denarius

Bust of Emperor Tiberius and famous "tribute" denarius of Tiberius

of Tiberius (e.g. Matthew 22:17-21; Mark 12:13-17; Luke 20:22-25; John 19:15). The date of his "fifteenth year" as described by Luke has significant bearing on the chronology of Jesus.

If Luke was counting from the time when Tiberius was made co-princeps with Augustus in AD 12, then the beginning of the ministry of Jesus would have been in about AD 26 or 27. The evidence for this view, however, may not be powerful enough to warrant a departure from the typical Roman system of reckoning. The primary evidence for an earlier beginning of the ministry of Jesus is found in a passage of Tertullian, written in the 2nd century AD. There, Tertullian stated that Jesus has been revealed since the twelfth year of Tiberius Caesar, perhaps indicating that Luke was counting from when Tiberius received shared powers in AD 12, but Tertullian counting from when Tiberius was sole emperor after the death of Augustus following September 18 of AD 14 (Tertullian, *Against Marcion,* Book 1, chapter 15). Yet, it is unclear if Tertullian was equating the time of the baptism of Jesus and the chronology in Luke with the revealing of Jesus.

Possibly relevant to this discussion are the coins issued by Pontius Pilatus in Judea, specifically coins bearing year 16 of Tiberius showing Empress Livia in contrast to coins bearing year 17 without Livia. If the death of Livia in AD 29 was reflected in her absence on coins, then year 16 or year 17 could have been her last year alive, meaning year 15 could coincide with either AD 27 or 28. There were coins of Tiberius beginning in AD 12, and he was granted equal powers with Augustus, but other evidence points to the fifteenth year of Tiberius universally referring to the period beginning in AD 14 when the Senate conferred upon him the official titles of his position as emperor.

For example, a chronologically significant coin from Antioch in Syria bears both regnal year 1 of Tiberius and year 45 of the Actian Era, which was AD 14. A passage of the historian Tacitus overlaps with this chronology as it recounts that the time when Caius Asinius Pollio and Caius Antistius Vetus began as consuls, January of AD 23, was in the ninth year of Tiberius (Tacitus, *Annals* Book IV).

A chronological marker in the Gospel of John, in an event set soon after the baptism of Jesus, also helps to pinpoint the correct date for the beginning of the ministry of Jesus. In an exchange on the Temple Mount, Jesus was told that it took 46 years to build the temple, which was a reference to the time when Herod the Great began a complete rebuild of the temple in Jerusalem (John 2:20). According to Josephus, Herod the Great began this construction project in the eighteenth year of his reign, which Josephus reckoned from the consulship of Agrippa and Gallus in 37 BC when Herod captured Jerusalem, had control of the region, and took the title of king (Josephus, *Antiquities* 15.380).

If the eighteenth year of Herod was 20 BC/19 BC, and if a full 46 years of construction had already taken place, this event with Jesus on the Temple Mount in the early days of his ministry would have been in about AD 28 (note that there is no "year 0" in the BC/AD system). Therefore, AD 28 in the fifteenth year counting from when Tiberius had exclusive powers and title of emperor appears to be the most likely year in which Jesus began his ministry. At this time Jesus was "about" 30 years old, or more specifically around 34 years old, depending on the exact date of his birth (Luke 3:23).

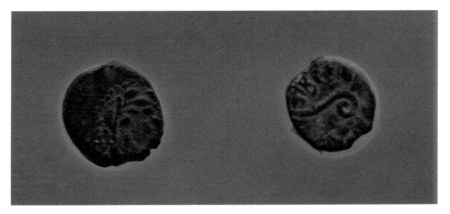

Year 17 coin of Pontius Pilate with lituus (augur staff), wreath, and name "Tiberius"

Tiberius, the most powerful political figure in the world during much of the life of Jesus, was the stepson of Caesar Augustus and the husband of Julia, daughter of Augustus. In AD 4, Augustus officially adopted him and he eventually became the obvious heir after the death and banishment of the other probable heirs. Tiberius was a successful general and political leader, but never seemed to have ambitions of political power. This carried over into his reign as emperor and his encouragement of Senate cooperation. Perhaps related to his introverted character, Tiberius retired to the island of Capri in AD 26, where he intended to remain in contact with Rome and manage the Empire. It is during this period that John would have been preaching, Jesus would have been baptized, and the public ministry of Jesus would have begun.

The Empire, meanwhile, was essentially ruled by Sejanus, commander of the Praetorian Guard. Sejanus took the opportunity to introduce modifications to the Praetorian Guard and obtain more power. He eventually became consul in AD 31, effectively ruling the Roman Empire (Suetonius, *The Lives of Twelve Caesars, Life of Tiberius* 65). There is a possibility that Pilate and Sejanus were somehow connected, as Pilate was appointed to replace Valerius Gratus (appointed by Tiberius) in AD 26, which is the year when Sejanus began exercising substantial control over the Empire. However, after several political purges, Sejanus was accused of a plot in AD 31 and subsequently executed (Josephus, *Antiquities* 18.181-250; Juvenal, *Satire* 10.67-72; Cassius Dio, *Roman History* 58.9-11).

After the AD 31 execution of Sejanus, things in Judea would have changed for Roman officials—cooperating with and pleasing the emperor would have been of utmost concern in those perilous times. This is the backdrop of what was a trap orchestrated by the Pharisees with the intent of depicting Jesus as treasonous toward the emperor (Matthew 22:15-22; Mark 12:13-17; Luke 20:19-26).

Pontius Pilatus, known also as Pilate, was a Roman politician of the early 1st century AD. Born in the Roman Empire as a citizen in the equites class, an aristocratic class below that of patrician, Pilate was eligible for many major political and military offices but could not achieve the rank of legate. During the early Empire period, the equites had a wealth threshold of 100,000 denarii, which was approximately equivalent to the annual salaries of 450 legionaries but less than half the threshold of the senatorial elite. While his praenomen (personal name) is unknown, his nomen (family name) of Pontius suggests that his family came from Samnium in southern Italy. His cognomen (additional name used to distinguish within a family) of Pilatus has an unknown origin, but appears to be derived from a word for javelin and related to the military.

According to one ancient source, his birthplace was likely the village of Bisenti, Italy (Eusebius, *Historia Ecclesiae*). The village, in the region of Samnium, contains the ruins of a Roman house suggested to be that of Pontius Pilate, but no evidence exists to substantiate the claim about the owner of the house. Pilate was married, and according to a source of late antiquity that might have been based on contemporary records or recent tradition, the name of his wife was Procula (*Gospel of Nicodemus*). The 3rd-century church father Origen also indicated that the wife of Pilate may have become a Christian (Origen, *Homilies on Matthew*).

After the exile of Archelaus in AD 6, Rome formed Judea Province and appointed a Roman prefect named Coponius to govern the area. Eventually, Pilate was appointed as the fifth prefect of Judea Province, replacing Valerius Gratus in AD 26 (Josephus, *Antiquities*; Luke 3:1). As a prefect, Pilate commanded more than a thousand Roman auxiliary soldiers, and he had full power over life and death in the province.

At the time of the early Roman Empire, a prefect governed smaller or less significant provinces, or assisted a legate by managing one part of a larger province. Judea seems to have been connected to Syria Province, but the prefect answered directly to the emperor. Additionally, prefects of Judea were able to appoint and depose high priests and control funds of the temple in Jerusalem (Josephus, *Antiquities* 18.34-35).

Further, because of a recent policy change only a few years before in AD 21, Pilate was able to take his wife with him during his time as provincial prefect, and this is why she is mentioned in the Gospel of Matthew (Tacitus, *Annals* 3.33-34; Matthew 27:19). During his tenure, Pilate was primarily based in Caesarea, which was the Roman capital of the province. While Jerusalem still retained importance, the prefects generally only resided there during major festivals.

In the years AD 27–31, Pilate had bronze *prutah* coins for Judea Province minted (Kindler, "More Dates on the Coins of the Procurators"). A *prutah*, the name apparently derived from an Aramaic word meaning "coin of smaller value," was the second smallest coin used in Judea Province. The coins minted by Pilate were decorated with Roman religious symbols, such as the lituus staff, the sipulum, and the patera libation bowl, and had inscriptions in Greek, the international language. The coins mention Tiberius Caesar and Julia rather than Pilate himself, since as a mere prefect of a province it would have been inappropriate by Roman standards for coins to bear his name. Similar to coins minted by other Roman officials, those coins issued by Pilate displayed pagan symbols, and perhaps also intended the symbols on the coins to help conform Judeans to Roman culture (Kanael, "Ancient Jewish Coins and Their Historical Importance").

Although referred to as a procurator in later Roman sources, the title for Pilate was "Prefect" according to an inscription commissioned by Pilate himself, an inscribed limestone block at the theater of the coastal capital city of Caesarea Maritima. The Latin inscription reads "Pontius Pilate, Prefect of Judaea" and makes mention of a dedication to Tiberius, although part of the inscription is no longer preserved.

Roman governors of Judea Province prior to AD 41 were prefects like Pilate, while beginning with Cuspius Fadus in AD 44, after Herod Agrippa I died and direct rule by Rome was reinstituted, these officials were appointed as procurators (Curran, 88; Josephus, *Wars* 2.111 and *Antiquities* 17.342; Cassius Dio, *Roman History* 55.27). The later Roman historian Tacitus mistakenly identified Pilate as a procurator (Tacitus, *Annals* 15.44).

The Pilate Stone found at Caesarea, noting Pontius Pilatus as Prefect of Judea

This inscription not only demonstrates that Pontius Pilate existed, but that he was a prefect of Judea and in that position prior to AD 41. According to Josephus, Pilate governed from ca. AD 26 to 36 (Josephus, *Antiquities* 18.35-89).

Recently, a 1st-century ring bearing the name "Pilato" (Pilatus), which had been excavated at the palace fortress site of Herodium near Bethlehem, was cleaned, analyzed, and published. The ring was discovered in a 1st-century AD archaeological layer dating to AD 71 or before, inside a room with other artifacts and coins of the period. It is a copper-alloy Roman ring with an oval seal section slightly less than 1 cm at its longest point. In the center of the oval is an amphora symbol, and this is encircled by six Greek letters spelling "Pilato," which is the Greek form of his name used in the Gospels and also equivalent to Pilatus in Latin. The letters are inscribed backwards so that they would be read left to right on a surface the ring would stamp.

Although Latin was used for most official Roman documents and inscriptions, in many of the provinces Greek was the common language, and the coins minted by Pontius Pilate in Judea also used Greek. Because the cognomen (third Roman name used to distinguish a branch of a family) of Pilatus is of Italian origin and is unknown from any other person in ancient Judea, and it dates to the 1st century, this ring almost certainly refers to Pontius Pilate, the prefect who interacted with Jesus. Most likely it was used by a lower-ranking Roman official performing tasks in the name of the governor during his tenure in Judea, rather than by Pilate himself.

When Pilate was made prefect of Judea Province in ca. AD 26, the emperor was Tiberius, who reigned from AD 14–37 (Luke 3:1). However, in AD 26, Tiberius also withdrew to the island of Capri, and the crafty commander of the Praetorian Guard and confidant of the emperor, named Sejanus, had eventually accumulated enough power that he began making many decisions for the emperor (Suetonius, *Life of Tiberius* 65). Due to this situation, Pilate may have obtained his appointment as prefect through his associate Sejanus rather than from Emperor Tiberius (Philo of Alexandria, *Embassy to Gaius* 159-160). Then when Sejanus was accused of a plot in AD 31 and subsequently executed, Pilate was once again accountable to Tiberius and probably in a precarious position (Josephus, *Antiquities* 18.177-182; Juvenal, *Satire* 10.67-72; Dio, *Roman History* 58.9-11).

Sections of a letter from Herod Agrippa I, preserved in the writings of Philo, describe Pontius Pilate as a man of inflexible disposition, ruthless, and obstinate with ferocious passions (Philo of Alexandria, *Embassy to Gaius* 301-302). The dark characterization of Pilate that Agrippa communicated could have initially been influenced by his perspective as a local ruler under the dominance of and in competition with the Romans, although Agrippa may have also slandered Pilate for political or familial reasons. Pilate fell out of favor with Emperor Tiberius due to problems in Judea and perhaps his association with Sejanus, while Agrippa was a loyal follower who sought to receive every favor from the Roman Empire, and in particular the new ruler Claudius. Pilate had also governed part of the area that the Herodian family of Agrippa once ruled, and Agrippa may have had motivations to demonize the prefects as fools and poor rulers so that he could retain his own power over the region instead of Roman officials.

Pilate had an irregularly long term as prefect, governing for over ten years and having his tenure exceeded only by his predecessor Valerius Gratus, who ruled a few months longer, out of all the other prefects, procurators, or legates in Judea from AD 6–135. Yet, he also encountered many problems and conflicts. Due to the religious tensions between Judaism and Roman polytheism, in addition to various independence movements and general distance from Roman rule, leadership in Judea Province was never simple. During his time as prefect, Pilate experienced at least five significant conflicts with the local population, or six if the trial of Jesus is included. Josephus recorded the first conflict, which occurred when Pilate offended the religious Judeans by bringing Roman standards bearing images of the emperor into Jerusalem, which they saw as a violation of the Mosaic Law's ban against graven images (Josephus, *Antiquities* 18.55-59; *Wars* 2.160-174; Exodus 20:4). As a result, a delegation was sent to Caesarea to request that the images be removed from the holy city. On the sixth day of protesting, Pilate sent soldiers into the crowd to disperse the people under penalty of death. However, the people threw themselves on the ground and prepared for death rather than violate their Law. This affected Pilate so much that he commanded the images of the emperor to be brought back to Caesarea from Jerusalem.

A second conflict arose when Pilate used funds from the temple treasury to construct a new aqueduct system bringing fresh spring water into Jerusalem. While probably within his authority as prefect to use the funds for a project that would likely serve the temple with another water source, many did not approve. Thousands who protested this use of funds and construction started a riot and yelled abuses at Pilate when he came to Jerusalem, prompting him to send soldiers into the crowd with clubs. However, the situation became dire as the soldiers exceeded their orders, and severe beatings from the soldiers plus trampling by the crowd resulted in the death of many of the protesters (Josephus, *Antiquities* 18.60-62; *Wars* 2.175-177).

A violent episode that probably occurred after the images of the emperor and the aqueduct riots involved the slaying of an unknown number of Galileans. Although the account is extremely brief, it appears that Pilate may have had some Galileans executed when they were offering sacrifices (Luke 13:1). This seems to have caused enmity between Pilate and Herod Antipas, since Galilee was under the jurisdiction of Antipas (Luke 23:8-12).

Another incident occurred in Jerusalem and involved golden votive shields. These shields, apparently inscribed with the name of the emperor, perhaps proclaiming Augustus or Tiberius divine or ruler of the world, were placed in the former palace of Herod in Jerusalem, which had become the Roman praetorium for Jerusalem (Josephus, *Wars* 2.301). The shields were met with objections and disapproval by many of the locals, similar to previous objections about the images of the emperor in Jerusalem (Philo of Alexandria, *Embassy to Gaius* 299-305). At first, Pilate refused to acknowledge complaints about the shields, and in light of the fact that even synagogues in Alexandria had similar ornaments in honor of the emperor, perhaps Pilate did not foresee any problem (Philo of Alexandria, *Embassy to Gaius* 133). The sons of Herod appealed to Tiberius, who ordered Pilate to transfer the shields to the temple of Augustus in Caesarea. Pilate carried out these orders and the situation was diffused.

The final major incident recorded resulted in Pilate being recalled to Rome and Marcellus replacing him as prefect of Judea in about AD 36. A liar, as Josephus called him, claiming to be the Samaritan Messiah, Marcellus led his followers to Mount Gerizim, promising to show them sacred vessels hidden by Moses on the mountain (Josephus, *Antiquities* 18.85-89). Probably attempting to prevent another rebellion led by a messianic claimant, Pilate blocked their road with cavalry and infantry, who then marched on the village of Tirathaba where the group had been waiting. This encounter resulted in many deaths, especially those who were leaders of the Samaritan group. Soon after, the Samaritan leadership sent an embassy to Vitellius, legate of Syria, and claimed that the group was not going to revolt against the Romans but had merely been fleeing from the violence of Pilate. Vitellius then ordered Pilate to go to Rome to answer these accusations before the emperor, and meanwhile sent Marcellus to preside over Judea as an interim prefect. However, Tiberius died in March of AD 37, before Pilate arrived back in Rome.

After Pilate returned to Rome, it is unclear how events unfolded. Eusebius recounted that according to one tradition Pilate had suffered misfortune after his return to Rome in the reign of Caligula, was exiled to Gaul, and eventually committed suicide in Vienne because of his depression (Eusebius, *Historia Ecclesiae* 2.7; cf. Orosius, *Historiarum Adversus Paganos*). Agapius of Hierapolis, a 10th century Christian historian writing in Arabic, recorded that Pilate killed himself in the first year of the reign of Caligula, about AD 37–38 (Agapius, *Universal History*). Although Agapius wrote nearly 900 years later, he accessed many earlier sources, such as the writings of Bardaisan and Papias in the 2nd century AD, and Josephus in the 1st century AD.

However, legal precedents from Roman history involving the change of emperors, and the amnesty that Caligula granted to magistrates, suggests that

Pilate was likely cleared of charges, especially since he merely faced accusations by the Samaritans (Suetonius, *Gaius Caligula*). Further, the statements of 2nd-century AD Roman writer Celsus serve to clarify this incident, as he recorded that in contrast to King Pentheus, Pilate suffered nothing for condemning to death a supposed god (Celsus, *The True Word*).

Rather than accounts of the punishment and death of Pilate, 1st and 2nd-century AD sources are silent about the matter. Additionally, the 2nd- and 3rd-century church father Tertullian claims that Pilate became convinced of the divine nature of Jesus and can be regarded as a Christian (Tertullian, *Apology*). The existing evidence, sparse as it is, suggests that Pilate was not exiled and did not die in Gaul early in the reign of Claudius, but instead probably lived out his days as a retired magistrate in Italy.

While primarily attested in the writings of Josephus, Philo, and the authors of the Gospels, Pilate is also mentioned in a letter of Paul and various early apocryphal and pseudepigraphical works (1 Timothy 6:13; *Gospel of Peter*). However, most of the apocryphal and pseudepigraphical writings cannot be regarded as the most reliable historical sources for Pilate. The *Acts of Pontius Pilate* is a work known first from a reference found in a letter from Justin Martyr to Emperor Antoninus Pius in the 2nd century AD (Justin Martyr, *First Apology*). A similarly named text appears later in a 4th-century AD apocryphal work, but it is unknown if this later existing text contains the older work that was referred to by Justin and Tertullian. It is possible that the Pontius Pilate sections were copied

Inscription of Lysanius, the tetrarch from Abila

from the earlier text, which claims to be material derived from the records in Jerusalem during the reign of Pilate. Because of the uncertainty involved, the material should be used with caution, acknowledging that the presently known *Acts of Pilate* may not be historical records from the 1st century AD. Yet, what we do know of Pilate and the Roman authority in Judea Province during the time of Jesus serves as useful historical context and illuminates the Gospel accounts.

Along with Tiberius, Pilate, Herod Antipas, Philip, and the high priests Annas and Caiaphas, a ruler named Lysanias, tetrarch of Abilene is also listed by Luke as being in power during the fifteenth year of Tiberius when the ministry of Jesus began (Luke 3:1). Although the most enigmatic and disputed of the political figures listed in this important chronological passage from Luke, Lysanias the tetrarch of Abilene does appear in both archaeological sources and ancient historical accounts. In the context of the death of Tiberius and succession of Caligula in AD 37, Josephus recorded that Herod Agrippa I was promised various lands including the "tetrarchy of Lysanias," which were associated with Abila (Josephus, *Antiquities* 18.237, 19.275, 20.138). The Lysanias who was tetrarch of Abilene in the early 1st century AD may have been the son of the tetrarch Zenodorus and grandson of the Lysanias executed by Cleopatra. While coins issued by Lysanias the tetrarch with his name and title on them have not been identified, two nearly identical inscriptions of the 1st century discovered at Abila seem to document this Lysanias whom Luke stated was a tetrarch during the time of Tiberius and Pontius Pilate.

The Greek inscriptions, containing a dedication and remembrance, were discovered carved into a rock hill along a road and on the wall of a temple. A translation of the best preserved inscription reads "For the salvation of the August lords and of all their household, Nymphaeus, freedman of Eagle. Lysanias the tetrarch established this street and other things." The text refers to Lysanias the tetrarch and the "August lords," which is thought to be a title for Tiberius and Livia. If so, this means the inscription would be no later than AD 29 when Livia died, and in agreement with the time frame in which Luke mentioned Lysanias ruling as tetrarch of Abilene.

After Herod the Great died and his kingdom was split among his heirs, Philip was made a tetrarch and ruled over areas east of Galilee called Gaulanitis, Batanaea, Trachonitis, and Auranitis (Luke 3:1; Josephus, *Antiquities* 17.21-27, 17.189). Unfortunately, much less is currently known about Philip the Tetrarch, who reigned from 4 BC to AD 34, than other Herodian rulers of his time. He was a son of Herod the Great and the half brother of Antipas and Archelaus who became fellow heirs of the former kingdom of Herod. Unlike Archelaus and Antipas, Philip was in power over a primarily Hellenistic area, and very few Judeans probably lived there (Luke 3:1).

Coins issued by Philip, which included his name and title "tetrarch," also reflect this religious and worldview difference, as the coins feature portraits of himself and the emperors Augustus and Tiberius, and images of pagan temples. One particularly relevant coin that dates to about AD 30 shows the head of Emperor Tiberius with his name and title on one side, and the image of a tetrastyle temple with "Philip tetrarch" on the other side. During his 37 years as a tetrarch, Philip erected temples, named places after Augustus and Tiberius and the imperial family, and remained on good terms with the Romans.

Of the immediate heirs of Herod the Great, Philip appears to have had the most peaceful rule, and unlike his brothers Antipas and Archelaus, he was never deposed or exiled. A few scholars do not consider Philip the Tetrarch part of the Herodian Dynasty, merely because there are no clear texts or currently known inscriptions demonstrating that he used the name "Herod." Nevertheless he was a son and heir of Herod the Great and received a piece of that former kingdom.

Annas was the acting high priest of Judaism from about AD 6–15, appointed when Judea became a Roman province and the prefect Coponius began his tenure as governor. His role as high priest lasted until the later prefect Valerius Gratus removed him from office. Annas is documented as the son of Seth who was appointed as high priest by the Romans following Joazar (Josephus, *Antiquities* 18.26-27). The discovery of an incredible 1st-century tomb in the Hinnom Valley south of ancient Jerusalem, surely the burial place of one of the most wealthy and powerful families around the time of Jesus, has also been tentatively identified as the tomb of Annas and his high priestly family through a comparison of descriptions in Josephus to the geography and archaeology of the tomb. A former high priest and father-in-law of the acting high priest Caiaphas, Annas was still considered a high priest according to the lifetime appointment system of the Mosaic Law, and he continued to retain significant influence even after being deposed (Numbers 35:25-28; Luke 3:2; John 18:13).

All of these political figures included by Luke not only allow a historical analysis that demonstrates accuracy in names, titles, and locations, but their overlapping chronologies also place the ministry of Jesus in a very specific time frame. If one factors these seven officials even without referring to the fifteenth year of Tiberius, the window of time in which all held those positions still only falls between AD 26–34 at the maximum. The additional information of the fifteenth year of Tiberius recorded by Luke and the 46 years of temple reconstruction mentioned by John allow an even more precise estimation for the beginning of the ministry of Jesus around AD 28.

JOHN AND THE BAPTISM OF JESUS

John the Baptist, or more accurately "John the Baptizer," was born just six months before Jesus to a priest named Zachariah and his wife, Elizabeth, and they lived in the hill country of Judah near Jerusalem (Luke 1:5-13). Zachariah is referred to in a 4th-century Greek inscription found in the "Tomb of Absalom," which claims that Zachariah the priest, father of John, was buried there.

John was a unique character in the 1st century, living in the wilderness, wearing camel-hair clothing with a leather belt, eating locusts and wild honey, and baptizing on the east side of the Jordan River (Matthew 3:4-6; Mark 1:4-6; John 1:28). He is compared many times in the Gospels to Elijah, who was described similarly and spent much of his time around the Jordan River, like John (1 Kings 17:5; 2 Kings 1:8; Matthew 17:9-13; Luke 1:13-17).

Although a small percentage of the Gospel narratives are dedicated to John the Baptizer, he appears in all four Gospels and in Acts, and multiple prophecies refer to John and preparing the way for Jesus. Initially, Zachariah is given a message from an angel that he will have a son named John who will turn many of the Israelites back to God, and he will be a forerunner to make the people ready for the Lord (Luke 1:11-17). In the Gospel of Luke, a reference is made to a prophecy of Malachi that this forerunner will turn the hearts of the fathers back to the children and the hearts of the children to their fathers, which is clearly linked to the prophetic and repentance ministry of John the Baptizer seen later in the Gospels (Luke 1:17; Malachi 4:6).

All four Gospels quote from the Book of Isaiah, implying that John was a voice in the wilderness that was making ready the way of the Lord (Isaiah 40:3; Matthew 3:3; Mark 1:2-3; Luke 3:4; John 1:23). Luke expands the quotation to include the next two verses of Isaiah, while Mark also has a verse from Malachi about the messenger going before (Malachi 3:1).

Jesus confirmed the ministry and role of John, and emphasized his importance in preparing the way (Luke 7:24-30). Like Jesus, John the Baptizer stated that merely being physical descendants of Abraham would not suffice (Luke 3:7-9; John 8:31-39). For the religious elite of Judea, this was a departure from what had become their traditional beliefs.

Just prior to the public ministry of Jesus, John was preaching the coming of the Messiah and baptizing people in water as a symbolic ritual that identified them with acceptance of the spiritual message John was communicating. It appears that the ministry of John was the first to employ baptism of a person by another person, and the association of baptism with God's message was a distinctive from the typical idea of ritual washing in Judaism of the day.

John often baptized people at the Jordan River in a place called Aenon near Salim (John 3:23). Eusebius near the end of the 3rd century wrote that Salim was about seven miles, or at the eighth milestone, south of Scythopolis of the Decapolis region (Eusebius, *Omomasticon* 40:1, 152:4). Others have suggested that the Salim east of Shechem or perhaps the Wadi Saleim, six miles northeast of Jerusalem, was the location. All of these locations were probably in the region of Judea, although the Gospels also specify that John used the east side of the Jordan River, in Perea, as a common place for baptisms. As Eusebius lived close to the time of the New Testament, his location may be more accurate than modern hypotheses. This would place many of John's baptisms in Judea Province but also near to the Galilee region where Jesus began his ministry. However, John also baptized in Bethany beyond the Jordan (east side of the Jordan

Bethany beyond the Jordan, traditional location of the baptism of Jesus

River), in the region known as Perea administered by the tetrarch Herod Antipas, and this is where the baptism of Jesus occurred (John 1:28).

Several 2nd-, 3rd-, and 4th-century AD documents mention John the Baptizer, but many of these are borrowing material from the Gospels, or in some cases even relating unreliable information (Pseudo-Clementines; the *Gospel of the Nazarenes*; the *Gospel of the Hebrews*; *Protevangelium of James*; Justin Martyr; Tertullian; Hippolytus; Origen; Epiphanius). However, in addition to the Gospels, the 1st-century AD historian Josephus refers to John. Josephus calls him a "good man" that persuaded the Judeans toward virtue and reverence to God, and even mentions John's baptisms (Josephus, *Antiquities* 18.116-117). John the Baptizer was instrumental in paving the way for Jesus, and his contribution and unique position have been remembered by the church throughout the ages.

According to the Gospel of Luke, Jesus was baptized by John the Baptizer prior to the beginning of the public ministry of Jesus (Luke 3:21-23). This happened in the fifteenth year of Tiberius Caesar, which seems to have been about AD 28. In the religious world of 1st-century Judea, baptism was usually viewed as a ritual washing to symbolically purify oneself, which could take the form of washing the hands or immersing the entire body in a ritual bath. The practice goes back to the Law of Moses in ancient Israel when washing with water was used to purify from a variety of types of uncleanliness or symbolized purification (Exodus 30:17-21; Leviticus 14:8-9; 15:5-27; 17:15-16; Numbers 19:10-13; 2 Kings 5:8-14; Ezekiel 36:25; Luke 11:37-41).

The scope of reasons for ritual washing expanded later in Judaism, and it became one of the primary practices of the religious elite (Josephus, *Wars* 2.150; 1QS 3:3-9, 5:6). Ritual washing was so common in Judea during the time of Jesus that baths were installed in many houses and public areas around the cities and villages, and stone vessels for ritual washing have been discovered in massive quantities. Many people eventually learned of John and his ministry of baptism, and even those who did not become Christians recognized that the baptisms of John were an outward symbol that took place after a change in the soul (Josephus, *Antiquities* 18.116-117).

Bethany beyond the Jordan (or Bethabara "place of crossing") was a site where John the Baptizer was preaching and baptizing, and most likely where the baptism of Jesus occurred (John 1:25-34). Excavations on the east side of the Jordan River at Al-Maghtas (meaning "immersion") uncovered an ancient Byzantine church that had been built in the 4th century AD to mark the place of the baptism of Jesus, although earlier remains from the 2nd century AD suggest that Christians may have revered the site and built a monument or baptismal area in the generation after the apostles. Located about 10 km southeast of Jericho and 9 km north of the Dead Sea, this site and specifically "Bethabara" is noted on the 6th-century Madaba Map. In the 3rd century, Origen also identified the location of the baptism of Jesus at Bethabara.

The ancient remains relating to baptism consist of water collection systems and baptismal pools, including one in the shape of a cross, demonstrating the association of the site with the baptism of Jesus. This "Bethany beyond the Jordan" should not be confused with the Bethany immediately east of Jerusalem on the Mount of Olives, which Jesus also visited. The reading "Bethany" is attested in the 2nd-century AD manuscript P66, and the vast majority of ancient manuscripts of John show the reading Bethany. The name Bethabara, which probably has its roots in the Bronze Age and Iron Age location named Beth-barah, may have been an alternate name or originally the name of the place on the west side of the Jordan River (Judges 7:24).

Today, the western side site is called Qasr el-Yahud, while immediately across the river on the eastern side is Al-Maghtas and the ancient church and baptismal structures connected to John the Baptizer and Jesus. The sites of Al-Maghtas and Qasr el-Yahud were part of a military zone and inaccessible for many years until mines were cleared and the areas opened for pilgrims. While all four Gospels include the baptism of Jesus, with Matthew and Mark even mentioning the Jordan River, only the Gospel of John specified the name of the place as Bethany beyond the Jordan.

TEMPTATIONS OF JESUS

Immediately after his baptism, Jesus went into the wilderness of Judea for 40 days (Mark 1:12-13). This was truly a period of extreme difficulty, as Jesus was in the middle of what was then and still is today a hot and arid wilderness, which during the 1st century was also occupied by wild beasts. The site of the temptation of protection, when Satan tried to make Jesus fling himself down from a great height and have the angels rescue him, was recorded at a place called the "pinnacle of the temple" (Matthew 4:5-7; Luke 4:9-12). This pinnacle of the temple is often understood as the top of the southeast tower or rooftop of the temple complex, overlooking the Kidron Valley below, which Josephus described as a dizzying height (Josephus, *Antiquities* 15.411-416). As a high tower or rooftop above the wall on the edge of the valley, the height was so great that no human could survive the fall.

The location of the temptation of power, at a very high mountain, is not specified in either of the Gospel narratives, nor does any other ancient text claim to know the exact location (Matthew 4:8-11; Luke 4:5-8). However, centuries old tradition claims it was at "the Mount of Temptation" in the Judean wilderness west of Jericho, towards Jerusalem. Geographically this is in the same region as the 40 days of fasting and the other temptations of hunger and protection. Yet, archaeological investigations determined that the Dok fortress from the time of the Hasmoneans was on top of this mountain, and it may have been in use through

Corner of the Temple Mount, possible location of the pinnacle of the temple

the time of Herod the Great and into the 1st century AD (1 Maccabees 16:15; Josephus, *Wars* 1.56; Josephus, *Antiquities* 13.230; *Copper Scroll* 265:19). While that fortress could have been abandoned by the time of the ministry of Jesus, it is also impossible to determine if the Gospel writers were even referring to this particular mountain.

NAZARETH TO CAPERNAUM

Although Jesus was born in Bethlehem of Judea, he was raised in Nazareth and is often referred to as "Jesus of Nazareth" (Matthew 2:23; 21:11; 26:71; Mark 1:24; 6:1; Luke 2:39; John 1:45-46). During his childhood and early adult years, Jesus lived and worked in Nazareth, but also demonstrated his vast knowledge and wisdom through the teaching and explanation of the Scriptures (Matthew 13:53-58; Luke 2:51-52). Early in the ministry of Jesus, just after the temptation in the wilderness, all four of the Gospels record that Jesus said a prophet is not without honor except in his hometown (Matthew 13:57; Mark 6:4; Luke 4:24; John 4:44).

In what appears to be the last time Jesus taught in Nazareth, he read from the scroll of Isaiah and stated that this prophecy of Scripture had been fulfilled (Isaiah 61:1-2; Luke 4:17-21). The Gospel of Luke gives the most extensive account of this episode, which ends with Jesus leaving Nazareth for the town of Capernaum after people in Nazareth rejected his claims and tried to throw him off a cliff (Luke 4:14-31).

Although it has been argued that there is no cliff at Nazareth from which Jesus could have been thrown off, there are multiple sites in and around Nazareth from which the people could have attempted to throw Jesus. Luke specifically calls this geographical feature a brow, crag, overhang, projection, or rim of a hill (Luke 4:29). Therefore, it was a hill with some type of steep drop-off. Luke also recorded that the people drove Jesus "out of the city," but it was still on the same hill that Nazareth had been built. This indicates that the slope or cliff should be outside the boundaries of the ancient town, but on the same large hill that was partially covered by the town. Since Luke is no more specific than that, there are varying ideas on where the cliff may have been. The traditional location, called Mount Precipice, is about 1.5 miles from the city center of Nazareth. While it appears to fit the broad description in the text of Luke, the cliff may have been located nearer to the ancient village but now built over and no longer visible.

After the attempted cliff execution in Nazareth, Jesus relocated to Capernaum during his ministry around the Galilee region (Matthew 4:13). It was from Capernaum, which was strategically located on the coast of the Sea of Galilee and on a major road, that Jesus traveled around the area while teaching and performing miracles.

THE SEA OF GALILEE

Jesus probably lived most of his life around the region of Galilee in relative obscurity. The Sea of Galilee area specifically, situated in northern Israel about 60 miles north of Jerusalem, is where Jesus spent the majority of his ministry. This freshwater lake is watered by underground springs, rainfall, and the Jordan River, which flows into it from the north.

It was known by many names throughout ancient times, ranging from Kinnereth in the time of the Israelite conquest of Canaan (Numbers 34:11), to the popular name Sea of Galilee in Roman times (Matthew 4:18), and finally the Sea of Tiberias later in the 1st century AD (John 21:1). There are also variants including Gennesaret and Ginosaur, while an Islamic-period name for the lake was Sea of Minya (Luke 5:1; Josephus, *Antiquities* 5.84; *Life* 349). The original name of the lake, Kinnereth, is derived from the word for lyre and is presumed to be due to the resemblance between the shape of the lake and the instrument. Although there was an ancient town named Kinnereth, it likely received its name after the lake. The most popular name for the lake, the Sea of Galilee, came from the name of the region, Galilee, which surrounds the lake (1 Kings 19:11). The rarely used name Sea of Tiberias appeared in the 1st century AD after Herod Antipas named the town of Tiberias for the Emperor Tiberius, and the lake retained this name through Roman times.

Mountains on the west of the lake rise to an elevation of about 4000 feet, while on the east the hills are only about 2000 feet high. However, due to the extremely low surface elevation of the lake, approximately 690 feet below sea level, the mountains and hills ascend high above the coastline. This low elevation also makes the Sea of Galilee the lowest freshwater lake in the world. The geography of the lake allows for sudden storms to occur, as the clash of hot air at the low elevation and cold air from higher in the mountains results in a weather system that can rapidly cause large waves (Matthew 8:23-27).

At 13 miles long, 8.1 miles wide, and about 150 feet deep, depending on droughts and water usage, it is the largest freshwater lake in the region. As such, the lake was a key component of the economy in the region during the time of Jesus, being beneficial as a source of fishing, irrigation for agriculture, fresh water, and travel.

The Sea of Galilee was situated on a major highway that connected Egypt to the Levant and Anatolia. The ancient Egyptians called this highway the Way of Horus, while the ancient Israelites called it the Way of the Philistines, and in the 1st century one of its names may have been the Way of the Sea (Exodus 13:17; Matthew 4:15). In modern times it is often referred to as the Great Trunk Road.

Since the Galilee area was productive for both farming and fishing, and also along a major highway used for trade, military, and travel, the lands around the Sea of Galilee were prime locations for villages and cities (Josephus, *Wars* 3.42-43, 516-519). Cities and towns situated around the Sea of Galilee during the time of Jesus include Capernaum, Bethsaida, Gennesaret, Magdala, Tiberias, Chorazin, Hippos, Tabgha, Philoteria, and Gadara.

Although most of the exposed architecture that has been excavated at Chorazin, including the impressive synagogue, dates to the 3rd century AD or later, recent excavations at Chorazin have uncovered archaeological materials and architecture from the 1st century, including 1st-century AD coins and pottery and a stone "podium" section apparently built in the 1st century, found buried underneath the ruins of the later synagogue. The town was also mentioned in the Talmud and noted for its wheat, which was acceptable for use in offerings at the temple in Jerusalem (Menahot 85a).

By the 1st century, settlements lined the shores on both sides of the lake, and at least 16 harbors had been built. Each coastal city or town probably had its own harbor, although they varied in size, with the largest extending over 600 feet into the water at Gadara. Because fish were abundant in the Sea of Galilee, and a major source of protein, fishing was the main industry of the lake. This is evident in the most common profession of fisherman for those men from Galilee who became disciples of Jesus (Matthew 4:18-22; Mark 1:16-20).

Fishing at that time was usually done with large nets, although hooks from the Roman period have also been recovered in archaeological excavations around the Sea of Galilee (cf. Matthew 17:24-27; Luke 5:1-11). The nets were attached to weights of clay or stone to make them sink below the surface of the water, although various types of nets were used. Although translations simply render "net" in all instances, there were actually three different types of nets designated by three different Greek words in the Gospels. There was a small, circular, handheld cast net (*amphiblestron*), a layered trammel or gill net (*diktuon*), which would be left floating in the water for several hours overnight, and the dragnet (*sagene*), which was pulled by the boat (Matthew 4:18,20; 13:47-48).

Since no cold storage existed, fish had to be salted and dried in order to keep them from spoiling. However, due to the fresh water sources, the area around the lake was also a significant producer of crops such as wheat, olives, and grapes. The location on the highway made tolls or taxes profitable, and Matthew was stationed in a customs house in Capernaum to collect duties (Mark 2:14).

Since settlements were located all along the shores and useful farmland was situated in the region, the area around the Sea of Galilee was densely populated. Estimates for the population of Galilee in the 1st century are tentative, but based on archaeological remains, ancient historical accounts, and comparative studies, the population of the whole Galilee region may have been around 200,000 people, while the population of the whole Herodian kingdom, including Galilee, Peraea, Judea, and Samaria, was likely less than 1 million during the Roman period. Because the population of Galilee was concentrated around the lake and in a few urban centers within close proximity, Jesus was able to teach and perform miracles in front of thousands of people during his early public ministry without traveling any great distance, often using boats to go from town to town.

Due to its fresh water sources, fishing, fertile lands surrounding the lake, and location on major roads, the area of the Sea of Galilee in antiquity was a major economic center. This caused the region to become highly populated with people of both Judean and Hellenistic culture, resulting in an area that was influential economically and ideologically while still being distant from the primary religious and political centers of Jerusalem and Caesarea. Because of this, the Sea of Galilee was a crucial place for the early ministry of Jesus.

Although the Sea of Galilee was heavily populated and the shoreline was dotted with towns and harbors during the time of Jesus, the ravages of time and water caused many of these structures to be barely visible or even lost under the waves. The remains today consist mostly of the foundations, which were covered by the sea until recently. The combination of a dam and a drought, however,

Galilee in the time of Jesus

dropped the water level to almost 4 meters lower than the typical level of the lake in the 1st century, from about 209.5 meters below sea level to about 213 meters below sea level. While problematic for water supply and agriculture, this did allow the discovery and archaeological analysis of many artifacts and structures from the Roman period, including harbors of many towns occupied during the time of Jesus. Currently, at least 16 ancient harbors have been discovered around the Sea of Galilee, such as at Capernaum, Tabgha, Gennesar, Magdala, Ein al-Fuhyeh, Tiberias, Sennabris, Beit Yerah, Gadara, Duerban, two near Hippos, Ein Gofra, Kursi, Kefar Aquvya, and Aish.

These harbors were built with the local black basalt stones, and the harbor of a town usually consisted of several piers that protruded out into the water, stopping the waves and providing calm and protected docking locations for the boats. Anchors, mooring stones, and fishing weights at the harbors have also been discovered. The known harbors are located all around the Sea of Galilee and demonstrate the prolific fishing industry during the time of Jesus, which appears obvious when reading the Gospels (Matthew 17:24-27; Mark 1:16-20; Luke 5:1-11; John 21:3-6). Josephus also noted this, stating that when counted, 230 fishing boats were found to be working on the Sea of Galilee on a particular day during his lifetime in the 1st century AD (Josephus, *Wars* 2.635).

ANCIENT CAPERNAUM, THE SYNAGOGUE, AND THE HOUSE OF PETER

Capernaum appears in all four of the Gospel narratives as the home of several of the disciples and the temporary home of Jesus during his public ministry. The town was located on the northwestern shore of the Sea of Galilee and generally regarded as inhabited from about the 2nd century BC to the 10th century AD, although the town of the 7th to the 10th century was built only on the east side of the Roman-period settlement. However, archaeological remains from as early as 2000 BC and as late as the 12th century AD have apparently been recovered at the site.

The name of the village, Kfar Nahum (Capernaum), means village of Nahum, although it has no definitive connection to the Hebrew prophet Nahum. While it contains significant remains from the time of Jesus and the early church, it seems that the town was not settled during the Israelite Monarchy period. In addition to being mentioned in all four Gospel accounts, the town is also referred to in the writings of 1st-century AD Roman-Judean historian Flavius

Josephus as a village on the Sea of Galilee, apparently near Tabgha and in the same area as Magdala (Josephus, *Life* 403-404; Josephus, *Wars* 3.519-521).

Capernaum appears to have been largest during the Roman and early Byzantine periods, and at the time of Jesus the town occupied about 10 hectares (nearly 25 acres). Although population estimates for Roman-period Capernaum are usually quite small and around 3000 people, due to the currently known size of the settlement, the population density of towns and cities in antiquity, and the possibility that more of the settlement has yet to be uncovered, the population of the Capernaum area in the 1st century AD may have been as high as 15,000. Magdala, while appearing to be a relatively small town from the currently known archaeological remains, supposedly had a population of about 40,000 people in the 1st century AD, although this ancient estimate could have been erroneous or an exaggeration (Josephus, *Wars* 2.608). In antiquity this was considered a large town, and since towns and villages lined the shore of the Sea of Galilee in the 1st century, the area would have seemed even more urbanized and highly populated.

Capernaum was connected to the coast of the Mediterranean via a highway that went west to the city of Ptolemais, or Acco (Acts 21:7). Another major road could be followed south to Jerusalem or north towards Damascus, while sailing east across the Sea of Galilee would bring one to the area of the Decapolis cities. Due to its location on the Sea of Galilee and major roads, fishing, agriculture, and trade made the town an important commercial center. This is further evidenced by the Roman customs house located at Capernaum and the presence of various tax collectors (Mark 2:14; Matthew 17:24-27). A centurion and another government official were perhaps located there (Matthew 8:5-13; 9:18). A Roman milestone found in the town, with an inscription honoring Emperor Hadrian, attests to its significance for the Empire in the early 2nd century AD.

The layout of the town also reveals Hellenistic and Roman influence, as it was mostly organized according to Roman urban plans with streets running north-south and east-west intersecting at 90 degree angles, and a Roman bathhouse was discovered during excavations. Although the house of a Roman centurion has not been identified, archaeological findings do indicate that a Roman presence existed in Capernaum. Due to its location, the town was home to a wide variety of professions, such as fishermen, farmers, artisans, merchants, government officials, soldiers, scholars, and religious leaders.

Ancient Capernaum at the time of the ministry of Jesus was the home of Peter, James, John, Andrew, and Matthew, although Peter and Andrew had moved there from their earlier home of Bethsaida (Mark 1:16-29; Matthew 9:9; John 1:43-44). Many of the disciples were fishermen and Capernaum was described as a fishing village in the Gospels, just as archaeological excavations have also revealed. Fish hooks and weights for fish nets, along with other lower-class household items such as basic pottery, weaving implements, and grain millstones have been discovered.

In addition to fishing, the area of Capernaum was an agricultural center that seems to have focused on the production and processing of olives and grain. Archaeological discoveries also indicate that glass vessels were manufactured at Capernaum. A jetty was constructed to prevent water from flooding the town and to form a harbor for boats, as can be seen by the protrusion of stone walls going out over 75 feet into the water to form a pier.

A synagogue at Capernaum is specifically mentioned in the Gospels of Mark, Luke, and John, and remains of two synagogues from antiquity have been found in the town (Mark 1:21; Luke 4:31-33; John 6:59). An impressive 4th- to 5th-century AD synagogue, dated by thousands of coins found beneath the pavement, still stands today. The main hall of this reconstructed synagogue measures 24.4 meters by 18.65 meters, and two inscriptions, one in Greek and the other in Aramaic, apparently commemorate those who helped construct the

Capernaum and the ancient synagogue

building. Coins mostly from around AD 350–400 found underneath the white synagogue indicate that it was constructed in the late 4th century or early 5th century. In fact, the coins seem to have been used as a component in the mortar—perhaps because they were Roman coins of Christian emperors.

Additionally, the Aramaic inscription from the synagogue and the column capitals used in the architecture were identified as 4th century or later. The main hall of the synagogue may have been constructed in the late 4th century, while the eastern wing could have been added in the early 5th century.

However, underneath this Byzantine-period white limestone synagogue, remains of a 1st-century AD black basalt synagogue were discovered, making it one of the oldest synagogues currently known. This synagogue from the time of Jesus and the apostles was dated primarily based on the 1st-century AD pottery found underneath the cobblestone floor. The Gospel of Luke states that the centurion paid for the building of this synagogue, which would place the construction in the early 1st century AD (Luke 7:1-5). Underneath the 1st-century AD structure, earlier coins and pottery were also discovered, restricting the construction of the building to a very precise time range.

The black basalt walls of this building are about 4 feet thick, demonstrating that this could not have been a private dwelling. This synagogue of the 1st century AD, underneath the white limestone synagogue, was just slightly smaller at 22 meters by 16.5 meters. As the black basalt structure does not line up exactly with the white synagogue, it is clear that the basalt blocks are remains of an earlier building and not foundations for the Byzantine-period synagogue. Sections of the basalt walls were preserved up to about 3 feet high, and examination revealed that they were plastered on the interior. The building is referenced by the 4th-century pilgrim Egeria, who would have heard about or perhaps even seen the ruins of the earlier basalt synagogue. Egeria also noted that the limestone synagogue was built in the same place as the 1st-century basalt synagogue. While only column fragments, the floor, and the foundations remain from the 1st-century AD synagogue, this material is sufficient for its identification.

A large octagon-shaped church was also built in Capernaum in the 5th century AD, during the Byzantine period. Similar to other churches of the period, it was constructed over or around a location of significance mentioned in the Gospels. This Byzantine church appears to have been constructed in two phases, first during the 4th century when the ancient church was expanded by means of a wall built around the area, then a new structure was built in the 5th century into a more formal church.

Remains of the black basalt 1st-century synagogue walls at Capernaum

The 4th century was a significant period of church building, as Emperor Constantine legalized Christianity, commissioned the building of many churches, and encouraged additional church building through his actions and policies. When the church was rediscovered during excavations at Capernaum, sections of the mosaic floor were still intact and a baptistery in the southern apse was found.

Underneath the Byzantine church, remains of an even earlier church were discovered, modified from a house that was originally built in the 1st century BC and changed into a house church in the second half of the 1st century AD. The use of black basalt building materials that were prevalent in the town during the 1st centuries BC and AD, along with pottery found in the house, allows this house church to be dated to the 1st century AD. The original walls of the house were much thinner than the later church, since this was the norm in domestic architecture, and it would have been covered by a thatch roof (Mark 2:1-5).

The house was the site of many works of Jesus, and in one instance, it sounds as if large crowds of people from the town continued to gather in front of the door of the house so that they could be healed by Jesus (Mark 1:29-34). This suggests that a large space was available in front of the house of Peter where people could gather. Excavations of the house demonstrate that it was along the main north-south street of the town, and a large open space did exist between the street and the doorway, which would allow a crowd to assemble in front of the house and all the way down the street as they waited to see Jesus.

Eventually, by around AD 50, it appears the house was treated differently from other buildings in the town. What has been identified as the original church room, with walls measuring about 7.5 meters, was the only room in the city with plaster floors and walls, which had been applied in the second half of the 1st century AD. This apparent meeting place also had a conspicuous absence of household ceramic remains, while storage jars and many oil lamps that would have been used for lighting have been discovered.

According to the excavators, Christian graffiti in Aramaic, Greek, Syriac, and Latin, mentioning the names "Lord Jesus Christ" and "Peter," along with symbols of the cross, the names of pilgrims who visited, the Eucharist, and various blessings and prayers were found and deciphered. While debate has surrounded the Peter inscriptions, one of the three proposed inscriptions mentioning Peter certainly contains the name Peter. Before AD 135 when Hadrian changed the Province, the walls were plastered and eventually this Christian graffiti was written on the walls. A total of 196 pieces of graffiti with letters or words have been identified. The graffiti on the walls of the church may have started earlier, but most of it appears to date from after AD 200.

Ruins of the house of Peter at Capernaum

The house has an extremely early tradition as being the home of Peter, documented in the 4th century AD during the pilgrimage of Egeria, who wrote that "in Capernaum, what is more, the house of the prince of the Apostles [Peter] has been turned into a church, leaving its original walls however quite unchanged." Later, the 6th-century Piacenza pilgrim visited Capernaum and referred to the church that had been built over the house of Peter (*Itinerarium Antonini Placentini*). Ancient rabbinical writings confirm that a group of Christians existed at Capernaum prior to the reign of Constantine (Midrash Rabba). The passages in Matthew and Mark indicate not only that Peter's house was in Capernaum, but that it was extremely close to the synagogue (Matthew 8:5-15; Mark 1:29). Indeed, the house is located very close to the entrance of the synagogue remains, about 90 feet to the south or a walk of less than a minute.

Years later, Capernaum was involved in the first Judean revolt against Rome, which Josephus also initially participated in, and many of the people were apparently defeated and killed by the Romans around AD 68, although the town was later repopulated and a new synagogue was eventually built in the 4th century (Josephus, *Wars* 3.519-531).

THE GALILEE JESUS BOAT

During the ministry of Jesus, he and his disciples often used boats to catch fish or as transportation to different cities or areas on the Sea of Galilee (Matthew 9:1; Mark 4:35-41; Luke 5:1-11; John 6:16-24). While ancient literary sources provide information about boats, and archaeological excavations have uncovered artwork, such as a mosaic from Magdala, depicting 1st-century boats from Galilee, the most illuminating discovery occurred along the shore of the lake.

In January of 1986, between the harbors of Gennesar and Magdala, two of the coastal towns during the time of Jesus, fishermen brothers Moshe and Yuval Lofan noticed what appeared to be the remains of an ancient boat encased in mud near the shore of the lake. A severe drought had caused the water level of the Sea of Galilee to decrease substantially, and a team of archaeologists and specialists in the preservation of ancient remains was called in to extract the boat without damaging it before the rising waters of the sea once again covered it. They spent 11 days and nights on the recovery project.

The boat measured about 26.5 feet long, 7.5 feet wide, and was preserved to a height of 4.5 feet, although the hull would have been slightly taller (8.8 meters long, 2.5 meters wide, and 1.25 meters high). To prevent decay and crumbling, the boat was encased in liquid polyethylene glycol and removed from the lake for further studies and preservation. Based on radiocarbon tests, pottery found in the boat, and analysis of the nails used in its construction, researchers concluded that the boat was used between about 50 BC and AD 50, or roughly the 1st century BC to the 1st century AD, covering the time of Jesus. While the boat was not complete, the hull was about 70 percent intact and the nails were barely rusted.

Research indicated that the boat had undergone repairs and had been in use for many years, but when the hull reached the point that it was no longer viable to repair, the owners removed other components, such as the deck and mast, and then allowed the hull to sink to the bottom of the lake. Once at the bottom, the boat was slowly encased in mud, which prevented it from being decomposed over time by bacteria.

The boat had been built from planks primarily of cedar, along with oak and at least eight other types of wood, suggesting repairs over many years. Originally it would have had a small cabin and a mast for a sail. The construction of the boat used mortise and tenon joints and iron nails, and was shallow drafted with a flat bottom, allowing it to float very close to the shore. Studies suggested that this boat would have used a crew of about five people consisting of four rowers and one to man the sail and steer the boat (Josephus, *Wars*). However, the 1st-century historian from Judea, Josephus, also recorded how these boats were able to hold at least 15 people. Therefore, a group of 13 men, such as Jesus and the 12 disciples, could have used a boat like this while traveling, fishing, and teaching on the Sea of Galilee. The carrying capacity of the boat was well over the approximately 2000 pounds that the men and their equipment would have weighed.

The 1st-century Galilee "Jesus boat" after its recovery and preservation

The boat was placed in a chemical bath for seven years before being put on display, but now it can be viewed in the Yigal Allon Center at Kibbutz Ginosar. Because of this discovery, an accurate reproduction of a 1st-century fishing boat was able to be constructed, based on the recovered boat and ancient artwork depicting ships from the period, and it serves as an incredible example illuminating the historical context of 1st-century Galilee and the life of Jesus.

SELECTED BIBLIOGRAPHY
(CHAPTER 3)

Anderson, Paul. "Aspects of Historicity in the Gospel of John: Implications for Investigations of Jesus and Archaeology." *Jesus and Archaeology*, ed. James Charlesworth. Grand Rapids: Eerdmans, 2006.

Barrett, Anthony. "Claudius, Gaius and the Client Kings." *Classical Quarterly* 40, no. 1 (1990).

Blomberg, Craig. *Jesus and the Gospels*. Nashville: B&H Publishing, 2009.

Bond, Helen. *Pontius Pilate in History and Interpretation*. Cambridge: Cambridge Press, 2004.

Brown, Francis et al., *Enhanced Brown-Driver-Briggs Hebrew and English Lexicon*. Oak Harbor, WA: Logos, 2000.

Chen, Doron. "On the Chronology of the Ancient Synagogue at Capernaum." *Zeitschrift des Deutschen Palästina-Vereins* 102 (1986).

Crossan, John Dominic, and Jonathan Reed. *Excavating Jesus: Beneath the Stones, Behind the Texts*. New York: HarperCollins, 2001.

Cohen-Tavor, Achia. Interview at Chorazin Excavations, 2020.

Directorio Franciscano Tierra Santa. https://franciscanos.org/tierrasanta/ts.html.

Franz, Gordon. "Ancient Harbors of the Sea of Galilee." *Near East Archaeological Society*, 1990.

Hendin, David. *Guide to Biblical Coins*. New York: Amphora, 2010.

Liddell et al. *A Greek-English Lexicon*. Oxford: Clarendon, 1996.

Loffreda, S. "The Late Chronology of the Synagogue of Capernaum." *Israel Exploration Journal* 3, no. 1 (1973).

Maier, Paul. "The Episode of the Golden Roman Shields at Jerusalem." *Harvard Theological Review* vol 62, no. 1 (1969).

———. "The Fate of Pontius Pilate." *Hermes* 99 (1971).

McRay, John. *Archaeology and the New Testament*. Grand Rapids: Baker Academic, 1991.

Meyers, Eric, and Mark Chancey. *Alexander to Constantine: Archaeology of the Land of the Bible*, vol. 3. New Haven, CT: Yale, 2012.

North, Robert. "Discoveries at Capernaum." *Biblica* 58, no. 3 (1977).

Nun, Mendel. "Ports of Galilee." *Biblical Archaeology Review* 25:4 (1999).

Peachy, Claire. "Model Building in Nautical Archaeology: The Kinneret Boat." *Biblical Archaeologist* 53, no. 1 (1990).

Piccirillo, Michele. "The Sanctuaries of the Baptism on the East Bank of the Jordan River." *Jesus and Archaeology*, ed. James Charlesworth. Grand Rapids: Eerdmans, 2006.

Reed, Jonathan. *Archaeology and the Galilean Jesus*. Harrisburg, PA: Trinity, 2000.

Ritmeyer, Leen. 'Akeldama' Potter's Field or High Priest's Tomb?" *Biblical Archaeology Review* 20:6 (1994).

Savignac, Raphaël. "Texte complet de l'inscription d'Abila relative a Lysanias." *Revue Biblique* 9.4 (1912).

Tzaferis, Vasillios. "New Archaeological Evidence on Ancient Capernaum." *Biblical Archaeologist* 46, no. 4 (1983).

Vardaman, Jerry. "A New Inscription Which Mentions Pilate as 'Prefect.'" *Journal of Biblical Literature* 81, no. 1 (1962).

Wachsmann, Shelley et al. "The Excavations of an Ancient Boat from the Sea of Galilee (Lake Kinneret)." *Atiqot* 19 (1990).

Wachsmann, Shelley. "The Galilee Boat: 2,000 Year-Old Hull Recovered Intact." *Biblical Archaeology Review* 14:5 (1988).

CHAPTER 4

Teaching, Travel, and Miracles

A fter the baptism of Jesus and the temptations in the wilderness, Jesus returned to Galilee where his first public teachings and miracles are recorded. The village of Cana in Galilee, a short walk from Jesus's home in Nazareth, is mentioned in the Gospel of John as the location of a wedding where Jesus performed his first public miracle, as the site of another miracle in which Jesus healed the son of a royal official, and the home of the disciple Nathanael (John 2:1-11; 4:46-54; 21:2). Only the Gospel of John mentions this village and those events, and additional information about Cana is extremely sparse.

THE VILLAGE OF CANA IN GALILEE

From John, it is known that Cana was in Galilee, but no other geographical details are given. The name Cana appears to derive from the Hebrew word meaning "reed" or "stalk of grain." Another town named Kanah is mentioned in the Book of Joshua and on a geographical list of Pharaoh Rameses II, but this town was in Phoenicia near Tyre, far to the northwest, and is now marked by the modern town of Qana, Lebanon. The 4th-century church scholar Eusebius seems to have conflated the two towns into one and thought that the Cana mentioned in the Gospel of John was near Tyre, while Jerome made notes on the writings of Eusebius that there were two towns called Cana (Eusebius, *Onomasticon*).

This Kanah in Phoenicia is disqualified on the basis of it not being located in Galilee, of Jesus later visiting the region of Tyre and Sidon and that geographical area being specified, and that it would be much farther than a three-day journey from Bethany beyond the Jordan (John 1:35–2:2; Matthew 15:21). Josephus also referred to Cana in Galilee on the plain of Asochis (the Beth Netofa Valley) as a military headquarters during the First Judean Revolt against Rome in the late 1st century AD, although he does not give additional details that can pinpoint the exact site (Josephus, *Life* 86, 207). The Plain of Asochis, and all of Galilee, was part of the area ruled by Herod Antipas, which explains the presence of the royal official from Capernaum who went to see Jesus at Cana (John 4:46-54).

As a result of the lack of information about the location of the village of Cana in Galilee, multiple ancient sites have been proposed as possibilities. While at least five have been suggested, two of the sites can be easily discounted. Qana in Phoenicia was located far outside of Galilee, while Ain Quana is located about one mile north of Nazareth and has no ancient tradition associating it with the Cana in the Gospel of John. A consensus has not been reached on the identification of the village of Cana, but the sites of Khirbet Cana, Kafr Kanna, and Karem a-Ras all have intriguing possibilities.

About 8.5 miles north of Nazareth and 5 miles northeast of Sepphoris is the site of Khirbet Cana (Khirbet Qana). This location has a tradition going back at least to the Crusader period in the 12th century, but probably as early

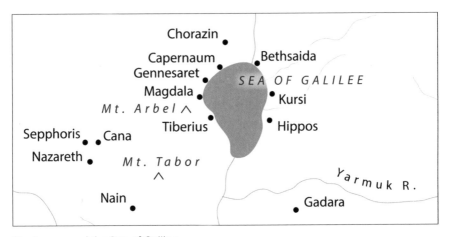

Region around the Sea of Galilee

as the 6th century. A significant ancient Byzantine-era find from the 6th century discovered at Khirbet Cana was a cave in which two stone water pots were found, apparently linking the site to the miracle of Jesus in which he turned water into wine.

At Khirbet Cana, archaeological excavations have also uncovered remains from the 1st century AD, including a glass-blowing factory, olive oil presses, typical houses of the period, ritual stone vessels, ritual baths, Maccabean coins, a Hebrew ostracon, many 1st-century stone-cut loculi tombs, and possibly a 2nd- or 3rd-century synagogue. The finds indicate that the site was a Jewish village in the Hellenistic, Roman, and perhaps Byzantine periods. Additionally, a cave next to the village appears to have been used as a place of worship, as a shelf that apparently held two stone vessels was found in the cave along with a sarcophagus lid or possibly an altar. While Khirbet Cana fits the general geographical and chronological requirements, more definitive evidence, such as an inscription or a Byzantine-period church, is absent from the site.

Kafr Kanna is another traditional site located along the ancient route that went from Capernaum to Ptolemais and also passed by Nazareth. Depending on the path taken, Kafr Kanna is about 4.7 miles northeast of Nazareth and about 4.6 miles east of Sepphoris, which is approximately 5 Roman miles for each. Therefore, in the 6th century, Theodosius may have identified Kafr Kanna or its area with "Cana of Galilee," since he reported that the distance from Cana of Galilee to Diocaesarea (Sepphoris) is 5 Roman miles, and the distance from Diocaesarea to Nazareth is 5 Roman miles (Theodosius, *The Layout of the Holy Land*).

The Arabic name of the town, Kana-el-Jalil (Cana of Galilee), does match the Gospel of John, but this could be either ancient name preservation or the result of pilgrims in antiquity identifying the site with the Cana mentioned in the Gospel of John.

The tradition associating Kafr Kanna with Cana of Galilee appears to be quite late, after the Crusader period, and first becomes apparent in the 17th century. However, it is possible that a much earlier tradition existed, as a Byzantine church was discovered in the town. Since Byzantine-period churches were often built at locations of significant events in the Gospels, it is likely that, during that period, the early church associated Kafr Kanna with a location mentioned in one of the Gospels. However, the archaeological remains at Kafr Kanna indicate that it was a village settled in about the 2nd century AD, and therefore it would have been unoccupied during the life of Jesus.

Immediately adjacent to Kafr Kanna, only 500 meters northwest of the center of that town, a site named Kerem a-Ras ("top of the vineyard") was recently excavated. Around AD 520, during the Byzantine period, Theodosius wrote that the distance from Cana of Galilee to Diocaesarea (Sepphoris) was 5 Roman miles, which matches the distance from Kerem a-Ras/Kafr Kanna to Sepphoris at approximately 4.5 miles or about 5 Roman miles (Theodosius, *The Layout of the Holy Land*). At this site, remains from the Israelite Monarchy, Persian, Hellenistic, Roman, and Byzantine periods were discovered, including a house from the 1st century AD and coins from the 1st century AD. At Kerem a-Ras, fragments of large, stone purification jars, the type mentioned in the Gospel of John, and ritual baths of the 1st century AD were also found (John 2:6-7). Discoveries demonstrate that during the 1st centuries BC and AD, the site was also a Jewish village. Interestingly, the neighboring site, Kafr Kanna, in which a Byzantine church was discovered, only became established in the 2nd century AD. This newly established settlement adjacent to the earlier settlement may have been due to the tension that occurred between Judaism and Christianity in the 1st and 2nd centuries.

Based on an examination of the archaeological ruins, the historical sources, and the pilgrim traditions, it appears most likely that Kerem a-Ras, adjacent to Kafr Kanna, was "Cana in Galilee" of the 1st century AD. The neighboring village of Kafr Kanna was then founded in the 2nd century AD, and later a Byzantine church was built there, possibly to commemorate the site of the miracle of water into wine that Jesus performed at the Cana wedding.

STONE JARS, RITUAL WASHING, AND WATER TO WINE AT CANA

Stone vessels were common in Judea for ritual purposes, since according to the Law of Moses stone would not become impure, unlike the often used pottery of ancient times (Leviticus 6:28; 11:33-36). Additionally, running water or living water was considered pure, and collection of water in a stone cistern could be used for purification purposes (Leviticus 11:36; 15:13). This "living water" could be stored in a large, stone water jar, which would function like a cistern holding ritually clean water, then later it could be used for purification.

While the use of stone vessels is not apparent from the Hebrew Bible and must be implied, sources in the Mishnah make it clear that this was the understanding during the Roman period. During the 1st centuries BC and AD,

Ritual stone vessels from the 1st century, recovery and preservation

purification rituals and stone vessels associated with this practice were extremely common in Judea and Galilee, since purification washing was a religious custom carried out frequently (John 2:6; 3:25; Mark 7:3-4). These stone vessels were made from a soft limestone that is found throughout the region and easy to carve.

The craftsmanship of the vessels varies widely, by hand or on a lathe, from crude and uneven to perfectly uniform with incised decoration. A few even contain inscriptions, such as a personal name or a chant.

The archaeological evidence indicates that there was an industry for producing stone vessels during this period centered at Jerusalem, where the priests, festivals, and temple necessitated more frequent use than other areas. In the houses of the elite, both bathtubs for regular washing and ritual baths for purification rituals have been discovered, demonstrating the distinctive uses. The primary purpose of these washing rituals was to become spiritually clean or holy, rather than physically clean.

While the standard belief and practice was that stone vessels made or kept materials ritually pure, there were sects of Judaism that had slightly different ideas about the ritual purity of these vessels (*The Temple Scroll; The Damascus Document*). The Gospel of John records that the six stone water jars contained two or three measures each, suggesting that the six were of slightly varying size (John 2:6).

Many of the stone vessels have been discovered all over the regions of Judea and Galilee from the 1st centuries BC and AD, and the large stone water jars have specifically been discovered in places such as Jerusalem and Cana. Yet, their general absence from Samaria and the predominantly Hellenistic and Roman areas of the region and their chronological distribution from the 1st century BC to their decrease in AD 70 and near disappearance after AD 135 further demonstrate their association with ritual in Judaism.

The stone jars are often referred to as a *krater* or a *kalal*, which is an Aramaic word used to denote a large stone jar for ritual washing (*Mishnah Parah* 3:3 and *Eduyot* 7:5). These large jars were usually about 26 to 32 inches high and 16 to 20 inches in diameter, agreeing with the size variance stated by John of 2 to 3 *metretas*, which was about 9 gallons or 34 liters.

Both John and Mark included explanatory notes on Judean purity customs, since many readers from other cultures would be unfamiliar with these ritual practices. However, the main point of these sections was not to educate on ritual customs of Judaism but to record significant events in the life of Jesus. In particular, the Gospel of John references the stone water jars and purification rituals in the context of the Cana wedding, where Jesus performed his first recorded miracle. Later in the Gospel of John, "living water" is mentioned multiple times. Jesus says in reference to eternal life that he gives living water, and those that drink of it will never again thirst (John 4:7-15; cf. John 7:38). Perhaps the stone water jars were used in the miracle as an earlier allusion to drinking the "living water" that Jesus would explain later.

Beyond the obvious miracle of turning water into wine that authenticated Jesus as sent from God, there may also be a connection between drinking the wine that Jesus gave them at the wedding and the wine at the Last Supper. The wine, which represented the atonement on the cross through the blood of Jesus, was clearly used during the Last Supper to foreshadow the death of Jesus on the cross, and then commemorated by drinking the wine representative of the blood of Jesus during the ritual of the Lord's Supper in the early church (Matthew 26:26-29; 1 Corinthians 11:23-26).

Regardless of the validity of these possible meanings of the water and the wine at the Cana wedding, stone water jars were regularly used in purification rituals during the 1st century. Additionally, many vessels of this type have been discovered in Judea and Galilee, and drinking wine from jars used for ritual purification would have sent a powerful message of spiritual purification to those in attendance at the wedding.

MERCHANTS AND
MONEYCHANGERS AT THE TEMPLE

After the Cana wedding, Jesus returned to Capernaum for a few days, but because Passover was approaching, he soon left for Jerusalem to observe the festival. The first Passover mentioned during the ministry of Jesus was recorded in the Gospel of John, but prior to the feast Jesus went into the temple where he saw moneychangers and merchants selling preapproved sacrificial animals. In the 1st century, the platform on which the temple stood was massive, enveloping an area of about 37 acres and providing ample space for various activities outside of the actual sacred areas of the temple.

Around two centuries earlier, in about 167 BC, the Seleucid king Antiochus IV Epiphanes desecrated the temple by sacrificing pigs on the altar (Josephus, *Wars* 1.32-34). The Hasmoneans revolted against their Greek rulers, rededicated the temple in 164 BC, and probably did repairs, but apparently did not substantially modify the structure or the enclosure. Beginning in about 20 or 19 BC during the reign of Herod the Great, the temple, the enclosure, and the mountain itself underwent massive construction and remodeling (Josephus, *Wars* 1.401; *Antiquities* 15.380-421). Herod essentially replaced every stone of the temple, including the foundations, meaning this manifestation of the temple could more technically be referred to as the third temple. Measurements indicate that the Temple Mount during the time of Herod was an irregular quadrangle of 280 meters by 485 meters by 315 meters by 460 meters. Josephus records the length of the east portico as 400 cubits (probably about 224 meters), and while he does not give the overall dimensions of the enclosure or mount, the sheer number of pillars mentioned further indicates the great size of the complex (Josephus, *Antiquities* 15.413-417; 20.221).

Josephus does, however, remark that the circumference of the walls was 4 stadia (Josephus, *Antiquities* 15.400). This would have been a circumference of approximately 740 meters according to standard Roman measurement, but up to 836 meters if using the Phoenician equivalent. Either way, these walls would have fit within the dimensions of the Temple Mount expansion. The measurements by Josephus may not have included the Royal Stoa and other similar structures, but only the temple courts proper, and thus the discrepancy.

Meanwhile, the Mishnah, compiled around AD 200 but accessing earlier writings, recorded the outer wall of the temple area to be about 500 cubits square (Mishnah, *Tractate Middot* 2.1). This figure, while appearing to contradict Josephus and the archaeological measurements, would fit well within the measured quadrangle and not necessarily conflict with the figures of Josephus,

Area where temple courts of the 1st century were once located in Jerusalem, and model showing the temple in the context of 1st-century Jerusalem

which could be referring to internal walls or specific sections. This figure of 500 cubits square would fit perfectly into the Temple Mount constructed by Herod, where the shortest side is about 280 meters or just over 500 cubits. Although initial construction lasted only about eight years, the renovations and repairs of this manifestation of the Jerusalem temple lasted until AD 63, and then was destroyed soon after in AD 70 (Josephus, *Antiquities* 15.5-6, 420-421; John 4:20; Luke 21:5-6).

After Herod the Great had expanded the size of the temple complex, merchants and moneychangers used open space and unoccupied areas to set up kiosks for sales and for the exchange of coins. The temple itself occupied only a small percentage of this area, so sections of the outer courts were often used to sell animals for the sacrifices or to change money into the proper type and denomination for paying the temple tax, but these transactions were basically done at extortionist prices (Mishnah *Kerithoth* 1.6-7; Mishnah *Megillah* 29).

Moneychangers were known throughout the ancient world, and it was not a highly respected profession anywhere. The moneychangers specifically would do their greatest business in the weeks before Passover, especially near the temple in the final several days, focusing on the exchange of foreign currency into the accepted silver Tyrian shekel for a surcharge (Mishnah *Sheqalim* 1.3). Although this coin was minted with pagan images, the purity of the silver, at 94 percent or higher, made it a more desirable choice for the temple tax than lower purity Roman silver coins.

The animals used for sacrifice also had requirements, but all those sold in the temple complex were apparently preapproved and ready for offering. A fragment of a ritual stone vessel inscribed with the word "offering" and depicting two birds was discovered in the debris by the southwestern wall of the Temple Mount, suggesting that it may have been located in the Royal Stoa area before the destruction of the temple. This further indicates that commerce related to the temple was taking place in the area of the Royal Stoa during the 1st century AD.

During the Feast of Passover, when the population of Jerusalem temporarily increased exponentially due to pilgrimage, the merchants with shops inside the temple complex could make huge profits. Typically, these kiosks were probably situated in and around the Royal Stoa at the southern side of the temple complex near the present location of Al-Aqsa Mosque. This was also the side of the complex where the main public entrance was located.

The Royal Stoa was apparently a magnificent structure, extending over 600 feet east-west across the Temple Mount with 162 columns arranged as 4 columns wide in the form of a basilica (Josephus, *Antiquities* 15.411-416; *Sanhedrin* 41.1). Resembling a marketplace in other Roman cities, and given its proximity to the temple, the Royal Stoa was the logical location for those seeking to profit from sacrifices and temple taxes.

All four Gospels contain an account of Jesus cleansing the temple area by driving out those selling sacrificial animals and exchanging money for the temple tax (Matthew 21:12-13; Mark 11:15-18; Luke 19:45-46; John 2:13-17). However, it appears as if the event in the Gospel of John occurred near the beginning of the public ministry of Jesus, since two or three more Passovers are mentioned before the crucifixion and a reference to the passing of 46 years after the reconstruction of the temple began, which indicates the event was about AD 28. Matthew, Mark, and Luke record a similar but later event that happened just after the triumphal entry in AD 33 (Mark 11:1-11; John 2:18-20; Josephus, *Antiquities* 15.380; Herod Year 20 Donation Inscription for Jerusalem Temple Pavement).

A stone inscription discovered near the southern side of the Temple Mount appears to relate to the expansion and remodeling of the Temple Mount begun by Herod the Great and continued by his successors into the time of Jesus and beyond. The Greek text commemorated a donation to fund construction costs for a stone pavement for one of the temple complex courts, and it mentions the high priest Simon son of Boethus who held that position from 23–5 BC. A reference in the inscription to year 20 of Herod the Great dates it to around either 20–19 BC when temple reconstruction began, or three years later, depending on which year 1 of Herod was being used.

The event in John is also distinct because only in this account did Jesus use a flagrum (a short whip made of at least two cords, usually with weighted ends), while in the three Synoptic accounts, Jesus spoke harsher words, saying that they have made the temple a "robber's den." This flagellum was apparently made on the spot out of materials such as rope or leather cords available there and would not have been the same as the brutal weapon or instrument of punishment typically used by the Romans.

Further, only John mentions a quote from Psalms, immediate questioning from witnesses, and reference to the destruction of his "temple" (meaning his body), but John does not include the quote from Isaiah, the healing miracles, or the praises from the people that the Synoptics record (Psalm 69:9; Isaiah 56:7).

When Jesus encountered these merchants, they may have gone even beyond the halls of the Royal Stoa and encroached upon the temple courts themselves,

The best-preserved of the temple warning inscriptions discovered in Jerusalem

which were considered holy places. The Gospel of John states that these people were "in the temple," suggesting the possibility that they had actually set up their shops in the outer temple courts (John 2:14). The temple courts were considered so sacred that according to a passage in Josephus and two inscriptions of the 1st century found in Jerusalem, if a foreigner passed into them, the penalty could be death.

Because they had defiled a holy place by exploiting people for monetary gain who were coming to the temple, Jesus temporarily put a stop to the sales and exchanges in the temple area and made a theological point that the temple was for the worship of God, not for commerce. Therefore, it appears there were cleansings of the temple by Jesus at the beginning and the end of his ministry.

JESUS AND THE SAMARITAN WOMAN AT THE WELL

The place known as Jacob's well, located in the town of Sychar in the region of Samaria and approximately 30 miles north of Jerusalem, was first mentioned in written sources by John, recording a visit to Samaria by Jesus and his disciples (John 4:5-6). Sychar seems to have been located at Al-Askar, and an archaeological survey discovered Roman-period, 1st-century materials there. It is probable that Sychar was a village adjacent to Shechem in the 1st century, and this is further suggested by the Arabic name of the village of Askar located just north of the site of Jacob's well.

According to the reports of Christians from antiquity, including the Bordeaux Pilgrim in about AD 333 and Eusebius in the middle of the 4th century AD, the site of the well was known after the time of Jesus (*Itinerarium Burdigalense*; Eusebius, *Onomasticon* 164). Eventually a Byzantine-period church in the shape of a cross was built around the well in about AD 380 to preserve and commemorate the site due to its association with Jesus teaching the Samaritan woman there (Jerome, translation of *Onomasticon*).

The well and the church also appear on the Madaba Map from just after AD 542. This church was located about a quarter of a mile southeast of the ruins of ancient Shechem in what is now the modern city of Nablus, which traces its name back to the Roman period when the city was renamed Flavia Neapolis in AD 72 and built over an early town of Samaria called Mabortha (Josephus, *Wars* 4.449). To the east of Mabortha, the city of Shechem (Sychem) occupied part of the area between Mount Ebal and Mount Gerizim, with the village of Sychar slightly farther east (Acts 7:16; John 4:5).

Jacob's well in the probable location of ancient Sychar

Archaeological investigations of Jacob's well revealed it to be carved directly into the limestone bedrock, which in antiquity might have been more than 135 feet deep, measuring about 4 feet in diameter at its opening then widening to 7.5 feet. It is clear from various measurements over the centuries that debris had piled up in the well, as a visit to the well around AD 670 by the bishop Arculf affirmed the great depth of well during his time, which may even have been significantly deeper than the more recent measurement of 135 feet. Water can still be drawn from the well today, as it seems to be fed by an aquifer.

While Jacob's well dates back to at least the 1st century when it is first mentioned by name, it may have originally been hewn from the bedrock centuries earlier. According to the book of Genesis, when Jacob returned to Canaan from northern Mesopotamia, he camped in front of the city of Shechem and purchased a plot of land that would have been to the east of the city. Since a water source was essential, it is logical that he would have dug a well on his land just as his father Isaac had done (Genesis 33:18-19; 26:25). Therefore, it is likely that this well had been named in association with the patriarch Jacob before the time of Jesus.

The Samaritans first appeared as a distinct group during the Persian period, but the origin of the Samaritans appears to have occurred immediately following the Assyrian conquest of the kingdom of Israel in 722 BC, when Assyrians and others were moved into the area along with a remnant of people from Israel who had not been deported to other areas of the Assyrian Empire (2 Kings 17:5-34; *Annals of Sargon II*; Josephus, *Antiquities* 9.288-291).

Early sources for the Samaritans include Ezra, Nehemiah, and the *Elephantine Papyri*, which date to the 5th century BC during the time of the Achaemenid Persian Empire (Ezra 4:8-17; Nehemiah 2:10; 4:2). Nehemiah, the *Elephantine Papyri*, and the 4th-century BC *Wadi ed-Daliyeh* papyri mention Sanballat, who was the governor of Samaria in the 5th century BC. The religious syncretism due to the influence of polytheists from Mesopotamia being transplanted to the area appears to explain why the Samaritans were later excluded from rebuilding the Jerusalem temple in the Persian period (Ezra 4:1-17).

Genetics studies of the Samaritan community indicates that their ancestors are from both ancient Israel and Mesopotamia. The Samaritans view themselves as descendants of Ephraim and Manasseh, which appears to be at least generally correct based on historical accounts and genetic studies.

Because the Samaritans were excluded from the rebuilding of the Jerusalem temple, they began to claim that Mount Gerizim was the holy mountain and that the true temple and place of worship was there (John 4:20-21; 4Q372). To accommodate the view that Mount Gerizim was the holy mountain, the ancient Samaritans made small modifications to the Torah, creating the Samaritan version of it, and regarded only those books as authoritative, rejecting the other books of the Hebrew Bible.

The Samaritans believe in one God, one prophet as Moses, one holy place as Mount Gerizim, the Samaritan version of the Torah as Scripture, and a future coming of the Messiah when the dead will be resurrected. The Samaritans celebrate the major feasts of ancient Israel recorded in the Law of Moses, and their practices are much more similar to how these feasts were celebrated in ancient times than the practices of Judaism.

According to Josephus, the Samaritans attempted to distinguish themselves from the Judeans during the period of Seleucid rule by claiming they were descendants of the Sidonians rather than the Israelites (Josephus, *Antiquities* 12.258). A historical survey makes it clear that neither group had any affinity for the other. Apocryphal literature of the 3rd century BC records the negative view of Samaritans that many Judeans had, equating them with Philistines and fools (Sirach 50:25-26). Conflicts between the people of Judea and the people of Samaria had been going on for hundreds of years, and this continued into the 1st century AD (Josephus, *Wars* 2.232-238; *Antiquities* 13.74-79, 18.29-30). This strife and division means that the parable of the Good Samaritan would have been surprising to many Judeans (Luke 10:30-37). There was a general disdain for Samaritans by the local inhabitants and especially the religious population throughout Judea, and even Romans in the 1st century recognized the Samaritans as a distinct religious and ethnic group.

The most sacred religious area for the Samaritans is Mount Gerizim, near Shechem, about 40 miles north of Jerusalem. Following the lead of earlier sources, Josephus mentioned Sanballat, but he also recorded the presence of a Samaritan temple on Mount Gerizim (Josephus, *Antiquities* 11.302-347). Although a few scholars had questioned the existence of the Samaritan temple, archaeological excavations have demonstrated that a temple existed on Mount Gerizim from the 5th century BC in the time of Sanballat I, which accords with Josephus mentioning its existence at least as early as the 4th century BC (Josephus, *Antiquities* 11.343).

The temple area, or sacred precinct, was initially about 315 feet by 315 feet, but in the 2nd century BC it was expanded to approximately 690 feet by 450 feet. Around 175–164 BC, Antiochus IV Epiphanes forced the conversion of the Samaritan temple into a temple dedicated to Zeus Xenios, and at the same time he attempted to convert the Jerusalem temple into a temple dedicated to Olympian Zeus (2 Maccabees 6:2).

After the Seleucids were defeated and the Hasmoneans gained power, John Hyrcanus attacked and destroyed the Samaritan capital city of Shechem in ca. 128 BC, including the Samaritan temple on Mount Gerizim. The Hasmonean period was a time of strife not only between Judeans and Hellenistic culture, but also between the Judean leadership of the Hasmoneans and divergent groups such as the Essenes and Samaritans.

Ruins on top of Mount Gerizim include a Byzantine church, under which are remains of the Samaritan temple

However, once the Romans took over the region, beginning in 63 BC, there was a time of relative peace, and during the life of Jesus, there was only one known serious incident, when Samaritans violently disrupted Passover in the years around AD 6–9. At this time, there was Samaritan worship occurring at Mount Gerizim, but there is no evidence that a Samaritan temple existed in the 1st century, and it was probably not rebuilt until the 4th century AD.

THE SERMON ON THE MOUNT

According to the Gospels, Jesus taught the Beatitudes near Capernaum on the northwest side of the Sea of Galilee (Matthew 5:1-2; 8:1-5; Luke 6:17-19; 7:1). The account in Matthew is also called the Sermon on the Mount, while the similar discourse in Luke is often referred to as the Sermon on the Plain. The difference in geographical description between Matthew recording a sermon on a hill and Luke recording that Jesus came down to a level place has been explained a variety of ways. While some have suggested historical or geographical mistakes in the Gospel accounts, others have attempted to explain the discrepancy as the sermon occurring on a level place at the top of a hill. An alternative understanding of the passage interprets "the mountain" as meaning "the mountainous district," and thus would apply to a hilly region above the coast of the sea (Matthew 14:23; 15:29; Mark 6:46; Luke 9:28; John 6:3).

However, it is also possible that there were two separate sermons with similar content—one discourse primarily to the twelve disciples on the mountain, and then another to a large crowd on the plain in the same area. The Sermon on the Mount in Matthew, which is much more extensive than the discourse in Luke, appears to be taught primarily to the Twelve but also with a crowd that had come up the mountain to hear Jesus. After the sermons, in both accounts, Jesus went to Capernaum and healed the servant of a centurion, placing the events in close chronological proximity.

The story of the healing of the leper comes before the sermon in Luke, but after the sermon in Matthew (Luke 5:12-14; Matthew 8:1-4). This would seem to place the sermon recorded by Luke in between the events of Matthew 8:4 and Matthew 8:5. Mark includes the event of the leper, then skips to the healing of the paralytic who was let down through the roof in Capernaum, which Luke also places before the sermon (Mark 1:39–2:5; Luke 5:18-20). This is eventually followed by the appointing of the twelve disciples in Mark (Mark 3:13-14). The appointing of the Twelve in Matthew is found after the Sermon on the Mount and in Luke after the Sermon on the Plain (Matthew 10:1-5; Luke 9:1).

Therefore, the sequence of events appears to be the Sermon on the Mount, the healing of the leper, the healing of the paralytic in Capernaum, the Sermon on the Plain, the return to Capernaum and healing of the Centurion's servant, and the bestowing of authority over unclean spirits and healing for the Twelve. This means that while the Sermon on the Mount and the Sermon on the Plain likely occurred in the same area, they were probably not at the same time nor on the top of the same hill.

Because of the ancient Byzantine-period tradition for the location of the sermon and its proximity to Capernaum, where Jesus was living at the time and where he went after delivering the sermon, Mount Eremos, a hill just above the Cove of the Sower, has generally been considered the "mount" for over 1600 years. This hillside on the northwest coast of the Sea of Galilee would accommodate crowds in the tens of thousands. Across the Sea of Galilee from this area to the east is Hippos, possibly the "city set on a hill" that Jesus referred to (Matthew 5:14). Alternatively, Mount Arbel, the most prominent mountain nearby and overlooking the sea, is only about a 7.5 mile (12 km) walk southwest of Capernaum and has also been proposed as a possible location for the sermon. Mount Arbel has a large, flat area that would also accommodate thousands of people. Another proposed site, the Horns of Hattin, seems less likely. Although the top of the Horns of Hattin is higher in elevation than Mount Arbel, it is also substantially farther inland and farther from Capernaum, about 11 miles (18 km).

Just southeast of Mount Eremos stands the current Church of the Beatitudes, completed in 1938. The current church sits near the ruins of a small Byzantine-era church dating to the late 4th century that had a mosaic floor and a cistern. However, this ancient church seems to have been associated with another event in the Gospels.

Around AD 380 during her visit to the Holy Land, the pilgrim Egeria referred to a cave up the slope of the mountain or hill to which Jesus climbed to deliver the sermon of the Beatitudes, and indeed in modern times a cave has been located on the slope of a hill above Tabgha. She located the place of the Beatitudes close to the Church of the Multiplication of the Loaves and Fishes in Tabgha, on a nearby hillside about 300 meters northwest of that church where there was a cave, but she did not state that a church was built at the site of the sermon (Egeria, *Itinerarium Egeriae*). Oddly, in the 5th century, Jerome was apparently unaware of the location of the Sermon on the Mount and suggested that it may have occurred on Mount Tabor or another high mountain in Galilee (Jerome, *Commentary on Matthew*).

Therefore, while we may not know the exact location, according to geographical information in the Gospels and information from the early church in the Byzantine period, the Sermon on the Mount appears to have taken place on a hill or small mountain near the 1st-century AD towns of Capernaum and Tabgha.

View of the Sea of Galilee from the Mount of Beatitudes

JESUS THE TEACHER

In writings going back to antiquity, Jesus has often been referred to as a wise teacher (Josephus, *Antiquities*; Serapion, *A Letter of Mara*; Matthew 9:11; Mark 10:35; Luke 3:12). Jesus used parables in his teaching methodology, logic in his debates, and many references to Scripture (Matthew 5:33-48; Luke 8:4-15). While parables and logic were employed by teachers throughout the Roman Empire, frequent citations of Scripture were utilized only by those few who considered the Bible to be of value. Jesus also typically taught in a conversational style rather than through lectures, in contrast to the famous orators of the Roman period, although the Sermon on the Mount appears to have been conducted in the format of a public speech (Matthew 7:28-29).

Around the time of Jesus, there were many famous teachers and philosophers who amassed followers, left behind writings, and influenced the worldview of many people in the Roman world and beyond. Was Jesus simply another famous intellectual, similar in method and belief to teachers, scholars, and philosophers of the time, or was he unique among all the teachers and thinkers of the Roman period?

In the ancient world, parables were a teaching tool. The word *parable* is an English transliteration of the Greek word *parabole*, which means "juxtaposition, comparison, illustration, analogy." In ancient Greek literature, the word could also have the connotation of moving side by side or indirectly, and therefore it could be used as an indirect way to teach a concept. Parables were fictional or illustrative stories, similar to a metaphor, and designed to teach a principle or lesson. The story of a parable often used comparison or hyperbole, and the story itself could be a model, analogy, or example of the intended lesson. By telling stories using the examples and situations familiar to people in a particular region and time, listeners could better relate to and understand what was being taught. Rhetoricians in antiquity also used parables to clarify or prove a point in an argument in a more interesting or more neutral way (Cornificus, *Rhetorica ad Herennium*).

Although parables do not explicitly state their intended meaning, the basic lesson is usually obvious. Parables are always short and focus on one principle or lesson, unlike allegorical stories, which may be long and complex. Much of the teaching of Jesus recorded in the Gospels is in the form of parables, which may have descended from both Greek and Hebrew rhetorical tradition.

In the Hebrew Bible, several stories similar to parables are found. These are called a *mashal*, and are essentially short stories intended to teach a moral lesson or a theological principle through allegory or comparison. This tradition continued on in later texts of Judaism, and by the time of Jesus the use of *mashal* was probably a common teaching tool that had been influenced by the use of the parable in rhetoric of Hellenistic culture.

While parables certainly exist in various works from antiquity, studies suggest that the uniqueness, frequency, and excellence of the parables in the Gospels are unparalleled. The settings for the parables of Jesus are usually in the context of daily life in ancient Judea, ranging from stories reflecting the rural society to the life of the elites, both of which the listeners would have been familiar with. Common situations, such as agriculture, fishing, shepherding, politics, religion, family, travel, hospitality, economics, and celebration are found in the parables. Within the stories and familiar settings, unfamiliar spiritual principles and concepts are taught, which in general the listeners would not have known.

The parables of Jesus are often preceded by a statement specifying that the story is a parable, and these parables, while having human characters, do not use names or directly refer to real people. For example, the story of the rich man and Lazarus is often mistakenly thought to be a parable even though the text does not say it is a parable, it is not in the context of other parables being taught, it teaches explicitly about the afterlife, and it names real people such as Lazarus, Abraham, and Moses (Luke 16:19-31).

Jesus's parables also often included the unexpected or use hyperbole. While Jesus indicates that he taught in parables to obscure those truths to certain people, it is also obvious that many of the listeners clearly understood what he was teaching (Matthew 13:10-17; 21:45). Another reason for teaching in parables may have been so that the religious leaders could not charge him with any crimes such as treason or blasphemy, since he was merely "telling stories" (Luke 11:53-54). Jesus also spoke in parables in order to fulfill prophecy from the Old Testament (Matthew 13:34-35; Psalm 78:1-4). Finally, parables are also a powerful tool in communicating a message to a person who may be opposed to the lesson if stated bluntly, but it allows the lesson to be taught free of prejudice due to the teaching technique.

A variety of interpretation methods have been used for the parables of Jesus over the centuries, with the two major schools being allegorical or metaphorical. During the medieval period, allegorical interpretation was extremely common, and extra or hidden meaning was often assigned to every character, item, place, and event in the parable. Since the Reformation, metaphorical interpretation of parables stressing a main point or principle being taught has been the most common method. In addition to an allegorical versus metaphorical idea, there are several interpretational principles that must be noted in order to have a proper understanding of the parable, such as historical context, audience, common symbolism, the importance of the conclusion, and that they concerned the kingdom of heaven (Matthew 13:11).

In the Gospels, although several parables are repeated and opinions vary on whether or not certain stories can be classed as a parable, there may be about 40 different parables of Jesus spread out through Matthew, Mark, Luke, and John. It has been calculated that approximately one third of the teaching of Jesus recorded in the Gospels is in the form of parables. However, the Synoptic Gospels contain the vast majority, while John recounts perhaps three, which some do not consider to be actual parables (John 10:1-18; 12:24; 15:1-11).

Slightly later writings from antiquity, such as the *Didache*, works of the apostolic fathers, *1 Clement*, the *Gospel of Thomas*, the *Gospel of Truth*, and the *Gospel of the Nazarenes*, repeat many of the parables that Jesus taught in the canonical Gospels, demonstrating widespread knowledge of these teachings even outside of orthodox Christianity as early as the beginning of the 2nd century AD. The parables of Jesus have continued to be a source of study, debate, and insight throughout the church, and even two thousand years later many of the stories are among the most well known in the world.

In Roman Judea near and during the time of Jesus, several influential teachers lived and wrote. Although parables were not common in the Old Testament, there is evidence of this style being used in rabbinical tradition, but appeals to rabbinical commentaries or the oral law were more common than the formulation of a logical argument in Roman-period Judea.

Gamaliel the Elder was a famous Pharisee and scholar of the Law during the 1st century AD. Gamaliel lived in Jerusalem until his death in about AD 50, so he probably saw and heard Jesus on multiple occasions. Although Gamaliel is not mentioned in the Gospels, he is mentioned in the Book of Acts as a respected teacher of the Law and the educator of Paul (Acts 5:34; 22:3).

Prior to Gamaliel, a renowned Jewish scholar named Hillel the Elder moved from Babylon to Jerusalem in about 30 BC and became a leader in the religious community for 40 years. Hillel established the Academy of Hillel, and Gamaliel studied under him. The Hillel school was often in conflict with the Shammai school, founded by Shammai, another prominent scholar of Judaism who lived about 50 BC to AD 30. However, their disagreements were generally over trivial interpretations of the oral law, and the two schools maintained friendly relations.

According to the Mishnah, Hillel said, "That which is hateful to you, do not do to your fellow. That is the whole Law." This stresses only the negative aspect of what Jesus instructed regarding love for others (Matthew 7:12; 22:37-40). Shammai was known for his extreme strictness in following and enforcing the religious laws, which is clearly seen in the attitudes and actions of many of the Pharisees in the Gospels, who lived only decades after him. The inquiry by a group of Pharisees asking Jesus about divorce may have been to see if he would side with either the school of Hillel or Shammai, since one of their main disagreements was the permissible reasons for divorce (Matthew 19:3-9).

As one of the Pharisees of 1st-century AD Jerusalem, Gamaliel was very knowledgeable about the written and oral Law, and concerned with not only keeping these commands but teaching them to others. According to the Mishnah, Gamaliel authored additional legal ordinances for the laws of Israel, including a few relating to marriage and divorce. He also is credited with stressing the importance of becoming educated and giving tithes accurately. His insistence to the Sanhedrin that they should not try to kill Peter and some of the other apostles, but leave the movement in the hands of God, may have influenced early readers to consider Gamaliel sympathetic towards Christianity (Acts 5:35-39).

According to claims of the 4th-century *Gospel of Gamaliel*, another of the many pseudo-Gospels or New Testament apocrypha, Gamaliel was an eyewitness to the resurrection of Jesus. No early evidence exists to corroborate this claim, but Gamaliel would have been in Jerusalem during the resurrection of Jesus and probably witnessed the crucifixion of Jesus.

A later follower of Gamaliel, Akiva Joseph, became a leader of the Pharisees and, according to the Mishnah, he participated in the Bar Kokhba Revolt of AD 132–136, recognized Simon bar Kokhba as Messiah, and was apparently executed by Emperor Hadrian.

Gamaliel, Hillel, Shammai, and Akiva were all scholars and teachers of the Law in the tradition of the Pharisees, employed alternative tactics, stressed different ideas, and opposed many of the teachings and claims of Jesus. Further, none of these men claimed to be God, performed miracles, or traveled the region ministering to the general populace.

Joseph Caiaphas, who also lived in Jerusalem during the 1st century AD and served as high priest ca. AD 18–36, was a prominent member of the Judean priestly community and a Sadducee in his ideology. Although a Jewish religious leader, Caiaphas as a Sadducee held views that were very different from the leaders of the Pharisees. For example, the Sadducees rejected the oral law that the Pharisees so prized and only accepted the written Law, did not believe in resurrection or the immortality of the soul, did not believe in the afterlife, did not believe in angels, and many of the Sadducees were extremely Hellenized, even adopting some religious beliefs of Hellenism. As a priest, Caiaphas was not a teacher, and it is obvious that his views were drastically in opposition to Jesus, as Caiaphas was one of the major proponents of executing Jesus (Matthew 26:3-4).

About the same time, outside of Judea but a part of the Diaspora, a famous philosopher named Philo lived and wrote in Alexandria. Although a practitioner of Judaism, Philo was a Hellenistic Jewish philosopher who attempted to syncretize and combine ideas of both Hellenism and Judaism. Philo adopted many ideas of Platonism, and was also influenced by Stoicism, so parts of his ideology were often in conflict with the various philosophies he adopted. He interpreted the Bible allegorically and viewed God as transcendent. While Philo would have agreed on more with the Sadducees than the Pharisees, he was far removed from the traditional views of the Scriptures. In contrast to Jesus, Philo produced many written works, focusing on syncretistic philosophy, and he was heavily involved in Roman politics of the day. Neither Caiaphas nor Philo were truly teachers, and their ideologies were far separated from the teachings of Jesus, demonstrating them to be poor examples for intellectual comparisons to Jesus.

Comparisons between Jesus and the Hellenistic and Roman academics living around the 1st century AD show that their differences far outweigh their similarities. Seneca the Younger (4 BC to AD 65) spent most of his life in Rome and became a teacher and eventually advisor to Emperor Nero. Seneca was a Stoic, like many philosophers of his day, focusing on logic, moral and intellectual perfection with the suppression of emotions, and determinism. He wrote many tragic plays, but also often wrote on morality, philosophy, and worldview (e.g., *Epistulae Morales ad Lucilium*; *De Vita Beata*; *Naturales Quaestiones*).

Another Stoic philosopher and teacher of the 1st century AD living in Rome, Gaius Musonius Rufus, was the mentor of the famous Epictetus. Musonius was exiled from Rome twice, and attempted to persuade the soldiers marching on Rome under Vespasian by speaking about the benefits of peace versus the dangers of war (Tacitus, *Histories*). There are copies of discourses of Musonius, but it is unknown if he wrote them down himself or if his students preserved them. He seems to have been primarily concerned with ethics, and in addition to standard views of the time advocated vegetarianism, the education of women in philosophy, and argued against infanticide.

His greatest student, Epictetus, was born a slave in Phyrgia, moved to Rome, began to study philosophy, and soon acquired his freedom. Eventually, Epictetus taught philosophy in Rome but was banished by Domitian in AD 93, so he relocated to Greece and founded a school. He is remembered as an exceptional orator, and his student Arrian compiled many of his teachings (Arrian, *The Discourses of Epictetus*). Epictetus believed in determinism, but also in personal responsibility and the necessity of ethics.

Agrippa the Skeptic was a philosopher who lived in the late 1st century AD. Although no works of his survive, his views were supposedly recorded by another skeptic named Sextus Empiricus in the late 2nd century AD. Classifying Jesus as a skeptic is also impossible when the details are compared. Other intellectuals of the time, such as Aenesidemus, Lucretius, and Plutarch also have little in common with Jesus, his teaching, or his character.

According to a few scholars, however, one 1st-century philosopher was allegedly an extremely close parallel to Jesus. Apollonius of Tyana, a Neopythagorean Hellenistic philosopher from Cappadocia, studied and taught throughout the 1st century AD. While the dates of his birth and death are uncertain, according to his 3rd-century AD "biography," which often reads more like Greek mythology, he was born about 3 BC and died about AD 97. The majority of information about Apollonius comes from this epic story, a sample of his writings found in Eusebius, and a few letters that may or may not have actually been written by him (Philostratus, *Life of Apollonius of Tyana*). Philostratus was requested to write about the life of Apollonius by the empress Julia Domna, wife of Emperor Septimius Severus, under whom Christians throughout the Empire were persecuted, although if Severus was directly responsible or not is debated (e.g. Eusebius and Tertullian record varying opinions). Further, their son Caracalla worshipped Apollonius, so the supernatural power and greatness ascribed to Apollonius may have been influenced by particular requests from the imperial family. Much of what is recorded in the biography is supposedly based on the memoirs of Damis, an otherwise unknown companion of Apollonius.

In the biography, Apollonius is described in terms so fantastic that many scholars question the accuracy of the entire work. According to Philostratus, Apollonius was a wandering teacher of philosophy and a fearless wise man with supernatural powers. He supposedly traveled around Greece, Asia Minor, Italy, Spain, North Africa, Mesopotamia, India, and Ethiopia. He was a Pythagorean, opposed animal sacrifice, believed that God was pure intellect, and had no desire for worship (Apollonius, *On Sacrifices*). He apparently did have students who carried on his beliefs for a time, as the pagan rhetorician Lucian criticized the entire school as fraudulent and full of charlatans (Lucian of Samosata, *Alexander the False Prophet*).

In Rome, Apollonius is said to have defied both Nero and Domitian when they had banned philosophers from being in the city. Other stories, such as Apollonius performing human sacrifice, predicting a plague, sensing the death of Domitian from hundreds of miles away, and being taken up to heaven at his death made him appear to have supernatural powers and blessing from the gods (Philostratus, *Life of Apollonius of Tyana*; Cassius Dio, *Roman History*). That he was a type of "magi" or magician is also claimed by a 3rd-century Neoplatonist who wrote that the miracles of Jesus were not unique since Apollonius also performed similar works (Porphyry, *Against the Christians*). However, since Porphyry was an anti-Christian philosopher writing after Philostratus had completed the biography of Apollonius, Porphyry probably used that information as his source. The 3rd- and 4th-century Christian scholar Eusebius considered Apollonius to have been a sorcerer who used demonic powers to perform magic. The few resemblances of Apollonius to the life of Jesus, if they are not coincidental, are possibly derivate material from the Gospels that had been circulating for around 150 years before the biography of Apollonius was written.

An examination of prominent teachers and philosophers during and near the time of Jesus reveals that all of them differed from Jesus in their beliefs and teaching. The various messiah figures of the time were not wise teachers but violent revolutionaries, and their following died out almost immediately with them. Although there are reports of magicians in the ancient world doing supernatural acts, none of the other teachers are reported to have performed miracles in the same scope as Jesus, and none claimed to be the one true God. While some of the prominent intellectuals of the time wrote down their own teachings while others left it to their students or followers, only the unique teachings of Jesus and his following continue on today.

THE POOL OF BETHESDA

Back in Jerusalem, perhaps to observe Passover, Jesus visited the Pool of Bethesda on the north side of the city where according to John a famous healing miracle was performed by Jesus (John 5:1-9). The description of the location notes the association of the pool with sheep, and although most translations mention the "sheep gate," there is no word "gate" in the original Greek text of John. Other sources from antiquity indeed mention the pool or the sheep pool. Eusebius in the 4th century mentioned the sheep pool but not the sheep gate, and he identified it as a place with twin pools (Eusebius, *Onomasticon*). The Bordeaux Pilgrim in the early 4th century AD called them the twin pools but mentioned no gate, while other writings of the 4th and 5th centuries also mention the site of the pool, demonstrating the ruins of the pool were known and visited during the Late Roman and Byzantine periods (e.g., *Itinerarium Burdigalense*; Cyril of Jerusalem, *Homily on the Paralytic at the Pool of Bethesda*). Josephus mentioned the area of Bethesda and noted that the neighborhood was north of the Antonia Fortress with a small valley in between, in an area of Jerusalem that became walled at the time of Herod Agrippa around AD 41–44 (Josephus, *Wars* 5.146-152). While the area was known in antiquity, the location of the Pool of Bethesda appears to have been lost by the 7th century AD, and only rediscovered through archaeological investigation at the end of the 19th century.

John also recorded a few details about the pool that are useful in its identification, such as its name, location in Jerusalem, relationship with sheep, distinct architectural design of five porticoes or stoas, use as a pool for bathing or washing, and association with healing (John 5:2-7). Once identified and excavated at the site adjacent to St. Anne's Church in Jerusalem, the ruins of the pool also further demonstrated the historical accuracy of the account in John.

Originally, a pool was constructed in the 8th century BC, probably during the reign of Hezekiah, and an upper pool seeming to be in the area of Bethesda

Pool of Bethesda model

is mentioned (2 Kings 18:17; Isaiah 36:2). Around 200 BC, during the time of the Seleucid Empire, an extension of the original pool was built to the east, essentially making a pair of twin pools about 13 meters deep, or an upper and lower division of one large pool system. The northern pool measures about 53 meters by 40 meters and collected rainwater. This was divided from the southern pool, measuring about 47 meters by 52 meters, by a wall running east-west about 6.5 meters wide.

These may have been constructed in order to collect water for the washing of the sacrificial sheep, as the temple was located just to the south of the pool and the association with the washing of the sacrificial sheep could be the origin of the "sheep pools" reference, although there was also a "sheep gate" in Jerusalem during the Persian period that probably still existed in the Roman period.

In the 1st century AD and the time of Jesus, this Pool of Bethesda existed as a system of two pools, with upper and lower sections. The Copper Scroll found at Qumran, dating to around AD 25–70, seems to mention the Pool of Bethesda in Jerusalem, calling it Beth Eshdathayin or "House of the Two Pools," and indicates that people used the smaller section for ritual washing. John refers to the pools of Bethesda and Siloam each as a *kolumbethra*, or a pool of water that could be used for bathing or washing. Steps had been built to descend into the pool, and during the 1st century, it seems to have been used for ritual

Steps of the Pool of Bethesda

washing and healing, rather than the older function of the washing of the sacrificial sheep.

John also described the pool as having five porticoes. Archaeological investigation has clarified what this odd five-portico construction meant. Excavations revealed a rectangular pool system bounded by porticoes on all four sides, with the fifth portico forming the dividing line between the upper and lower pools. The 4th-century church leader in Jerusalem, Cyril, must have been aware of the architecture of the pool before a church was built on the site as he correctly noted the arrangement of the five porticoes to be surrounding the pool on four sides, with the fifth portico forming a division between the upper and lower section.

The memories of the healing miracle at the Pool of Bethesda seem to have persisted for decades after Jesus, because during the reign of Hadrian in the early 2nd century AD, the emperor had a shrine or temple to Asclepius, the Greek god of healing and medicine, built at the southeast side of the pools. This was part of his campaign to defile or erase sites associated with Jesus and Christianity by building Roman temples on top of them, such as also happened at the location of the Nativity and the tomb of Jesus and possibly the Pool of Siloam. During excavations, significant finds included a marble foot with an inscription to Asclepius that "Pompeia Lucilia dedicated" as thanks for being cured. This offering was discovered at the small temple built over part of the pool and dates to the reign of Hadrian in the early 2nd century AD.

Another artifact discovered in a cistern nearby, referred to as the Bethesda Vase, is an exquisite Roman-period vase decorated with snakes. This further suggests connection to Asclepius since this god was depicted with his snake entwined staff and he was regularly associated with snakes. In fact, rituals at shrines or temples to Asclepius often included those hoping for healing entering the Asclepion, undergoing ritual cleansing, offering sacrifices, drinking a potion, then descending into the *abaton* ("inaccessible place," probably associated with the underworld) where they would fall asleep in a room full of snakes, waiting for a dream from Asclepius. When they awoke, they would tell their dream to the priest who would interpret it for them and prescribe a healing treatment. If healed, the patients would make an offering in the form of a body part that was healed, such as the marble foot discovered at Bethesda.

Christians in Jerusalem had continued to pass down the memory of the location, despite the pagan shrine erected at the pool, and finally in the 5th century during the time of Bishop Juvenal of Jerusalem, a Byzantine church was built there to commemorate the healing miracle that Jesus performed.

GADARA AND THE
DEMONS CAST INTO SWINE

Kursi was the location of a monastery, church, and harbor on the east side of the Sea of Galilee in antiquity. During the time of Jesus in the 1st century AD, it seems that there were no settlement remains up on the hill, while in the Byzantine period, this place became the location of a monastery and a church. Since the ancient name for this settlement has not been found on any inscription at the site, scholars usually identify Kursi as a place within the country of the Gerasenes, Gadarenes, or Gergesenes, mentioned in the Gospels as the area where Jesus cast out a legion of demons into swine that then jumped into the lake (Matthew 8:28; Mark 5:1; Luke 8:26,37).

All of the passages demonstrate that the event occurred on the eastern side of the Sea of Galilee from the Capernaum area, as Kursi certainly is. Yet, connecting the casting out of the demons specifically to the site of Kursi requires links to the geography, structures, and place names used in the passages. The "steep bank" not only fits Kursi, but is particular to that area, and tombs referred to in the accounts have also been found.

However, a major difficulty in the identification of this site is that the place name used in the Gospels varies among many of the ancient manuscript copies. As a result, scholars have suggested numerous theories. The reading "country of the Gerasenes" must be related to the Decapolis city of Jerash, but this city was located about 37 miles to the south and east of the Galilee region, making it unlikely that it would have had any association with the site on the eastern shore of the lake. The place name Gergesa is unknown before it was mentioned by Origen in the 3rd century AD, and although it is repeated by Eusebius and appears to have linguistic affiliation with Kursi, perhaps even representing the name of the town, it seems to be the most poorly attested variant in the ancient Gospel manuscripts and may not fit as well with "territory of" description found in all three accounts.

Because Gadara is not too distant from Kursi, especially the apparent harbor of Gadara near Tel Samra at Kibbutz Ha'on only about 7 miles (11 km) south of Kursi, it may be plausible to associate the "land of the Gadarenes" extending as far as the area of Kursi. Or, perhaps the Byzantine church was simply built in the general area but not on the exact location.

Josephus placed the cities of Hippos and Gadara in close proximity and remarked that the territory of Gadara extended to the Sea of Galilee (Josephus, *Life* 42). Since the city of Hippos has been identified and excavated, located just to the north of the site of Kursi, the reading "land of the Gadarenes" seems to be supported by the majority of the evidence.

The name for the site, Kursi, which is Aramaic and means "seat," is seemingly not found in the Gospels. This name was preserved in a village that had been located nearby, but which seems to trace back to the village of Kursi mentioned in the Talmud from late antiquity. The Talmud records a Kursi that was included in a list of pagan towns during the Roman period, which agrees with the accounts about the area and people in the Gospels. Therefore, it is possible that Kursi (transmitted into Greek as Gergesa) was the ancient name of the village near the time the miracle happened. Surveys and excavations indicate that there may have been a village located on the shore of the lake, about 300 meters from the Byzantine church, around the time of Jesus.

This Byzantine church at Kursi was constructed during the 5th century to commemorate a miracle of Jesus performed in the area. Correlation with the Gospel account suggests it was probably the casting out of the legion of demons into the swine. The church was constructed with two aisles and a nave, separated by two rows of columns, with a decorative mosaic floor with 296 design elements consisting of geometric designs, plants, and animals, such as birds, fish, pomegranates, and grapes. Unfortunately, most of the designs were destroyed during the Islamic period. The church also had a baptistery, and a dedicatory

Kursi church and cliffs

inscription on the mosaic floor at the entrance to the baptistery dates the construction of this addition to AD 585. Another chapel was found to the south of the church, and some type of structure had been built around a large boulder that may have been associated with the event recorded in the Gospels.

Additionally, a monastery and a bath complex was discovered, suggesting that an inn or hostel was located there in the Byzantine period for pilgrims to stay in as they journeyed to sites in the Holy Land. Recently, an eight-line Aramaic inscription dating to about AD 500, carved into a piece of marble about 140 cm by 70 cm, was found at the site. The inscription is fragmentary, but the words *amen* and *marmaria* (possibly meaning "son of Mary" or "marble") are visible. While theories about the inscription claim that it was a synagogue dedication and that the people practiced Judaism, it could be a Christian inscription. Untranslated, it merely demonstrates that Kursi was occupied into the 6th century AD by Aramaic speakers.

It is possible that these people practiced Judaism, although many local Christians also would have spoken Aramaic, and the presence of a church and monastery, combined with the fact that the Sassanid Persians destroyed the site in AD 614, demonstrates that the village was primarily occupied by Christians through this period. The church was rebuilt, but after the earthquake of AD 749 destroyed it once more, it was abandoned.

No remains from the Roman period have been recovered at the site of the church, but it is possible that a nearby town existed during the time of Jesus. This is in agreement with the tradition that it was the location where Jesus cast out the demons into the swine that plunged into the Sea of Galilee, and it would also explain why the location was referred to as the "land" or "territory" of the Gadarenes in the Gospels rather than the name of a particular town.

A harbor from the 1st century was discovered about 300 meters west of the church, and excavations there demonstrate that a village from antiquity was situated on the shore, also possibly during the 1st century AD. Therefore, it could have been the place where Jesus and his disciples landed after crossing over from the west side of the lake (Mark 5:1).

The people living in this region on the eastern side of the Sea of Galilee were part of the Decapolis, and generally Hellenistic in culture and religion rather than Judeans following the Mosaic Law. This is attested by the herd of swine mentioned in the passage, the attitude of those in the area towards Jesus not as a blasphemer of God but a miracle worker, and the mention of the people of the demoniac and the Decapolis region (Mark 5:13-20).

The church at Kursi, which may have been built up the hill from a village also known as Gergesa, certainly commemorates a significant event recorded in the Gospels, and was probably built at the place remembered as the location where Jesus cast out the legion of demons into the swine and then sent the formerly demon-possessed man into the Decapolis region to proclaim what Jesus had done.

THE DECAPOLIS

The Decapolis cities, located near and to the east and northeast of the Jordan River and the Sea of Galilee, were a group of ten cities in the Roman period that may have been semiautonomous. The name is derived from the number and description in Greek: *deca* (ten), *polis* (city). Most of the cities were originally founded during the Hellenistic period after Alexander the Great had conquered the region in ca. 323 BC. Eventually these cities gained a measure of independence after the Romans under Pompey conquered the region in ca. 64 BC and they were released from the authority of the Hasmoneans, which had resulted in cultural and religious tensions between Judaism and Hellenism.

However, both Hippos and Gadara were included in the kingdom of Herod the Great, and all of the cities must have had governmental oversight through a regional authority that led back to Rome. Inscriptions, coins, and historical writings demonstrate that the region of the Decapolis came into being after Rome conquered the area, but possibly as late as the early 1st century AD. Ancient city lists of the Decapolis come from writings of Pliny the Elder, Josephus, Ptolemy, Eusebius, Epiphanus, and Stephan of Byzantium.

The ten cities of Pliny, perhaps the original ten, were Damascus, Canatha, Hippus, Dion, Raphana (also known as Abila?), Gadara, Scythopolis, Pella, Gerasa, and Philadelphia (Pliny the Elder, *Natural History*). Raphana is sometimes identified as Abila, which is a city name found on later lists. All of these cities except Scythopolis were located on the eastern side of the Jordan River, and Sycthopolis (formerly Beth-Shean) was apparently also the largest city of the Decapolis (Josephus, *Wars* 3.446).

A combination of the different lists shows an eventual total of 17 or 18 cities, since the additional cities of Helopolis, Abila (Raphana?), Saana, Hina, Abila Lysanius, Capitolias, Edrei, and Samulis may have gained a semiautonomous status and joined the group over time (Ptolemy, *Geography* 5.14-22).

A variant in Mark also mentions the country of Gerasenes, which appears to be connected to the area of the Decapolis city of Gerasa or Jerash (Mark 5:1). However, the original reading for this passage relating to a Decapolis city may be "Gadarenes," connected to another Decapolis city named Gadara and attested in many ancient manuscripts of the Gospels (cf. Matthew 8:28; Byzantine text Mark 5:1 and Luke 8:26).

An inscription from the time of Emperor Hadrian in about AD 134, found near Palmyra, mentions Abila of the Decapolis. The earliest literary mention of the Decapolis seems to be found in the Gospels, where the term "Decapolis" is recorded, even though the specific cities are not listed (Matthew 4:25; Mark 5:20; 7:31). Jesus fed the 4000 in this general area, healed a deaf man, cast out demons, and presumably taught (Mark 5:1-20; 7:31–8:10).

Although no evidence exists that these cities formed any type of formal coalition or league, they were informally connected by their independent status, geography, and shared Hellenistic culture. Many of the coins from the cities mention concepts such as freedom, autonomy, and sovereignty, indicating that they exercised a degree of independence in their governing status at a local and regional level. An inscription on a coin issued by Scythopolis, rather than mentioning the Senate or Pompey, honored General Gabinius who had helped free and then rebuild the city. In contrast, Judea Province had Roman coins issued under the prefects and then procurators which honored the emperor.

Jerash

While maintaining a degree of autonomy, the cities were still ultimately under the authority of the Roman Empire and attached to various provinces or kingdoms depending on the time period, such as the Herodian kingdom, Syria Province, Arabia Petraea, and Syria Palaestina, although they appear to have functioned in a way similar to city-states on the local level. The Decapolis cities were usually located on major roads and often at crossroads, had natural fortifications, and were supplied with significant water sources. These attributes contributed to their economic prosperity and their ability to retain at least a degree of autonomy.

During the Roman period, the cities also had their layouts redone according to the style of Roman cities with a grid-style street system built around a central *cardo* (main north-south street in a Roman city), and typical Roman structures such as stadiums, theaters, agoras, temples, Roman baths, and aqueducts were built.

These cities were also very Hellenistic in their culture and religion, although they were influenced by the ideas of the surrounding local Semitic populations. However, the majority of the influence was pagan and polytheistic, and these were not cities in which those practicing Judaism would typically live.

One inscription from around AD 90 and the reign of Emperor Domitian mentions a Roman administrator of equestrian rank, such as a prefect or procurator, in Decapolis of Syria, suggesting that the region had its own separate Roman administrator within Syria Province, similar to Judea. There is debate as to whether the Decapolis should be considered only a geographical term referring to a group of cities in the region that shared a common Hellenistic culture and had a degree of autonomy or a subsection of a province that existed as a more distinct administrative unit. However, prior to AD 106 when the Decapolis cities were split between multiple provinces and likely the term became geographical, the Decapolis may have been a separate administrative and semiautonomous area.

While it is known that Jesus preached and performed miracles in the Decapolis region, the Gospels never record any problems with the authorities or with religious leaders from that area. In light of the polytheistic Hellenistic culture of the day, which was rapidly adopting gods from regions all over the Empire, the religious community in the Decapolis region likely would not have had a problem with Jesus performing miracles or claiming to be God, or a god as they would initially interpret him due to their polytheistic worldview. Yet, the message and miracles of Jesus appear to have significantly affected the Decapolis region and paved the way for the early church in the area.

According to Eusebius, during the beginning of the First Judean Revolt against Rome and prior to the AD 70 destruction of Jerusalem, many Christians fled from Judea Province and the surrounding regions into the Decapolis, and in particular to the city of Pella (Eusebius, *Ecclesiastical History*). In later years, Pella was a major center of Christianity and the entire region of the Decapolis became predominantly Christian as evidenced by early church writings and the many Byzantine-period church buildings that have been discovered in the ruins of those ancient cities.

BETHSAIDA

The ancient town of Bethsaida in the Galilee region, probably meaning "house of fishing," was situated on the northeastern shore of the Sea of Galilee, but its exact location has been debated. Three disciples of Jesus came from Bethsaida of Galilee—Andrew, Peter, and Philip—which was a fishing town on the coast of the Sea of Galilee that is usually identified as the same location (John 1:44; 12:21). The healing of a blind man happened at Bethsaida, the feeding of the 5000 took place somewhere in the vicinity of Bethsaida, and Jesus walked on water when the disciples were on their way across the lake from Bethsaida to the Capernaum area (Matthew 14:13-34; Mark 6:31-53; 8:10-26; Luke 9:10-17; John 6:1-25). Jesus also chastised Bethsaida for the unbelief of its people, along with the town of Chorazin, which was located only about 2.5 miles (4 km) to the north of Capernaum (Matthew 11:21-22; Luke 10:13).

Josephus noted that the city of Bethsaida was on the Sea of Galilee, located near the Jordan River, and in lower Gaulanitis (Josephus, *Life* 398-399; *Wars* 2.168, 3.515). It was a fishing village or town until Philip the Tetrarch expanded it and renamed it Julias around AD 30, after Julia, the daughter of Augustus, who was his only biological child (Josephus, *Antiquities* 18.28). This location in the realm of Philip the Tetrarch rather than Herod Antipas may be why Jesus and the disciples made their way across the lake to the area of Bethsaida soon after the execution of John the Baptizer by Herod Antipas.

Eusebius mentions the city in the 4th century AD, suggesting that it was still occupied in the Byzantine period (Eusebius, *Onamasticon*). Bethsaida is also mentioned as being six miles from Capernaum according to a 6th-century writer (Theodosius). A Byzantine church may have also been present at the site as late as the 8th century, over a location thought to be the home of Peter and Andrew (Huneberc, *Hodoeporicon of Saint Willibad*, Simon of Basora).

Unfortunately, there was no ancient name preservation of Bethsaida at any village in the area.

Currently, the most popular archaeological identification with ancient Bethsaida is a site called Et-Tell, although an alternative candidate El-Araj to the south has been recently studied, surveyed, and excavated. A third proposed site, Messadiyeh, has produced no evidence and has ceased to be regarded as a viable candidate.

Some scholars have also proposed that there were two different cities named Bethsaida—a Bethsaida Julias and a Bethsaida of Galilee (cf. John 12:21). Although a possibility, no evidence from ancient texts or archaeology yet exists to support this hypothesis. While Josephus mentions that Bethsaida was located in lower Gaulanitis, which had been part of the tetrarchy of Philip, John may have included Galilee as a geographical rather than political description. While suggestions have even been made that the two nearby sites, El-Araj on the shore and near the river, and Et-Tell about 1.5 miles (2.4 kilometers) northeast of the shore and near the river, were two parts of one city, this seems implausible due to their distance of about 1.5 miles from each other.

Et-Tell is currently the site that most refer to as Bethsaida. It is located about 1.5 miles northeast of the current shore and approximately 23 feet (7 meters) higher than the level of the lake in ancient times. It was apparently a city with a long history, as excavations have yielded remains from the Early Bronze Age, Iron Age, Persian period, Hellenistic period, Roman period, and medieval times, although with fewer remains from the 1st century AD and the time of Jesus than might be expected and no discovered remains from the Byzantine period, which may also be problematic.

Finds of interest from the Roman period include a possible Roman or Hellenistic temple, a house, lead and basalt weights probably used in fishing, iron hooks, basalt anchors, and a clay seal depicting two people standing in a boat with fish underneath. The main problem with the identification of this site as Bethsaida is its distance from the lakeshore and its higher elevation in contrast to known coastal towns from the 1st century, such as Capernaum, Magdala, Tiberias, and Kursi, suggesting that during the 1st century it was nowhere near the shore and thus would not match the ancient descriptions of Bethsaida.

However, advocates in favor of Et-Tell as Bethsaida claim that the lake extended much farther north in the 1st century and that a cataclysmic geological event along with a landslide in AD 363 raised the level of the ground all around the city from the shore level to its current level, changed the course of the Jordan River, and filled in the lake near the site with silt.

While it may be possible that the lake extended farther north in ancient times due to extreme buildup of sediment, if the lake in the 1st century did extend up to the site, the city still would not have been on the shore like the other known coastal towns on the Sea of Galilee because of its substantially higher elevation. Therefore, the supporters proposed a geologic event that raised the entire area of the city, including the alleged dock, 23 feet above the ancient sea level. Yet, this cataclysmic event appears to have left structures intact, leaving behind no evidence of the supposed event. Rather, the archaeology of the site indicates consistency in the topography from ancient times.

Further, scientific analysis of the sediment suggests that the area in front of Et-Tell had been covered by land, not water, at least as early as the 1st century BC, and this appears to be confirmed by the geographical description of the area in Josephus. The cataclysm explanation seems to be based merely on the idea that Et-Tell must be Bethsaida, regardless of the geographical problems.

If the ancient city had an acropolis and also a lower section that did extend down to the level of the water, there has not yet been any evidence found to indicate this. However, the fact that 1st-century settlements have been discovered south of Et-Tell on the shore of the lake would seem to refute the

Excavated structures at El-Araj, the possible location of Bethsaida

hypothesis that the lake extended north all the way to Et-Tell in the 1st century. Alternatively, the site of Et-Tell could have been another town located near the lake but not on it, like Hippos. Another possible problem with identifying Et-Tell as Bethsaida is its prominence during ancient times, especially the Iron Age, and yet no written material prior to the Roman period mentions a Bethsaida or any city with a similar name.

El-Araj is located on the shore of the lake, near the Jordan River, and its elevation is approximately the same as other 1st-century AD coastal towns such as Capernaum, Magdala, Kursi, and Tiberias. Although earlier assessments of El-Araj claimed that the site emerged in the Byzantine period, and therefore was not in existence during the 1st century AD, archaeological investigation has demonstrated that it was first settled during the late Hellenistic period about the 2nd century BC, occupied during the Roman period and the time of Jesus in the 1st century AD, and then continued into the Byzantine period.

Architectural fragments made of limestone and basalt, typical of public buildings, were also discovered at the site, along with mosaics. Earlier explorations at El-Araj had revealed pottery and coins from the 1st century AD, including coins issued during the time of Pontius Pilatus. Recent excavations discovered stone vessel fragments used in purification rituals of Judaism, a Roman bathhouse, and a Byzantine church visited by Bishop Willibald of Bavaria around AD 725 probably built to commemorate the home of Peter and Andrew.

Therefore, the site of El-Araj fulfills necessary requirements of occupational period and location for Bethsaida according to ancient texts such as the Gospels, Josephus, and early church fathers, although it is currently lacking definitive evidence such as an inscription mentioning the name of the city.

SELECTED BIBLIOGRAPHY
(CHAPTER 4)

Alexander, Yardena. "'Cana in Galilee': A Jewish Settlement in Kerem a-Ras, near Kafr Cana of the Second Temple Period." Israel Antiquities Authority.

Anderson, Paul. "Aspects of Historicity in the Gospel of John: Implications for Investigations of Jesus and Archaeology." *Jesus and Archaeology*, ed. James Charlesworth. Grand Rapids: Eerdmans, 2006.

Anderson, Robert. "The Elusive Samaritan Temple." *Biblical Archaeologist* 54, no. 2 (1991).

Arav, Rami. "Bethsaida—A Response to Steven Notley." *Near Eastern Archaeology* 74, no. 2 (2011).

———. "Bethsaida." *Jesus and Archaeology*, ed. James Charlesworth. Grand Rapids: Eerdmans, 2006.

———. "Et-Tell and El-Araj." *Israel Exploration Journal* 38:3 (1988).

Bahat, Dan. "Jesus and the Herodian Temple Mount." *Jesus and Archaeology*, ed. James Charlesworth. Grand Rapids: Eerdmans, 2006.

Barton, George. "Parables Outside the Gospels." *Biblical World* 33, no. 5 (1909).

Brown, Francis et al., *Enhanced Brown-Driver-Briggs Hebrew and English Lexicon*. Oak Harbor, WA: Logos, 2000.

Bull, Robert. "An Archaeological Context for Understanding John 4:20." *Biblical Archaeologist* 38, no. 2 (1975).

Croy, N. Clayton. "The Messianic Whippersnapper: Did Jesus Use a Whip on People in the Temple (John 2:15)?" *Journal of Biblical Literature* 128, no. 3 (2009).

Ehrman, Bart. *Did Jesus Exist? The Historical Argument for Jesus of Nazareth*. San Francisco: HarperOne, 2012.

Evans, Craig. *Jesus and His World: The Archaeological Evidence*. Louisville: Westminster, 2012.

Feldman, Steven. "The Case for el-Araj." *Biblical Archaeology Review* 26:01 (2000).

Gibson, Shimon. "Excavations at the Bethesda Pool in Jerusalem." Bouwen, ed., Sainte-Anne de Jérusalem. La Piscine Probatiquen de Jésus À Saladin. Proche-Orient Chrétien Numéro Spécial.

Huffman, Norman. "Atypical Features in the Parables of Jesus." *Journal of Biblical Literature* 97, no. 2 (1978).

Hultgren, Arland. *The Parables of Jesus.* Grand Rapids: Eerdmans, 2000.

Isaac, Benjamin. "The Decapolis in Syria, a Neglected Inscription." *Zeitschrift für Papyrologie und Epigraphik Bd.* 44 (1981).

———. "A Donation for Herod's Temple in Jerusalem." *Israel Exploration Journal* 33, no. 1/2 (1983).

Kopp, Clemens. *The Holy Places of the Gospels.* New York: Herder and Herder, 1963.

Lapp, Paul, and Nancy Lapp, eds. *Discoveries in the Wadi ed-Daliyeh. The Annual of the American Schools of Oriental Research* 41, 1974.

Liddell et al., *A Greek-English Lexicon.* Oxford: Clarendon, 1996.

Magen, Yitzhak. "The Dating of the First Phase of the Samaritan Temple on Mount Gerizim in Light of the Archaeological Evidence." *Judah and the Judeans in the Fourth Century BCE*, ed. Lipschits, et al. Winona Lake, IN: Eisenbrauns, 2007.

———. "Jerusalem as a Center of the Stone Vessel Industry during the Second Temple Period." H. Geva, ed. *Ancient Jerusalem Revealed.* Jerusalem: Israel Exploration Society, 1994.

———. "The Sacred Precinct on Mount Gerizim." *Bible and Spade* 14:2 (2001).

Mare, Harold. "Abila of the Decapolis Excavations, Northern Jordan." https://bibleinterp .arizona.edu/excavations/Abila_of_the_Decapolis, 2004.

Masterman, E.W.G. "The Pool of Bethesda." *Biblical World* 25, no. 2 (1905).

Mazar, Benjamin. "The Royal Stoa in the Southern Part of the Temple Mount." Proceedings of the American Academy for Jewish Research 46-47 (1979–80).

McCollough, C. Thomas. "Searching for Cana: Where Jesus Turned Water into Wine." *Biblical Archaeology Review* 41:6 (2015).

McRay, John. *Archaeology and the New Testament.* Grand Rapids: Baker Academic, 1991.

Menninga, Clarence. "The Unique Church at Abila of the Decapolis." *Near Eastern Archaeology* 67:1 (2004).

Metzger, Bruce. *A Textual Commentary on the Greek New Testament.* New York: United Bible Societies, 1994.

Netzer, Ehud. *The Architecture of Herod, the Great Builder*. Grand Rapids: Baker Academic, 2008.

Notley, Steven. "Et-Tell Is Not Bethsaida." *Near Eastern Archaeology* 70, no. 4 (2007).

———. "Reply to Arav." *Near Eastern Archaeology* 74, no. 2 (2011).

Notley, Steven, and Mordechai Aviam. "Searching for Bethsaida: The Case for El-Araj." *Biblical Archaeology Review* 46:2 (2020).

Parker, S. Thomas. "The Decapolis Reviewed." *Journal of Biblical Literature* 94, no. 3 (1975).

Pentecost, J. Dwight. *The Parables of Jesus*. Grand Rapids: Kregel, 1998.

Quintus Curtius Rufus, *Histories of Alexander the Great*.

Reed, Jonathan. *Archaeology and the Galilean Jesus*. Harrisburg, PA: Trinity, 2000.

Richardson, Peter. "Khirbet Qana (and Other Villages) as a Context for Jesus." *Jesus and Archaeology*, ed. James Charlesworth. Grand Rapids: Eerdmans, 2006.

Segal, Arthur, and Michael Eisenberg. "Sussita-Hippos of the Decapolis: Town Planning and Architecture of a Roman-Byzantine City." *Near Eastern Archaeology* 70, no. 2 (2007).

Spijkerman, Augustus. *The Coins of the Decapolis and Provincia Arabia*. Jerusalem: Franciscan, 1978.

Swanson, James. *Dictionary of Biblical Languages with Semantic Domains*. Oak Harbor, WA: Logos, 1997.

Zangenberg, Jurgen. "Between Jerusalem and the Galilee: Samaria in the Time of Jesus." *Jesus and Archaeology*, ed. James Charlesworth. Grand Rapids: Eerdmans, 2006.

CHAPTER 5

Fame and Opposition

Before Jesus began his ministry and while he was still working as a crafts-man based in Nazareth, Herod Antipas the tetrarch decided to move his capital city from Sepphoris to a new site on the western shore of the Sea of Galilee. Sepphoris was near Nazareth, and therefore it is possible, even probable, that Jesus visited Sepphoris. Excavations at the city have shown that during the time of Jesus in the 1st century, stone vessels and immersion baths (*miqvah*) for ritual purification in Judaism were used, and there was a lack of pig bones found indicating adherence to the Mosaic Law.

Because the Sepphoris theatre was possibly enlarged during the time of Jesus by order of Herod Antipas, it has been proposed that Joseph and Jesus and perhaps his brothers worked on this project. But Joseph and Jesus would almost certainly decline to work on a Hellenistic, pagan theatre ordered by a ruler that later sought to kill Jesus and whom Jesus later denigrates in his teaching. Working at Sepphoris also would have been unnecessary, as there was sufficient work in Nazareth and other nearby villages such as Cana.

THE CITY OF TIBERIAS

In about the year AD 18, Antipas began construction on his new capi-tal. This city, Tiberias, was built and named in honor of the current emperor, Tiberius, and populated with the poor, soldiers, settlers from outside the area, and the wealthy who were more friendly to Hellenism and Rome (Josephus, *Antiquities* 18.36-38). In order to make the appearance of Tiberias grand, and to aid its economic strength, Antipas built houses for and gave land to the poor who were relocated to the city, so effectually there would be no poor people in Tiberias.

Previously, the capital city of Antipas had been located at Sepphoris, in the hills to the west and near the villages of Nazareth and Cana, and while Sepphoris remained the largest city in Galilee, its status as principal place in Galilee was replaced by Tiberias, which may have grown to a population of around 30,000 people in the 1st century (Josephus, *Life* 37-38). The city of Tiberias had the advantages of being a more central location than Sepphoris for Antipas to rule his territories of Galilee and Peraea, it was located on the shore of the lake, and it was also a completely new city that he could design and populate according to his liking. The city was probably completed and officially founded in about AD 23, according to numismatic evidence.

Tiberias was built on land previously occupied by a graveyard, in violation of purity laws in Judaism, but apparently it was such a prime location that Antipas was willing to go against tradition and risk offending a segment of the population of Galilee. However, there were synagogues in Tiberias, and fragments of stone vessels and ritual baths have been found, demonstrating that at least part of the population practiced Judaism to some degree, although many also likely adopted facets of Hellenism.

Agrippa I, brother-in-law to Antipas, appears to have been appointed the *agoranomos* (market overseer) of Tiberias for a few years around AD 30, according to the records of Josephus and an inscribed weight found at the city. This was a political stepping stone for Agrippa I, a Herodian with Roman citizenship and a Roman name connected to Emperor Claudius, apparently opposed to Jesus, and who later ruled the entire area as a king for the Romans and persecuted Christians.

Tiberias was comparable to other Hellenistic and Roman-style cities throughout the Empire in regard to its layout, buildings, and government. It was allowed to mint its own coinage, elect an archon and committee of 10 along with a city council of 600, and was recognized as distinct from the rest of the Galilee region even during the First Judean Revolt when it sided with Rome and was spared (Josephus, *Wars* 3.446-461).

The city had a grid layout of streets intersecting at 90 degree angles, and the typical Roman north-south *cardo* and east-west *decumanus maximus* (the main

The ancient theatre of Tiberias

north-south and east-west streets in Roman cities), connecting it to Sepphoris and Caesarea Maritima in the west, Scythopolis and Jerusalem in the south, and eventually all the way to Syria Province in the north.

Similar to many Roman cities of the region, no city wall was built when Tiberias was founded. This was probably done for both economic and political reasons, saving time and resources and assuring that the city could not fortify itself against the Romans in the case of rebellion. Eventually, however, during the reign of Septimius Severus around AD 200, a wall was constructed.

Buildings in 1st-century AD Tiberias included a stadium, a synagogue, Roman baths, a marketplace, a harbor, a mint, a theatre, two towers, and a palace (Josephus, *Wars* 3.539; *Life* 65-68, 85, 277). Based on the surface area of the city, it was probably the second most populous in the Galilee region. The mint, an important marker of economic and political power, stamped coins with "Herod Tetrarch" and the name of the city enveloped in a wreath. The theatre, situated at the base of Mount Berenice, would have seated about 5000 people. Antipas, the tetrarch of Galilee, was based here during the ministry of Jesus (Matthew 14:1; Mark 6:14; Luke 3:1).

The palace of Herod Antipas, built in the style of a Roman villa, including an imported marble floor and decorated columns, appears to have been the definition of luxury (Luke 7:25). The request for the execution of John the Baptist came at a birthday party for Antipas, which seems to have been held at this palace in Tiberias. The city was probably the location where John's head was delivered, although he had been imprisoned earlier at Machaerus and likely also executed at Machaerus (Matthew 14:6-12; Josephus, *Antiquities* 18.119).

The city of Tiberias is mentioned only once in the Gospels (John 6:23), and Jesus may have avoided visiting the city to elude the grasp of Antipas, who had imprisoned and executed John the Baptizer, and was on the hunt for Jesus (Luke 13:31-35; 23:8-12).

THE BEHEADING OF JOHN THE BAPTIZER

During the preaching of John the Baptizer, which included the foretelling of the coming Messiah and messages against sin, he spoke out against certain actions of Herod Antipas. In addition to other unnamed wicked things Antipas had done, John publicly opposed Antipas for marrying Herodias, the wife of his brother Herod Philip (Matthew 14:3; Mark 6:17-18; Luke 3:19-20; Josephus, *Antiquities* 18.109-113).

Herod Antipas the tetrarch had been married to Phasaelis, the daughter of Aretas IV, king of Nabatea, but while at Rome, Antipas stayed with his brother Philip (probably son of Mariamme II) and fell in love with the unavailable Herodias. Subsequently, Antipas divorced Phasaelis and married Herodias. This eventually caused a war between Antipas and Aretas IV in which the army of Antipas was totally destroyed (Josephus, *Antiquities* 18.113-115).

John proclaimed that the marriage between Antipas and Herodias was against the Law of Moses (Leviticus 20:21). But for speaking out against this violation, John was locked up in prison by Antipas at a fortress called Machaerus, rebuilt by Herod the Great, which was located on top of a high hill on the northeastern side of the Dead Sea (Josephus, *Antiquities* 18.119; Matthew 14:3-4).

Machaerus was supposedly the second most fortified place in the region, behind Jerusalem (Pliny, *Naturalis Historia* 5.15-72). Josephus referred to Machaerus as a place on the borders of the dominions of Aretas IV and Herod, a fortress, and subject to Aretas. Machaerus had originally been built by Alexander Jannaeus, second king of the Hasmonean dynasty, in about 90 BC as an eastern border outpost. The Romans partially destroyed the fortress when Pompey was overseeing the conquest of the region, but it was later rebuilt by Herod the Great, who upgraded it into an extravagant palace fortress in 30 BC. Upon the death of Herod the Great, control of this palace fortress and the surrounding territory of Perea apparently passed to Herod Antipas the tetrarch. Ruins of the fortress remain to this day, although a prison room has not been located.

Herodias seems to have become particularly angry at John the Baptist for speaking against them and wanted to silence and execute John for this. However, Antipas was afraid of John because he was a righteous and holy man who also had substantial influence over the people. So, for a while, Antipas kept him imprisoned but also kept him safe, and often enjoyed listening to John (Mark 6:19-20).

Josephus framed the situation from a different perspective, viewing the public denunciation of Antipas as a problem that could undermine the tetrarch politically. Since both of the marriages had serious political implications, John preaching publicly about the law of God and the immoral choices of Antipas could have been interpreted as sedition or inciting rebellion against the tetrarch.

While John the Baptizer was in prison, he heard about some of the miraculous works of Jesus. Although he had met Jesus previously, baptized him, and proclaimed that Jesus was the prophesied Messiah, he had his disciples ask Jesus if he was "the Coming One, or are we to look for someone else?" (Matthew 11:12-3). Apparently, while in prison, John had begun to have doubts about

The fortress palace of Machaerus, where John the Baptizer was imprisoned and probably executed

Jesus and wanted to hear answers directly from Jesus himself. Jesus sent a message back to John that the blind, the lame, the deaf, and the diseased are healed, the dead are raised up, and the gospel is being preached (Matthew 11:4-5; cf. Isaiah 35:5-6). After sending the message to John, Jesus preached a lesson related to the life of John in which Jesus spoke against Antipas without naming him, but called him a reed shaken by the wind and a man in soft clothing (Luke 7:24-27).

This description was completely the opposite of the prophet John, a man living in the wilderness with clothes of camel hair who ate locusts and wild honey. The insult of a "reed shaken by the wind" that Jesus used was probably a reference to coins of Herod Antipas with the iconography of a reed on them, issued around AD 20 and in use during the life and ministry of Jesus. Perhaps it was only coincidence, but Antipas later changed the iconography on his coins from a reed to a palm branch.

At a birthday celebration for Antipas, probably around AD 31, there was a large banquet for the civil leaders, military commanders, and elites of Galilee. Salome, the daughter of Herodias, danced as entertainment at this party. Her dancing pleased Antipas and the dinner guests so much that Antipas promised her that he would give her anything she wanted up to half of his kingdom. Salome consulted her mother on this matter, and Herodias advised that she should ask for the head of John the Baptizer. Salome made the request, and Antipas felt compelled to keep his oath, even though he was distressed that he would have to execute John. Therefore, Antipas gave the command, and John was executed by beheading in the prison. The head of John the Baptist was then brought back on a platter, given to Salome, and Salome gave it to Herodias (Matthew 14:1-12; Mark 6:14-29; Luke 9:7-9).

The Synoptic Gospels and Josephus refer to the execution of John the Baptizer, and Josephus adds specific information that John had been imprisoned in Machaerus, where he was probably executed and his head subsequently brought back to Tiberias in Galilee for Salome (Josephus, *Antiquities* 18.110-119). Salome, the daughter of Herodias and stepdaughter of Herod Antipas the Tetrarch, in an odd and complicated web of familial relationships, was both a granddaughter and great-granddaughter of Herod the Great. She also married one of her uncles and subsequently one of her cousins. Salome first married Philip the Tetrarch, then sometime after his death in AD 34 she married Aristobulus of Chalcis, becoming queen of Chalcis and Armenia Minor. A few ancient manuscripts of Mark suggest that she may have also had the name Herodias, like her mother, but was typically called by her other name, Salome (or Shlomit), to avoid confusion.

An extremely rare coin from Chalcis, only three of which are currently known, shows a portrait of Salome on a coin issued by her husband Aristobulus around AD 56. The obverse shows the head of Aristobulus with the Greek inscription "King Aristobulus" and the reverse shows Salome with the Greek inscription "Queen Salome."

Salome, daughter of Herodias, depicted on a coin of her husband, Aristobulus of Chalcis

Although a courtyard excavated at Machaerus has alternatively been suggested as the location of the birthday banquet and dance, this idea appears unlikely when evaluated with what is known about Herod Antipas, his kingdom, and the story of John the Baptizer. Tiberias was the capital city and the location of the main palace for Herod Antipas, the writings of Josephus indicate that the fortress of Machaerus was not as significant a location for Antipas and was not referred to as a grand palace, and the narrative in the Gospel of Mark specifically states that the banquet was given for the leaders of Galilee, indicating that the celebration occurred in Galilee at the capital city of Tiberias.

News of the beheading spread to the followers of John, who then took and buried the body, then went and told Jesus and his disciples (Mark 6:29-32). The fact that Herod Antipas feared the great influence John had over the people, and that many attributed the defeat and destruction of the army of Herod Antipas by Aretas as repayment from God for an unjust execution of John, demonstrates the significant effect John and his ministry had on the region (Josephus, *Antiquities* 18.119).

Into the time of the church in the Byzantine period, John continued to be regarded as an exemplary believer and early martyr for Jesus and Christianity. Evidence from at least as early as the 4th century, such as his traditional burial place at Sebaste, an inscribed depiction of what appears to be John the Baptizer found in a cave near Ein Kerem, and many ancient works of art portraying John in events from his life, suggests that he was seen as an important figure by early Christians, and memory of his words and deeds lived on in the Gospels and several other texts from antiquity, despite his imprisonment and execution ending a relatively short life.

VISIT TO TYRE AND SIDON

The Roman province of Syria was established in 64 BC, and Tyre was one of the most important cities with its harbor and commerce, including the famous Tyrian purple dye made from the murex sea snail. Sidon was located nearby to the north. While Antioch was the capital of the province, the ancient cities of Tyre and Sidon were still influential in the 1st century, and Jesus visited the region of Tyre and Sidon at least once (Matthew 15:21-28; Mark 7:24-30).

Excavations at Tyre have revealed a major road and many tombs from around the time of Jesus, and tombs from this period have also been discovered at Sidon. Although the area was primarily pagan, some followers of Jesus were from there, perhaps as a result of an earlier visit or because word had spread north about the teaching and miracles of Jesus (Mark 3:7-8; Luke 6:17-19).

Tyre was also the place where the famous Tyrian shekel was minted, which ironically was used to pay the temple tax in Jerusalem even though there were images of the pagan god Melqart (associated with Herakles) and an eagle on the coin. This valuable silver shekel or *tetradrachma* likely circulated in Judea at least as early as the 2nd century BC, although new coins continued to be minted (Mishna *Bekhoroth* 8:7). This coin was of higher silver content than typical coins and for that reason it came to be commonly used for paying the temple tax because the purity of silver was highly valued. A half *shekel* or two *drachma* coin with the same iconography and inscription was also minted and circulated, although there was an additional fee assessed on a half-shekel payment.

These coins would be sold in exchange for common Roman currency so that the temple tax could be paid with a "proper" or accepted coin. Although bearing an image of a pagan deity prohibited by the Law of Moses, this coin was the standard used for the temple tax and exchange transactions in the Jerusalem temple courts during the Hasmonean and Roman periods. On a visit to the temple, Jesus overturned the tables of the corrupt moneychangers containing these coins and halting the transactions (Matthew 21:12; Mark 11:15-17; John 2:13-16).

By the time of Jesus, the practice of paying the temple tax had been going on in some form for over a millennium, but it had not been instituted as a yearly or regular tax until either the Persian period or later (Josephus, *Antiquities* 3.194-195). Documents from Qumran indicate that the community there continued to understand the tax as a single payment rather than annual (Magness, "Two Notes on the Archaeology of Qumran").

According to the Mishnah, even after AD 70 when the temple was destroyed by the Romans, the temple tax continued on for a short period, perhaps with the thought that the temple would be rebuilt. Regardless of where an Israelite man was living, in the Roman period he was responsible to submit the annual temple tax to Jerusalem as part of the religious, cultural, and national law (Philo, *The Special Laws*; Mishna *Shekalim*).

After the Ifsya hoard was discovered and analyzed, it was found to contain 3400 Tyrian shekels, 1000 half-shekels, and 160 Roman denarii, which equates perfectly with payment of the temple tax and the 8 percent additional payment mentioned in the Mishnah required of those who pay with a half-shekel. It seems that the Romans required these coins to continue to be minted with the pagan imagery, even for those coins made primarily for the purpose of paying the temple tax.

In Capernaum, Peter was asked about this two drachma tax, which was equivalent to the shekel of the sanctuary (Matthew 17:24-27; cf. Numbers 3:44-48 LXX). Jesus told Peter that when he would open the mouth of the fish, he will find a standard coin (*stater*), which he can then use to pay the tax for both of them. It is usually assumed that this coin would be a Tyrian shekel. The Roman *stater* was a standard coin that could be the equivalent of four drachmas, and the Tyrian *tetradrachma* was this value. Discoveries of coin hoards consisting mostly of Tyrian *tetradrachmas* from the 1st century have been found throughout the region of ancient Judea, suggesting the widespread use of the coin for the annual tax. Although the passage indicates that Jesus probably had not been paying this additional tax previously, he chose to have Peter pay for both of them in this instance so that they would not cause offense to the tax collectors.

A silver Tyrian shekel depicting Melqart-Herakles and an eagle

MAGDALA

The town of Magdala was located on the western coast of the Sea of Galilee in the 1st century, and the name has been preserved until today as Al-Majdal. Magdala, which seems to also be referred to in the Talmud as Magdala Nunnaya, means "Tower of Fish" in Aramaic, while according to Roman documents of the period it was called Taricheae in Greek, meaning "Salted Fish" (Pesahim 46a; Josephus, *Life*; Strabo, *Geography*; Pliny, *Natural History*). The town was north of Tiberias and south of Capernaum, near Mount Arbel. Pliny mistakenly located Magdala south of Tiberias, but since he was a native of Italy, it is not surprising that he could have made a minor geographical error in his report on Judea.

Archaeological excavations at Magdala suggest that it was founded as early as the 3rd century BC, during the period of Seleucid rule in the region, and reached its peak in the Roman period before being destroyed in the First Judean Revolt around AD 66–70. The Roman general and later emperor Titus defeated the town of Magdala, resulting in the death and slavery of thousands. The town never fully recovered and much of it was left abandoned, which resulted in excellent preservation of extensive ruins from the 1st century AD.

The Gospel of Matthew mentions that Jesus took the boat to the boundary or region of Magdala, perhaps indicating the boundary of the town area (Matthew 15:39). Although some early manuscripts copied this place name as "Magadan," no evidence exists for this name or site in ancient Galilee. In the Gospel of Mark, the parallel passage states that Jesus took the boat into the district of Dalmanutha, which is otherwise unknown but may have been a regional name for the area that Magdala was located in (Mark 8:10). It is possible that Dalmanutha is a Greek transliteration of the Syriac word for harbor.

Mary Magdalene, or Mary of Magdala, appears to have been from this town (Matthew 27:56). According to several sources from antiquity and the medieval period, a Byzantine-period church had been built at Magdala in or around the house of Mary Magdalene, although the ruins of this building have not yet been found (Theodosius; Epiphanius the Monk; *Life of Constantine*; Eutychius of Alexandria).

Many towns were situated around the Sea of Galilee during the time of Jesus, and fishing was the main source of income around the lake. This is underscored by the fact that most of the disciples of Jesus from Galilee were professional fishermen (Matthew 4:18-22; Mark 1:16-20). Like other coastal towns, the main economy of Magdala must also have been fishing, which is further supported by the Aramaic and Greek names of the town. Fish caught in the Sea of Galilee would have been taken back to the town to be salted for preservation, then presumably shipped to other cities and regions (Strabo, *Geography*). This salted fish industry was probably the origin of the alternate name for the town, Taricheae. Other discoveries at the town, such as commercial buildings located by the port, weights for fishing nets, a 1st-century mosaic depicting a Galilean fishing boat found in a house, and pools used for the processing of fish, all demonstrate the importance of the fishing industry at ancient Magdala and the entire Sea of Galilee area.

Early excavations at the site also revealed a large public building with rows of Doric columns on three sides, five steps on the fourth side, a water channel around the building, and a pool beyond the steps. Initially, this was identified as

The 1st-century AD boat mosaic from Magdala

a synagogue from around the time of Jesus. However, subsequent studies convincingly argued that it was instead a Hellenistic or Roman type of fountain house. Like other towns of the area, Magdala in the 1st century was influenced by Hellenistic and Roman culture, as evidenced by architecture, inscriptions, and material culture.

Yet, a synagogue of the 1st century was also discovered on the west end of the town. This synagogue is located near the main entrance to the city, similar to the architectural layout of Gamla. This is now one of several 1st-century synagogues discovered in Judea and Galilee, but its state of preservation from the 1st century is also one of the best due to the fate of the town.

The main room of this synagogue is surrounded by stepped benches, and the building featured a mosaic floor, pillars, and fresco painted walls. A second room, identified as a study room, is adjacent to the meeting room of the building. Discovered inside the main room of the synagogue was an intricately carved stone decorated with a menorah, ritual water jars, pillars, palm trees, and various geometric and floral designs.

Several scholars think the carvings represent aspects of the temple in Jerusalem, and provide a religious link between the synagogue and the temple. The overall shape of the stone also resembles what is often called the "Seat of Moses" from the Chorazin synagogue to the north. These stones may have been used as a table for the scrolls of the Hebrew Bible, with the books of Moses as foundational. Jesus mentioned the scribes and Pharisees placing themselves in the Seat of Moses, implying that they attempted to equate their authority and teaching with the Law of Moses (Matthew 23:2).

The remains of this 1st-century AD synagogue, which may have also functioned as a type of community center, gives detailed insight into what synagogues in Galilee looked like during the time of Jesus.

MARY MAGDALENE AND JESUS

Mary Magdalene, or Mary from the town of Magdala, was one of the female disciples of Jesus mentioned by name in all four Gospels. It is unknown how old Mary was, or if she had a husband or children, but she was a dedicated follower of Jesus even after the crucifixion (Mark 16:1). Although the conversion of this Mary is not specifically recorded in any of the Gospels, Luke mentions that seven demons had been cast out of her, and it can be suggested that Mary believed in and started following Jesus after this significant event (Luke 8:1-3;

cf. Mark 16:9). This occurred while Jesus was living in Capernaum, which was only a short walk or boat ride from nearby Magdala.

Although the Gospels and other early Christian writings mention nothing suggesting that Jesus had a romantic relationship or was married, occasionally claims are made that Jesus had a wife and that this woman might have been Mary Magdalene. The idea appears to have originated with speculative reconstructions drawn from pseudepigraphal and Gnostic books such as the *Gospel of Mary* and the *Gospel of Phillip*. The *Gospel of Mary*, which exists in a 5th-century AD Coptic manuscript and two Greek fragments of the 3rd or 4th century AD, suggests that Jesus loved Mary Magdalene more than the twelve disciples, although it never records anything about a marriage or romantic relationship. The *Gospel of Phillip*, found in a 4th-century AD Coptic manuscript, appears to expand on this, claiming that Mary Magdalene was the companion of Jesus, and fragmentary reconstructions have alleged that when the text mentioned that someone kissed her on the mouth, it was Jesus.

Building upon these inventive ideas of a romantic or marriage relationship between Jesus and Mary Magdalene, a hypothesis with the Talpiot tomb or "Family Tomb of Jesus" claims that the bones of Jesus were found in a family tomb, along with Mary Magdalene as the wife of Jesus. Supposedly indicated by ossuary inscriptions, geology, and DNA, this hypothesis fails when scrutinized.

In 1980, during construction and the resulting salvage excavation, ten ossuaries (bone boxes typically carved out of limestone) from Roman-period Judea, dating to approximately the 1st century BC through the 1st century AD, were discovered in a tomb in the Talpiot region of Jerusalem, south of the Old City. Ossuaries are found in many burial caves throughout the region spanning the 1st century BC into the 2nd century AD. Of the ten ossuaries discovered in the tomb, five were inscribed with Aramaic and one was inscribed with Greek, while the other four were blank. One of the blank, undecorated ossuaries was broken and the fragments were eventually lost. The results were published, but the discovery never gained widespread interest until a documentary was made claiming the tomb was that of Jesus of Nazareth and his family, and that Jesus and Mary Magdalene were married with children. However, nearly all scholars have disagreed with this hypothesis, regardless of their worldview, because those conclusions stretch and even conflict with the data.

The names found carved on the six inscribed Talpiot ossuaries were extremely common names for the Roman period in Jerusalem and the surrounding area. The use of a stone ossuary, a box or chest for secondary burial of human skeletal remains, was common in Judea from the late 1st century BC until about AD 70. The inscriptions on the ossuaries are as follows: 1) "[unknown] son of Joseph," which had been suggested as reading "Yeshua/Jesus son of Joseph" but several scholars follow the more probable reading of "Hanun son of Joseph" or admit that the first part of the inscription is mostly indecipherable; 2) "Mariamne/Mary" and "and Mara/Martha," which was a second inscription added on the "Mariamne" ossuary later by another scribe; 3) "Judas/Judah son of Jesus"; 4) "Yoseh/Josek," which appears to differ in spelling with the name of Joses the brother of Jesus in the Gospel of Mark, and is a diminutive of Joseph; 5) "Maria/Mary"; 6) "Matia/Matthew."

According to a study of personal names, Joseph accounts for approximately 8.3 percent of male names for this period and region, Mary was used by about

Ossuaries of "Judah son of Jesus" and "[unknown] son of Joseph" from the Talpiot tomb

21.3 percent of females, Martha about 6.1 percent, Judah about 6.2 percent, Jesus about 3.8 percent, and Matthew about 2.4 percent. It was claimed that these names represented Jesus of Nazareth, his father Joseph, his mother Mary, his wife Mary Magdalene, his son Judas, his brother Yose, and a friend or relative named Matia. The supposed Jesus reading, however, is more likely "Hanun" or another name. And, according to ancient sources, Jesus was rarely referred to as "Jesus son of Joseph," but instead ancient inscriptions and manuscripts mentioning him usually include titles or Nazareth.

The alleged Mary Magdalene inscription refers to two people sharing the ossuary, Mariamne and Mara. No ancient sources, including Gnostic gospels, specifically claim that Jesus of Nazareth was married or had a son. The names found on the ossuaries were also extremely common in Judea for the time, and by themselves suggest nothing other than that the tomb was used by Jews during the Roman period. Moreover, the tomb was probably in use decades before the life of Jesus, when the families of Joseph and Mary lived in Nazareth and Bethlehem, not Jerusalem.

The mitochondrial DNA evidence from the Talpiot tomb was also completely meaningless for the Jesus family hypothesis, since the only test conducted showed that bones from the "[unknown] son of Joseph" ossuary did not share a mother with one set of bones from the "Mariamne and Mara" ossuary, not that the people whose remains were tested were married—which a DNA test cannot show.

Further, there were skeletal remains of an estimated 17 people in the ossuaries and another 18 or more on shelves or the floor of the tomb. It is typical of these ossuaries to contain skeletal remains of many people, and since these types of tombs in the Jerusalem area were used for at least a century, if not more, the names on the ossuaries may represent people that were separated by several generations. In another tomb, for example, there were 15 ossuaries but skeletal remains of 88 people representing four or five generations.

There are also no ancient Christian markings on the Talpiot tomb, such as anchors, fish, crosses, and ships that might indicate it had any ancient tradition associated with Jesus or early Christianity, and there is absolutely no reference to the tomb as being related to Jesus in any text from antiquity.

Eventually, those promoting the idea of the Jesus family tomb began to suggest that the James ossuary, with the inscription "James son of Joseph brother of Jesus" also originally came from the Talpiot tomb in order to include a clearer association with Jesus of Nazareth. An earthquake in the Jerusalem area in AD 363 likely sealed the tomb with debris, although looting of the tomb may have occurred prior to this in the late Roman and early Byzantine periods. Because the ossuaries had been encased in soil for many centuries, a geological study was done, using samplings from the ossuaries themselves to determine the origin of the James ossuary, and whether it can be directly related to the Talpiot tomb ossuaries. To do this, the Talpiot ossuaries, the James ossuary, and an additional 12 random ossuaries were sampled for the study. Since limestone artifacts, such as the ossuaries, would absorb the soil and trace elements of the tomb environment they were placed in, the study attempted to show that the James ossuary came from the Talpiot tomb. The results demonstrated that the limestone and the chemical elements analyzed on the James ossuary display similar chemical signatures. However, the data indicates only that the ossuaries could have originated from the same limestone quarry in the Jerusalem area. Soil in the Jerusalem area does not vary widely, and therefore, many tombs and many ossuaries from different locations carry similar signatures. The similarity in limestone and soil merely demonstrates that the ossuaries were quarried and then buried in the area of Jerusalem, not that the ossuaries were buried in the same tomb.

The excavators of the tomb, both in their reports and in subsequent statements, stated there were only ten ossuaries, there were no additional imprints in the ground indicating an ossuary that had somehow been stolen, and the ossuaries were all buried and not visible under the accumulated earth. Further, the owner of the James ossuary purchased the artifact in the 1970s, years before the Talpiot tomb was opened, and photographic evidence confirms this. Additionally, the person he bought the James ossuary from said that it came from the area of Silwan, not Talpiot. All this data demonstrates that the James ossuary could not have been in the Talpiot tomb, and that this particular tomb is not the tomb of Jesus, nor was it ever regarded as such.

In addition to an extrapolation of Gnostic gospels and unsubstantiated claims about a tomb of Jesus, Mary Magdalene, and their family, a small papyrus fragment from the antiquities market was published that contains the words "Jesus said to them my wife…" This fragmentary Gospel of Jesus's Wife was initially considered by some scholars as an authentic ancient text. However, further examination revealed an ever-increasing majority of scholars claiming that it was a forgery.

At least two separate evaluations pointed out that the fragment appears to have copied and rearranged phrases and sentences from a modern text of the

Gnostic *Gospel of Thomas*, and perhaps additional Gnostic writings of antiquity. Other scholars questioned the letter forms, suggesting that the style does not match known Coptic documents from antiquity. Further, because the papyrus came from the antiquities market rather than an archaeological excavation or in situ discovery, many questions were unanswered about its origin.

The most recent tests have concluded that the papyrus material is from antiquity, dating to between the 7th and 8th centuries AD, and that the carbon composition of the ink is consistent with ancient ink types. Yet, analysis demonstrated an odd and significant similarity in composition to another unprovenanced "ancient" papyrus fragment of the Gospel of John. This led to the suggestion that the document may have been forged using an ancient papyrus fragment and techniques to recreate ancient ink, and probably copied from a section of the *Gospel of Thomas*. Although the debate has not been absolutely settled as to the authenticity of the papyrus, even if authentic, the papyrus would not be historically accurate or significant.

The papyrus fragment may have originated in Egypt, and the epigraphy and language used (a Coptic dialect called Lycopolitan) attempts to place it in the period of the 4th to 6th centuries AD. It measures approximately 4 cm by 8 cm and contains eight partial lines written in Coptic, a descendent of the ancient Egyptian language but with a script resembling Greek. The eight lines have been translated as: "…not me. My mother gave to me li[fe]…the disciples said to Jesus…deny. Mary is worthy of it…Jesus said to them my wife…she will be able to be my disciple…let wicked people swell up…as for me I dwell with her in order to…an image…"

On the reverse side, only a few words are legible that contribute nothing to the context or understanding of the document. The most notable lines contain references to disciples and Jesus, mention of Mary, Jesus mentioning "my wife," and "I dwell with her." If simply reading the phrases as one continuous narrative, these lines appear to suggest that the author claimed Jesus of Nazareth had a wife, had disciples, was associated with someone called Mary, and perhaps dwelt with a woman.

However, it should be noted that only parts of each sentence are represented and the entire papyrus is without context, so very little information can actually be understood. It does appear that the Jesus being referred to is Jesus of Nazareth, the Christ, since disciples of Jesus are mentioned and there may be some type of spiritual reference about punishment for the wicked.

The Mary that appears is not specified, and it could be any Mary mentioned in the New Testament or even someone else named Mary. Mary Magdalene is usually specified as Mary Magdalene or Mary of Magdala, while the mother of Jesus, with no title or place of origin attached and an early reference to "my mother," is the more likely candidate.

The words "…Jesus said to them my wife…" along with "I dwell with her" appear to suggest that the text claims Jesus was married. However, there are a number of problems with this idea. "Jesus said to them" may be the end of one sentence and "my wife" may be the beginning of the next sentence. The line "I dwell with her" may not be referring to Jesus at all, but to the author of the papyrus. Yet, even if it is assumed that Jesus is saying "my wife" and stating "I dwell with her" referring back to the earlier line, this does not necessarily mean the author of the papyrus was claiming that Jesus was married.

The Coptic words for woman and wife can be the same, and thus Jesus may be only saying "my woman" and referring to a female he is talking to or about, which could be the "she will be able to be my disciple."

If the phrase is actually referring to Jesus having a wife, there is a common precedent found throughout the New Testament for this type of metaphorical language referring to the church. For example, the church is referred to as "the bride, the wife of the Lamb [Jesus]" (Revelation 21:9). The papyrus may be following this metaphorical use and talking about the church as his wife and that God will "dwell" with the church—another common idea presented in the New Testament (cf. Romans 8:11; 2 Corinthians 6:16; Revelation 21:3).

Finally, even if it is assumed that the papyrus is authentic and is stating that Jesus had a human wife, because of the late date and origin of the papyrus this still does not substantiate the claim that Jesus of Nazareth had a human wife. The papyrus presumably comes from the 4th century AD or later, at least 350 years after Jesus died, and from Egypt—a region where Gnosticism developed in the 2nd century AD and often viewed Jesus as simply human or one who had achieved some form of divinity, but distinctly different and heretical in comparison to how Jesus is presented in the Bible.

In this era, many Gnostic pseudo-gospels have surfaced with outlandish claims completely contrary to all the accounts of Jesus from the 1st and 2nd centuries AD. In that environment, finding a papyrus that made claims making Jesus seem more human and less divine is to be expected. Yet, the idea that Jesus had a wife is completely contrary to the original and contemporary source documents about his life. The sensational claim that this papyrus proves Jesus had a human wife can be disregarded on many grounds—date, theological environment, lack of context, unclear meaning, metaphorical uses, and contradiction of the primary sources.

Although almost certainly a modern forgery, if ancient it would still be irrelevant in that it provides no historical evidence that Jesus of Nazareth had a wife or that this wife was Mary Magdalene. Therefore, the ancient evidence demonstrates that although Mary Magdalene is mentioned several times in the Gospels, she had no special or romantic relationship with Jesus as some Gnostic or modern works have claimed. Rather, Mary Magdalene was simply an early convert and dedicated follower of Jesus.

CAESAREA PHILIPPI

The city of Caesarea Philippi (distinguished from Caesarea Maritima) was located about 25 miles north of the Sea of Galilee and near the southwest base of Mount Hermon and had been renamed in honor of the emperor and the tetrarch Philip, who ruled the area. Jesus and the disciples visited the area at least once, and the significant "Peter's confession" occurred there (Matthew 16:13-20; Mark 8:27-30). The event was also recorded by Luke, although he does not mention the location (Luke 9:18-22).

In earlier times, the town of Baal-gad was located in the region, and it has

Sacred cave at Paneas (Caesarea Philippi), perhaps referred to as a gate to Hades

been suggested that the site may have had a shrine to one of the gods of Canaan such as Baal-Hermon who was associated with the nearby mountain of Hermon (Joshua 11:16-17; Judges 3:3; 1 Chronicles 5:23).

Following the conquests of Alexander the Great and the spread of Hellenism, a large cave at the site became a shrine to the god Pan, and the place came to be called Paneas. Pan was the Greek god of nature, the wild, shepherds, flocks, goats, rustic music, and associated with fertility. Pan was represented as a being with the legs, hooves, and horns of a goat, and the torso, arms, and head of a man. The use of a religious shrine at Paneas as early as the 3rd century BC is evidenced by its mention in an account about the time of Antiochus III in addition to artifacts at the site and an inscription dedicated "to Pan and the Nymphs" beneath a niche adjacent to the cave.

The shrine to the god Pan existed at the city from the 3rd century BC to the 5th century AD, when the population and government was so thoroughly Christian that the pagan shrines at the site were finally abandoned. Thus, the shrine had a long history of use before the 1st century AD, and there were probably worshippers of Pan going to the site during the time of Jesus (Polybius; cf. Pliny, *Natural History* 5.16).

After the region was conquered by Rome in 63 BC and control of the area eventually passed to Philip the Tetrarch upon the death of his father, Herod the Great, Philip had a city built there in about 2 BC, first naming it Caesarea Paneas and then Caesarea Philippi in honor of Emperor Augustus and himself (Josephus, *Antiquities* 18.28). Coins from his reign in the early 1st century AD have been found that read "Philip Tetrarch" in Greek, just as Luke referred to him when mentioning a list of government officials at the time of Jesus (Luke 3:1).

Caesarea Philippi became the capital city of the region that Philip the Tetrarch ruled and his official residence. Philip had constructed a palace, which is located west of the larger and more magnificent palace of Agrippa II. When Agrippa I became king of the region for a brief four-year reign in the time of Caligula, control of Caesarea Philippi passed to him. Later, when Agrippa II took power, the city was enlarged in AD 61 and temporarily renamed Neroneas for Emperor Nero until about AD 68 (Josephus, *Antiquities* 20.214). Other cities in the eastern Empire were also called Neroneas, as suggested by numismatic evidence, but names connected with Nero did not survive long due to his unpopularity, which culminated in his suicide. During the time of Agrippa II, much building was done in the city, including a large palace built with marble that has partially survived the centuries.

The Roman-period city was quite extensive and included an impressive cardo, bridges, aqueducts, baths, houses decorated with mosaic floors, clay pipes for sewage, temples, the palace, and the propylaea gateway. Eventually, the name reverted to Paneas near the end of the 2nd century AD, then morphed to Banias when the primary language of the area transitioned to Arabic after the Islamic conquests.

Originally, the rock face and cave may have been a shrine to a Canaanite god, then later adapted for the Hellenistic god Pan, although this is only a suggestion based on the large cave with a spring—features often used in a religious context in ancient times—in addition to the centuries-long tradition of a shrine. Evidence for worship at the site from the Hellenistic period to the Byzantine period includes animal bones and ceramic offerings, and for centuries the cult shrine referred to as "the Panion" existed without any adjacent town (Polybius, *Histories* 16.18; Josephus, *Antiquities* 15.10.3; Eusebius, *Ecclesiastic History* 7.17).

Niches in the rock hillside next to the cave apparently housed statues of Pan that were probably crafted out of stone or metal. Over one of the niches a Greek inscription mentions the god Pan and the nymphs. The massive cave that descended deep into the earth was even regarded by many pagans as a gateway to Hades, and because of this, associations with the underworld were strong at the sanctuary. Then, in 2 BC, Herod Philip established a city near the cultic sites. During the time of Jesus, shrines and temples to Pan and a temple to Augustus were located near the cave. By the 2nd century AD there was also the court of Pan and the Nymphs, the Temple of Zeus and Pan, the Nemesis Court, the Temple of Pan and the Goats, and another unidentified building, but these were not all present when Jesus and the disciples visited the area.

Evidence from the pottery found there suggests that people had ritual meals at the sanctuary, perhaps using the food that they had sacrificed to the gods, and that they dedicated miniature lamps as offerings. Slightly after the time of Jesus, coins from the late 1st century AD during the reign of Agrippa II struck in the mint of Caesarea Philippi attest to the town being modified again and named in honor of the Caesar and the god Pan, using the place name Paneas (Meshorer, "A New Type of Coins of Agrippa II"). Images on the various coins include Herod Philip, Emperor Augustus, a temple to Augustus at the city, the sacred cave at Paneas, and the god Pan, which helped to decipher the archaeological remains found at the site.

Being a pagan, polytheistic city, multiple deities were worshipped in the sacred area, although Pan was the primary god. An altar found in the sanctuary at Caesarea Philippi had a dedicatory inscription in Latin to Jupiter Olybraeus, who seems to have been a god connected with the area of Cilicia. Ruins of a temple to Augustus, built by Herod the Great out of white marble in 19 BC, were also found at the site (Josephus, *Antiquities* 15.363-364). This temple at "Panium" is mentioned as being next to the cave of Pan, which had a deep cavern underneath, full of water from an underground spring that is also one of the sources for the Jordan River.

At Caesarea Philippi, Jesus made a famous statement to Peter and the disciples that connected to the geographic and religious setting there, referring both to the bedrock and the cave: "I also say to you that you are Peter, and upon this rock I will build My church; and the gates of Hades will not overpower it" (Matthew 16:18). Noting that Peter (*petros*) means "stone" and *petra* means "bedrock" or "massive rock formations," also evident in the name of the ancient city of Petra, and the history of the cave being regarded as an entrance or gate to Hades, the examples would have been obvious to listeners or readers who had been to Caesarea Philippi. As the city was also extremely pagan during the time of Jesus, his statements about "the living God" and that the "gates of Hades" not overcoming the church would have been even more striking.

Carved niches for the worship of Pan and the massive rock face at Caesarea Philippi

THE MOUNTAIN OF TRANSFIGURATION

The location for the transfiguration of Jesus was described as a "high mountain" (Matthew 17:1-2; Mark 9:2; Luke 9:28-29; cf. 2 Peter 1:16-18; John 1:14). It was here that Jesus was transformed (*metamorphoo*) in front of Peter, John, and James. However, none of the accounts specify on which mountain this event occurred, leading to speculation about the possible site. While modern scholars have suggested a variety of possibilities, Mount Hermon became the most widely accepted due to its status as the highest mountain in the region and its proximity to Caesarea Philippi, where Jesus and the disciples had been previously. Arguments against this include a six-day period between the Caesarea Philippi episode and the departure for the Mount of Transfiguration, which seems to have taken an additional two days to reach, and that all of the known ancient Christian writings and traditions place the event on Mount Tabor.

While some scholars have attempted to disqualify Mount Tabor on the allegation that there was a town or fortress on the top of the mountain due to remnants of a 3rd-century BC fortress built by Antiochus the Great and a reference in the writings of Josephus, this information may have been misinterpreted. The 3rd-century BC fortress was apparently abandoned and may not have been in use for many years, since during the revolt, Josephus went to Mount Tabor and had a wall built at the top in a period of 40 days (Josephus, *Wars* 2.573, 4.54-56; *Life* 188). These accounts state that new construction of a small fortress was done at the top of Mount Tabor more than 30 years after the time of Jesus, suggesting that the place was probably vacant earlier in the 1st century AD.

Therefore, Mount Tabor would have been a viable candidate for an uninhabited mountaintop at the time of Jesus. In the 3rd century, the scholar Origen of Alexandria stated that the transfiguration of Jesus happened on Mount Tabor (Origen, *Commentary on Psalm 58*). In the 4th century, Cyril, the bishop of Jerusalem, and the prolific author Jerome also recorded that Mount Tabor was the location of the transfiguration (Cyril, *Catechetical Lectures*; Jerome, *Epistles*). Its mention by Eusebius of Caesarea in the 4th century may place it either at Mount Tabor or Mount Hermon, as both locations are mentioned and interpretations differ, but he may have been referring to the transfiguration at Tabor and the meeting of the other disciples by Hermon (Eusebius, *Commentary on Psalms*). A church commemorating the transfiguration was built at the top of Mount Tabor in the Byzantine period, probably in the late 4th century AD, and by 570 AD there were three churches on the mountain (Pilgrim of Piacenza). All of the early Christian writers appear to have associated the mountain of the transfiguration with Mount Tabor, though the identification is tentative since none of the Gospel accounts specify a location.

THE POOL OF SILOAM

While again in Jerusalem, and probably in the final year of his ministry, Jesus performed a miracle associated with the Pool of Siloam, which caused considerable controversy, especially with the sect of the Pharisees. After approaching a blind man and placing clay over his eyes, Jesus instructed the man to go wash in the Pool of Siloam. When the formerly blind man returned with the ability to see, the Pharisees were critical of the healing both because of the miraculous element and that it had been done on the Sabbath (John 9:1-22).

The Pool of Siloam was located near the southeast corner of Jerusalem, near the turning point of the wall, but inside the walls of the city unlike the Pool of Bethesda, and the records of Josephus were an important reference for correctly locating the remains of the pool (Josephus, *Wars* 5.140-145). The name Siloam, from the Hebrew verb *shalach*, meaning "sent," apparently designated an area or neighborhood of ancient Jerusalem, which was also mentioned by Luke but had been in use since at least the 8th century BC and the time of the kingdom of Judah (Luke 13:4; cf. Isaiah 8:6; Nehemiah 3:15).

Although the Pool of Siloam was a prominent feature in Jerusalem and in use during the time of Jesus, it eventually became covered over after the destruction of the city in AD 70 and subsequently lost to history for centuries. Because the area of the Pool of Siloam was at the low corner of southeast Jerusalem, down the slopes from the rest of the city that rises to the north and the west, deposits of debris and mud running down the slope after the destruction of the city probably covered the area relatively quickly. This is indicated by confusion of the exact location of the 1st-century Pool of Siloam already in the 5th century when a church was constructed nearby, and likely even in the 2nd century when Jerusalem was rebuilt as Aelia Capitolina.

Archaeological excavations in the neighborhood of Siloam found an upper pool that was originally constructed in the time of Hezekiah in the 8th century BC, apparently in conjunction with the carving of an approximately 1750-foot (533 meters) water tunnel connecting to the Gihon Spring, and used in subsequent periods (2 Kings 20:20; Isaiah 22:9; cf. Nehemiah 3:15).

The upper Pool of Hezekiah came to be traditionally considered the Pool of Siloam at least as early as the 5th century AD, when the Byzantine empress Aelia

Eudocia commissioned a church to be built there, which was typical of sites associated with Jesus during the Byzantine period. The church was destroyed by the Persians in AD 614, but ruins of the church indicated to archaeologists that the Pool of Siloam in the time of Jesus had been located there, since in many places Byzantine churches correctly marked the locations of significant events connected to the life of Jesus.

Archaeological investigations found remains from the 2nd and 3rd centuries AD at this upper pool under the Byzantine ruins, yet no material was found from the 1st century, indicating that the site had been incorrectly identified as the Pool of Siloam during the time of Jesus. In this case, the confusion was probably a result of the covering of the lower pool after the destruction of Jerusalem.

However, a few scholars did propose a solution that the 1st-century Pool of Siloam was slightly southeast of the "upper pool" due to descriptions in Josephus and an analysis of the geography, but that it had been covered over. This was unconfirmed until 2004 when the lower Pool of Siloam in use during the time of Jesus was rediscovered by accident as a result of repair work on the sewer system about 200 feet southeast of the upper pool. While only partially excavated, it is likely that the entire pool is intact.

Based on partial excavations, the Pool of Siloam was approximately 225 feet (70 meters) long and roughly rectangular in shape, with another estimate suggesting 190 feet by 160 feet (60 meters by 50 meters). However, with corners measuring slightly over 90 degrees it is more correctly described as a trapezoid, just as the Pool of Bethesda in northern Jerusalem. The stones used in construction were white limestone quarried locally and cut into rectangular blocks. Excavations also revealed a design of three sets of five steps leading down into the pool, with an open area just above the lowest set of steps, which may have been built to accommodate varying water levels.

The rest of the pool has yet to be excavated as much of the land above the pool is covered by an orchard that the Greek Orthodox Church identifies as the king's garden (Nehemiah 3:15). From the upper pool, a channel ran to the lower pool, where the water was held in what seems to have been a ritual washing pool in the 1st century AD. As the Gihon Spring was the source of water for the pool, it would have been an obvious choice for ritual washing due to the "living water" that flowed into the pool.

The extensive size of the pool has led many to suggest that it may have been used by pilgrims visiting Jerusalem for the three major annual feasts before they walked up to the temple. This is also supported by the discovery of a massive

The 1st-century Pool of Siloam in southern Jerusalem

1st-century street consisting of steps that led up to the Temple Mount, providing easy access from the pool and the southeastern part of the city.

Artifact discoveries at the pool, such as a bell that could have been part of the priestly attire and an engraving of a menorah, also indicate ritual use of the pool. This accords with records in the Talmud about a tradition performed during the Feast of Tabernacles in which a priest would take a golden vessel to the Pool of Siloam, fill it with water, bring it back to the temple, and then pour the water on one of the sides of the altar as a libation offering while another priest poured a wine libation offering on the other side (Sukkot 4.9).

In the 2nd century, it is possible that the upper pool, apparently still visible, was turned into the Nymphaeum, or Shrine of the Four Nymphs, by Hadrian during the building of Aelia Capitolina (*Chronicon Paschale* 119). While this would be consistent with the pattern of Hadrian building pagan temples and shrines over sites associated with Jesus, the numismatic and ceramic evidence indicates that the lower pool was not in use from AD 70 until its recent rediscovery, but remains from the 2nd century AD were discovered at the upper pool. Perhaps the Nymphaeum covered the upper pool section of the Pool of Siloam and that is why the Byzantines later built a church on that location rather than at the "lost" lower pool.

In the soil in one corner of the pool, several coins were found ranging from the time of Alexander Jannaeus (ca. 104–76 BC) to the first Judean Revolt against Rome (ca. AD 66–70), with the latest coin bearing the inscription "four years to the day of the Great Revolt," indicating AD 69 as the year. While the pool was under construction, coins minted by Alexander Jannaeus were placed in the original plastered steps, indicating the approximate date of construction or at least showing that it was built no earlier than his reign. These were later overlaid with stone in the remodeling of the pool that probably occurred either in the time of Herod the Great and his extensive building projects, or Herod Agrippa I who continued in the legacy of his grandfather.

Along with coins, pottery of the 1st century was also discovered in excavations of the pool, and together these demonstrate that the lower pool was in use from at least the 1st century BC until the fall of Jerusalem in AD 70, meaning this was the Pool of Siloam that Jesus referred to.

JESUS AT JERICHO

Jericho in the time of Jesus was not located within the ruins of those famous ancient walls known from the story of Joshua. Instead, a newer Jericho had been built nearby those fallen walls at a place known as Tulul Abu el Alaiq, about one mile to the south and slightly west. Although mentioned six times in the Gospels, the 1st-century BC and AD archaeological remains of Jericho are currently known primarily from palaces and large public structures (Matthew 20:29; Mark 10:46; Luke 10:30; 18:35; 19:1). However, multiple written sources from the Hellenistic and Roman periods also confirm this Jericho that existed in the 1st century (1 Maccabees 9:50; 16:11-17; Strabo, *Geography*; Josephus, *Antiquities*).

Located about 13 miles northeast of Jerusalem and 825 feet below sea level, Jericho was warm in the winter, and therefore ideal for a winter palace, but scathingly hot in the summer. In the Hellenistic period, the Hasmonean palaces were built south and west of the current city center. The ruins of the older Hasmonean palace, measuring about 165 feet by 165 feet, was no doubt impressive at the time, but not on par with the preferences of Herod the Great.

Houses from the Hellenistic and Roman periods were also discovered nearby, along with ritual baths, demonstrating that the residents of Jericho followed purity laws of Judaism. Herod the Great built his own new palace complex in three phases just east of the Hasmonean palace, on both the north and south sides of the Wadi Qelt. On the north side of the wadi (a ravine, channel, or seasonal riverbed), Herod expanded a palace that had originally been constructed by the previous ruling dynasty of the Hasmoneans. When Herod finished additions to the complex, Jericho had four palaces, a gigantic pool, aqueducts, a theatre, a stadium, and perhaps a gymnasium.

Three large swimming pools were built in this area—one about 100 feet long, 60 feet wide, and 12 feet deep, another 300 feet long and 130 feet wide, and the largest a massive 575 by 475 foot pool that could be described as a small lake. Water was supplied by multiple springs in the region and brought in by aqueducts. This water supplied not only the pools and baths, but extensive and impressive gardens, including valuable balsam trees and palm trees that Herod had planted at his palace complex. According to a 1st-century description, the area of Jericho was utilized as a successful agricultural area about 100 stadia, or nearly 11.5 miles, in length (Strabo, *Geography*).

Later in his reign, Herod built a second impressive palace on the north side of the Wadi Qelt, using an architectural design called opus reticulum (concrete masonry lined with cubes set at a 45 degree angle giving the appearance of a net) and decorating the buildings with opus sectile (materials such as marble cut into specific shapes and placed into floors and walls to form a pattern or picture), mosaic floors, wall frescoes, and Ionic and Corinthian capitals. The structures in the palace complex included a triclinium and a Roman bath.

To the north, closer to the town, a stadium or hippodrome over 1000 feet long and 280 feet wide had been constructed. The stadium (or hippodrome) also appears to have had a theatre integrated into its north end and functioned as a hybrid structure. This stadium at Jericho was also the holding site for many leaders of Judea that Herod the Great planned to have executed upon his death, although the order was not carried out by his sons. An adjacent building might have been a gymnasium, but only the foundations remain. Tombs from the Roman period have also been found all around the area, further indicating a populated town during the 1st century.

The lack of discovered architectural remains from the town suggests that Jericho in the time of Jesus was composed of houses spread throughout the large plain used for agriculture rather than packed densely into an urbanized structure.

The city of Jericho was the site of the healing of the blind man Bartimaeus and another unnamed blind man on the road, the location for the parable of the Good Samaritan, and the town of Zacchaeus the chief tax collector turned

Ruins of the palace complex at 1st-century Jericho

follower of Jesus. Zacchaeus, who was described as rich, may have lived in a villa on the outskirts of Jericho, although it would have been modest in comparison to the nearby palaces of Herod the Great (Luke 19:1-2). An ancient sycamore tree stands at a monastery in modern Jericho, built over the Byzantine-period town, and serves as a reminder of the sycamore tree Zacchaeus climbed in order to see Jesus.

The alleged discrepancy with the healing of Bartimaeus while Jesus was leaving Jericho as described in Matthew and Mark versus approaching Jericho in Luke, could be explained linguistically or historically. Luke could have been referring to one of the blind men approaching Jericho, perhaps sitting down to rest and beg on his journey between cities, as the Gospel of Luke does not specify that it was Jesus approaching Jericho.

Unfortunately, certain translations could have created additional confusion by erroneously supplying "Jesus" when the original Greek text translates only as "he" and is in the context of a narrative from the perspective of "a man who was blind" who continues to be referred to only with a pronoun, while Jesus is specifically named (Luke 18:35-43).

Alternatively, the verb translated "was approaching" is often rendered as "being near" or "being close," and therefore the passage referring to Jesus being near Jericho while leaving may be a viable option (Luke 18:35; cf. Luke 19:1; Matthew 3:2).

Scholars have also suggested that Matthew and Mark recorded Jesus leaving the ruins of ancient Jericho, while Luke recorded Jesus approaching 1st-century Jericho, although it should be noted that mentioning the long-abandoned ruin rather than the contemporary town of Jericho seems an unlikely scenario.

SELECTED BIBLIOGRAPHY
(CHAPTER 5)

Arndt, W., F.W. Gingrich, F.W. Danker, and W. Bauer. *A Greek-English Lexicon of the New Testament and Other Early Christian Literature*. Chicago: University of Chicago Press, 1996.

Avi-Yonah, M. "The Foundation of Tiberias." *Israel Exploration Journal* 1, no. 3 (1950-51).

Batey, Richard. "Did Antipas Build the Sepphoris Theater?" *Jesus and Archaeology*, ed. James Charlesworth. Grand Rapids: Eerdmans, 2006.

Berlin, Andrea. "The Archaeology of Ritual: The Sanctuary of Pan at Banias/Caesarea Philippi." *Bulletin of the American Schools of Oriental Research* 315 (1999).

Bonnie, Rick, and Julian Richard. "Building D1 at Magdala Revisited." *Israel Exploration Journal* 62, no. 1 (2012).

Brown, Francis et al. *Enhanced Brown-Driver-Briggs Hebrew and English Lexicon*. Oak Harbor, WA: Logos, 2000.

Gibson, Shimon. *The Cave of John the Baptist*. New York: Doubleday, 2004.

Gibson, Shimon. "Is the Talpiot Tomb Really the Family Tomb of Jesus?" *Near Eastern Archaeology* 69 (2006).

Hirschfeld, Yizhar, and Katharina Galor. "New Excavations in Tiberias." *Religion, Ethnicity and Identity in Ancient Galilee*, ed. Zangenburg et al. Tubingen, Germany: Mohr Siebeck, 2007.

Hirschfeld, Yizhar. *Excavations at Tiberias 1989–1994*. Jerusalem: IAA, 2004.

Hoehner, Harold. *Herod Antipas: A Contemporary of Jesus Christ*. Grand Rapids: Zondervan, 1980.

Horseley, Richard. "Archaeology and the Villages of Upper Galilee." *Bulletin of the American Schools of Oriental Research*, no. 297 (1995).

Isaac, Benjamin. "Dedications to Zeus Olybris." *Zeitschrift für Papyrologie und Epigraphik* Bd. 117 (1997).

Kadman, Leo. "Temple Dues and Currency in Ancient Palestine in Light of Recent Discovered Coin-Hoards." *Israel Numismatic Bulletin* No. 1 (1962).

Kelso, James. "New Testament Jericho." *Biblical Archaeologist* 14, no. 2 (1951).

King, Karen. "Jesus said to them, 'My wife…': A New Coptic Papyrus Fragment." *Harvard Theological Review* 107 (2014).

Kokkinos, Nikos. *The Herodian Dynasty*. London: Spink, 2010.

Leeper, J.L. "Sources of the Jordan River." *Biblical World* 16, no. 5 (1900).

Liver, Jacob. "The Half-Shekel Offering in Biblical and Post-Biblical Literature." *Harvard Theological Review* 56 (1963).

Liddell et al. *A Greek-English Lexicon*. Oxford: Clarendon, 1996.

Magness, Jodi. "Two Notes on the Archaeology of Qumran." *Bulletin of the American Schools of Oriental Research* 312 (1998).

Manns, Frederic. "Mount Tabor." *Jesus and Archaeology*, ed. James Charlesworth. Grand Rapids: Eerdmans, 2006.

McRay, John. *Archaeology and the New Testament*. Grand Rapids: Baker Academic, 1991.

Meyers, Eric. "The Jesus Tomb Controversy: An Overview." *Near Eastern Archaeology* 69 (2006).

Meyers, Eric, and Mark Chancey. *Alexander to Constantine: Archaeology of the Land of the Bible*, vol. 3. New Haven, CT: Yale, 2012.

Netzer, Ehud. *The Architecture of Herod, the Great Builder*. Grand Rapids: Baker Academic, 2008.

Paton, Lewis Bayles. *Jerusalem in Bible Times*. Chicago: University of Chicago, 1908.

Pfann, Stephen. "Mary Magdalene Has Left the Room: A Suggested New Reading of Ossuary CJO 701." *Near Eastern Archaeology* 69 (2006).

Rahmani, Levi. "Ancient Jerusalem's Funerary Customs and Tombs." *Biblical Archaeologist* 44 (1981).

Reed, Jonathan. *Archaeology and the Galilean Jesus*. Harrisburg, PA: Trinity, 2000.

Sabar, Ariel. *Veritas: A Harvard Professor, a Con Man and the Gospel of Jesus's Wife*. New York: Doubleday, 2020.

Seyrig, Henri. "Irenopolis–Neronias–Sepphoris." *Numismatic Chronicle and Journal of the Royal Numismatic Society* 15, no. 45 (1955).

Stein, Alla. "Gaius Julius, an Agoranomos from Tiberias." *Zeitschrift für Papyrologie und Epigraphik Bd.* 93 (1992).

Tabor, James. "Testing a Hypothesis." *Near Eastern Archaeology* 69 (2006).

Teasdale, Andrew. "Herod the Great's Building Program." *BYU Studies Quarterly* 36 (1996).

Zangenberg, Jurgen. "Archaeological News from the Galilee." *Early Christianity* 1 (2010).

Zapata-Meza, Marcela. "Migdal 2015 Preliminary Report." *Hadashot Arkheologiyot* 129 (2017).

Zapata-Meza, Marcela, and Rosaura Sanz-Rincón. "Excavating Mary Magdalene's Hometown." *Biblical Archaeology Review* 43:3 (2017).

Bethany, the Triumphal Entry, and Gethsemane

D uring the time of Jesus, Bethany was a village located about 1.5 miles directly east of the ancient walls of Jerusalem on the Mount of Olives. Stated in ancient terms, Bethany was about 15 stadia (approximately 1.7 miles) from Jerusalem, which was probably measured in walking distance (John 11:18). This Bethany is distinguished from "Bethany beyond the Jordan," which was the site of the baptism of Jesus located east of Jericho (John 1:28).

BETHANY AND LAZARUS

The meaning of Bethany is not known with certainty, but it may be derived from Aramaic *beth anya* translated as "house of the poor" (*Bethania* in Greek). Some scholars have also suggested equating Bethany with Ananiah of the Persian period (Nehemiah 11:32). Archaeological excavations indicate that the area of Bethany was used for tombs starting in the Late Bronze Age, then was settled at least as early as the 6th century BC, including the village of the Roman period.

Houses, wine presses, and cisterns have been excavated from antiquity, although none of the houses could be identified with anyone mentioned in the Gospels. Jesus visited Bethany many times, and followers such as Simon the Leper, Mary, Martha, and Lazarus lived there (Matthew 26:6; John 11:1). One of the residents of Bethany visited by Jesus, Simon the Leper, reflects the presence of a leper colony during the 1st century, which was confirmed by reference to this leper colony of Bethany in the Temple Scroll from Qumran (11QTemple 46; Matthew 26:6; Mark 14:3).

Several 1st-century ossuaries recovered in a tomb on the Mount of Olives near Bethany had names such as Martha, Mary, Lazarus, and Simon, among many others, inscribed on them. While no evidence connects these burials to the people mentioned in the Gospels, the inscriptions do demonstrate the use of these names in the area of Bethany during the 1st century, reflecting an accurate historical context for the location and people mentioned in the Gospels.

Jesus interacted with many people in Bethany, but near the end of his ministry, the event at this village east of Jerusalem that drew the most publicity was the raising of Lazarus (John 11:1-46). The Arabic name for the town, el-Azariah, meaning "the place of Lazarus," helped to preserve the historical memory of the event and location.

There is a particular tomb in Bethany that has been honored and preserved over the centuries due to its association with this miracle of Jesus. The tomb, cut into the limestone bedrock and originally sealed with a large stone, has a small passageway leading to the main burial chamber measuring about eight feet by eight feet, which matches the brief description in the narrative (John 11:38).

Interior of the 1st-century tomb of Lazarus in Bethany

This tomb has been tentatively dated by archaeologists to the 1st century AD on the basis of similar typology, the presence of other 1st-century AD tombs nearby, the archaeological findings from the Roman period at the village, and that the original 4th-century Byzantine church was built adjacent to the tomb.

Further, written records from about AD 330, 333, and 381 claim that people in the area had regarded the place as the tomb of Lazarus from the 1st century, even before Christianity had been legalized and before a church had been built by the tomb (Eusebius, *Onomastikon* 58.15; Bordeaux Pilgrim, *Itinerarium Burdigalense*; Egeria, *Itinerarium Egeriae*). According to Jerome, in his translation of Eusebius, by the end of the 4th century a church had been built next to the tomb to commemorate an important event in the life of Jesus. The location, date and type of tomb, ancient tradition, and written records together indicate the possibility that this may have been the tomb of Lazarus.

After Lazarus died in Bethany and was placed in the tomb, his family, friends, and many in the community believed that he had passed into the afterlife or underworld. While in general the Sadducees did not believe in the afterlife, although some seem to have adopted Hellenistic ideas about life after death, the majority of the population in Judea during the time of Jesus believed that a person descended into the underworld after death (Josephus, *Antiquities* 18.16; *Wars* 2.165; Philo, *On Dreams*). Whether a person ascribed to Judaism or Hellenism, there were similar ideas about the existence of the afterlife or underworld, and even the same Greek word was used.

For example, in the 1st-century AD Caiaphas tomb on the outskirts of ancient Jerusalem, a coin for the boatman Charon was found in one of the skulls of the entombed. In Hebrew, *Sheol* was the word for underworld, while *Hades* was the Greek term and was used to translate Sheol in the Septuagint. In Hellenistic thought, Hades was not only the underworld, but it was the name of the god who ruled the underworld. The Romans called this god Pluto, and similar to ancient Greek ideas, they believed Hades to be both a place of reward and punishment (Virgil, *Aeneid*; Homer, *Odyssey*).

In the Hebrew Bible/Old Testament, Sheol is described as a place where the dead go, under the earth, dark, with gates, a place that both the sinners and the righteous go and is controlled by God (Job 17:16; Psalm 49:14-15; 89:48; 139:8; Isaiah 38:10; 1 Samuel 28:13-14). It was also recognized as distinct from heaven, where God and the angels reside (Deuteronomy 10:14; 1 Kings 8:27; 22:19; Nehemiah 9:6; Psalm 68:33; Isaiah 63:15).

The beliefs about Sheol or Hades persisted into the 1st century, although

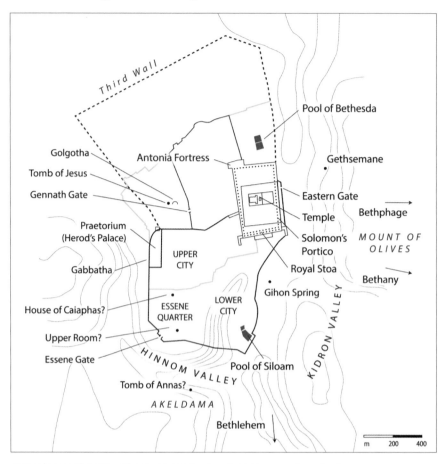

Jerusalem in the time of Jesus based on archaeology and ancient sources

Aerial view showing Bethany, Bethphage, Gethsemane, and Jerusalem

variants existed within Judaism (Josephus, *Antiquities* 18.14-16; John 11:24). The major differences between views of the underworld in Hellenistic and Roman thought versus the Bible include entrance to Paradise through good works, great feats, or ingenuity; the personification of Hades and aspects of the underworld as gods; that it was possible for people to leave Hades through their own power versus entrance to Paradise by faith in God; Hades as merely a name for the underworld that God controls; and the underworld as inescapable by humans.

Jesus himself taught about Hades, also dividing the underworld into Paradise and Gehenna, which were separate places within the underworld for the righteous and the sinners (Matthew 5:21-22; 11:23; 16:18; 23:33; Luke 10:15; 12:4-5; 16:22-23; 23:42-43). Gehenna, a name derived from the Valley of Hinnom south of Jerusalem, had also morphed into a word used for the punishment section of the underworld due the Tophet being located in that valley around the 7th century BC during the kingdom of Judah, and perhaps also its later use in the Roman period as a garbage dump where refuse was often burned (2 Kings 23:10). Therefore, people in the time of Jesus associated Gehenna with burning and the underworld.

The belief in the underworld and its two compartments is detailed in a teaching of Jesus recorded in the Gospel of Luke, in which an unrighteous and unbelieving rich man died and went to Gehenna, but Lazarus died and went to Paradise, where Abraham also resided (Luke 16:19-31). On the cross, Jesus told the criminal who believed in him that he would go to Paradise after he died (Luke 23:39-43). According to writings of the apostles Peter and Paul, Jesus descended into Hades, where he proclaimed his victory over sin (1 Peter 3:18-20; Ephesians 4:9-10).

Teachings in the Gospels and both the Old and New Testament state that believers would eventually go to heaven, the realm of God, and Hades, which had become the holding place of sinners, would be cast into the lake of fire (Genesis 5:24; 2 Kings 2:11; Job 19:25-27; Psalm 49:15; John 14:1-6; 2 Corinthians 5:6-8; 1 Thessalonians 4:13-14; Revelation 20:13-14). When Lazarus died in Bethany, most of the people there believed that he had gone to Paradise after death, but that it was impossible for him to return from the grave, making the miracle performed by Jesus even more astonishing and unsettling than any he had done before.

MIRACLES OF JESUS

The Gospels record many different miracles that Jesus performed throughout his public ministry over the course of a few years in Judea, Galilee, and

Samaria. These miracles varied from transforming or multiplying food and drink to healings, controlling nature, and even raising the dead (Matthew 9:20-30; Mark 2:3-12; 6:47-52; Luke 9:12-17; John 2:1-11; 11:38-45). His miracles, which defied the physical laws of the universe, were primarily used to validate the claims of Jesus Christ as sent from God and to demonstrate his divine nature (Matthew 8:16-17; 9:2-8; John 4:46-54; 6:14).

The Gospels describe miracles with words such as *dunamis* (power), *semion* (sign), and *teras* (wonder). The term "miracle" comes from the Latin word *miraculum* (wonder) during the Roman period, which came to be used in early Christian literature to describe supernatural acts of God. While Jesus is usually acknowledged as a brilliant teacher with vast knowledge and wisdom, his claims that he was God were validated by miraculous works that demonstrated his power over matter, the angelic realm, and life itself.

However, modern skeptics have often accused the Gospel accounts of being unhistorical religious propaganda that falsely attributed miraculous acts to Jesus, which in a purely naturalistic worldview would be impossible, and therefore supposedly never happened. If God, a being who created the universe, did not exist, and if Jesus was merely a man, then these miraculous works would have been impossible. Yet, multiple writers from the ancient world, even those that opposed Jesus, acknowledged that he performed miracles and thereby confirm the miracles of Jesus recorded in the Gospels as historically accurate.

The philosopher, pagan, and opponent of Christianity named Celsus, who lived in the 2nd century AD, wrote an extremely critical work attacking Christianity and Jesus, to which the church father Origen responded in defense. In one passage, Celsus claimed that while Jesus was in Egypt, he somehow acquired miraculous powers which he later used in Judea to demonstrate his claims that he was a god (Celsus, *The True Word in Origen, Contra Celsus*). Therefore, Celsus confirms that knowledge of Jesus and his miracles had spread throughout the Roman Empire, even to pagan skeptics of Jesus, and he acknowledged that Jesus performed supernatural, miraculous works, but attributed them to Egyptian magic. Another early document of possible relevance is a magical text of 80 lines called the "charm of Pibechis," who was an Egyptian magician or sorcerer possibly also known as Apollobex. Part of the instructions describing a method to casting out demons uses a formula appealing to "the god of the Hebrews, Jesus" (PGM IV.3007-3086). The magical papyri to which it belongs were compiled and date to around AD 300, but the origins of some of the incantations go back to earlier in the Roman period.

This reference to Jesus in a charm for casting out demons would have been influenced by oral and written reports of the deeds of Jesus in the 1st century, and the charm appears to have adopted a viewpoint similar to the Sons of Sceva in Ephesus, who attempted to cast out demons by invoking the name of Jesus during the time of the apostle Paul (Acts 19:13-19). A ceramic cup found in the ancient harbor of Alexandria with an inscription dated to the 1st century AD might make reference to Christ as a magician or sorcerer, although the association with Jesus is tentative. It is uncertain if this cup inscription refers to Jesus Christ, but it is a possible 1st-century mention of Jesus in a pagan context, which indicates widespread knowledge of his miracles. Around the same time, when the former-pagan-turned-Christian scholar Justin Martyr wrote a letter to Emperor Antoninus Pius in about AD 150, he also mentioned the miracles of Jesus. Antoninus Pius succeeded Emperor Hadrian, who attempted to replace many Christian sites with pagan shrines and temples. Although Antoninus Pius was a traditional Roman polytheist, he seems to have been an emperor who was not oppressive to Christians (Cassius Dio, *Roman History*). In his letter, Justin used the opportunity to argue the legitimacy of Christianity to the emperor by presenting evidence and referring him to accessible Roman records about the life of Jesus that were recorded during the time of Pontius Pilate in Judea. In one section of this letter, Justin wrote that if the emperor would read the Roman records, which he referred to as the *Acts of Pontius Pilate*, he could see that Jesus performed various miracles (Justin Martyr, *Letter to Emperor Antoninus Pius*).

It seems that each Roman prefect or procurator kept records about major events that occurred in the province they governed, and the records of Pontius Pilate while in Judea Province, which apparently included information about Jesus and miraculous acts that he performed, were still accessible to the Roman government.

The Mishna, a component of the Talmud, which was compiled around AD 200 but contains much historical information from earlier times, appears to preserve a few events associated with Jesus that were likely recorded in the 1st century. One passage in particular mentions how Jesus allegedly practiced sorcery or magic and led Israel astray, which is an obvious reference to the miraculous, supernatural works that Jesus performed (Sanhedrin 43a; Sanhedrin 107b; Sotah 47a). The accusation that his power was derived from an evil source rather than God is evidenced in the claims of the Pharisees, scribes, and other opponents of Jesus as recorded in the Gospels (Matthew 9:31-35; 12:22-29; Mark 3:20-30; Luke 11:14-20; John 7:20-25; 8:48-59; 10:19-21).

Remains and reconstructions of the 1st-century southern steps leading up to the temple complex in Jerusalem, where Jesus likely encountered both followers and adversaries

Finally, Flavius Josephus, a native of Judea born about AD 37 and an official Roman historian from about AD 75–99, may have mentioned Jesus performing miracles. In a short passage summarizing the life of Jesus, historian Flavius Josephus wrote that Jesus did works described as incredible, paradoxical, or contrary to normal expectation (Josephus, *Antiquities* 18.63). These "incredible" works are consistent with the description of supernatural or miraculous works in other Greek language sources, suggesting that Josephus was also aware of and referred to miracles of Jesus (2 Maccabees 3:30).

Occasionally, the Pythagorean philosopher Apollonius is compared to Jesus as another miracle worker of the Roman period, but an examination of the alleged miracles of Apollonius and the source for his life and adventures demonstrates that the accounts of Apollonius were not eyewitness testimony nor were the types of miracles equivalent. The *Life of Apollonius of Tyana* was written by Philostratus around AD 220, although Apollonius was probably born around AD 15–20 and died after AD 96, meaning the record of his life was composed by one author approximately 130 years after his death.

Apollonius, who was a vegetarian, taught that God did not want worship, prayers, or sacrifices, and that God could be reached only through the intellect. He was primarily based around Asia Province (western Turkey) and Greece, but apparently also traveled to Syria, Rome, and possibly even India. Apollonius may have appeared before Emperor Domitian around the 90s AD, was only a teenager when Jesus was crucified, and likely never even visited where Jesus walked, although he almost certainly came into contact with Christians later in the 1st century AD.

The "miracles" of Apollonius, such as ordering the stoning of a blind beggar who was supposedly a demon in order to stop a plague in Ephesus, bringing a girl "back to life" when she was still breathing, and supposedly claiming to perceive that Domitian had been assassinated in Rome while he was present in Ephesus were quite distinct from the miracles of Jesus, and mention of the wondrous works of Apollonius are absent from 1st- and 2nd-century writings.

Significantly, people in and near the time of Jesus did not deny that he performed miracles, although they had ample opportunities. Rather, four separate sources from a variety of viewpoints in antiquity, dating back to the 1st and 2nd centuries—Celsus, Justin, Josephus, and the Mishnah—attest to the fact that Jesus performed miracles, just as the Gospels record.

WITHDRAWAL TO EPHRAIM

After Jesus brought Lazarus back from the grave, word quickly spread throughout the Jerusalem region about him and his miraculous deeds. Many in religious leadership positions, including certain Sadducees, Pharisees, and the acting high priest Caiaphas, were concerned that the growing number of Jesus followers would eventually result in the Romans coming and taking over their nation and removing them from power. A plan was devised to capture and kill Jesus "that the whole nation not perish," and therefore Jesus avoided appearing in public and withdrew to a town near the wilderness called Ephraim (John 11:47-54).

This town of Ephraim that Jesus went to is also mentioned in ancient texts of Maccabees, Josephus, and Eusebius, but the location is not known with absolute certainty. Josephus recorded that Vespasian took the two small cities of Bethel and Ephraim, which means that around AD 70 there was a town of Ephraim in the area of Bethel, north of Jerusalem (Josephus, *Wars* 4.9.551). This Ephraim (Aphaerima) may also be mentioned in the context of being added to Judea out of Samaria around 145 BC, and was perhaps a fortified town on the road (1 Maccabees 11:27-34; cf. 1 Maccabees 5:46; 2 Maccabees 12:27; 2 Chronicles 13:19).

However, the most geographically specific references to a town of Ephraim in this region are preserved in the writings of Eusebius. According to the *Onomasticon*, a town called Ephraim where Jesus and his disciples went was near the wilderness, about 20 miles north of Jerusalem and 5 miles east of Bethel (Eusebius, *Onomasticon* 28:4, 86:1, 90:18). This criteria, including distances from Bethel and Jerusalem, and on an ancient road, matches almost precisely the location of modern Taybeh. Although a 5th-century Byzantine church is known at Taybeh, archaeological investigations there have not yet uncovered a 1st-century town, and other locations in the region have been proposed as an alternative.

THE TRIUMPHAL ENTRY OF JESUS

The triumphal entry of Jesus into Jerusalem was a momentous event recorded by all four Gospel writers (Matthew 21:1-16; Mark 11:1-11; Luke 19:28-46; John 12:12-19). The name of the event, derived from the Roman triumph celebration, is not found in the Gospels but was suggested as an appropriate description for a king or ruler entering his capital city during a procession of his subjects or followers.

On the eastern slope of the Mount of Olives was a small village called Bethphage, where Jesus sent two disciples to obtain the colt he would ride for his triumphal entry into Jerusalem (Matthew 21:1; Mark 11:1; Luke 19:29; Eusebius, *Onomasticon*). The name Bethphage is derived from Aramaic *beth pagy*, meaning "house of unripe figs," although the translation "house of eating" has also been suggested, and the place is mentioned multiple times in the Talmud. About a 1.2 mile (2 km) or less walk from the eastern walls of Jerusalem, Bethphage was on the way to Jerusalem from Bethany.

The modern village of Al Tur probably is situated over the ancient site, although the nearby village of Abu Dis, farther to the south and closer to Bethany, has also been suggested. Today, the Church of Bethphage stands within the boundaries of what is thought to be ancient Bethphage. This church was built upon a Crusader-period church of the 12th century, and while a Byzantine-period mosaic floor was discovered at the proposed site of Bethphage, there is no clear archaeological evidence of a Byzantine church.

The 8th-century writing of Epiphanius Hagiopolita in Jerusalem seems to place the village of Bethphage at this location, but he did not mention a church there. Discoveries around the area of ancient Bethphage, including pottery, coins, tombs, ossuary pieces, cisterns, a mosaic floor, and a Byzantine winepress, indicate that the village was probably occupied from about the 2nd century BC to the 8th century AD. While no identifiable buildings of the 1st century have yet been excavated in Bethphage, its location just east of Jerusalem and occupation during the time of Jesus is known, providing further insight into the geography and culture of the Gospel narratives.

On the Sunday before the crucifixion, Nisan 9 (March 29) of AD 33, Jesus of Nazareth approached Jerusalem from the east, crossed the Kidron Valley, and eventually entered the temple complex and the city through the Eastern Gate, also known as the Susa Gate. While opinions have differed as to which gate Jesus used to enter the city, since Mark records that "Jesus entered Jerusalem and came into the temple area" (Mark 11:11), and this entering into both Jerusalem and the temple could be done only through the Susa Gate, it seems to be the most likely scenario. It has even been suggested that Ezekiel alluded to the entrance of God through the Eastern Gate, which was closed and sealed when the city was besieged and then destroyed in AD 70 (Ezekiel 44:1-3).

As Jesus rode towards the city on a donkey, the people spread cloaks and branches on the road in front of him while shouting "Hosanna," quoting a Psalm, and proclaiming that Jesus was the king, descendant of David, and one

The Kidron Valley, the eastern walls of Jerusalem, and the retaining walls of the Temple Mount

sent from God (Psalm 118:26). This entrance into Jerusalem riding on a donkey or colt was prophesied in Zechariah, then quoted by Matthew and John and alluded to by Mark and Luke (Zechariah 9:9; Matthew 21:4-5; John 12:14-15; cf. Genesis 49:11 for a possible connection).

As to the alleged discrepancy about whether Jesus rode on a donkey, a colt, or both, it seems that Jesus instructed the disciples to obtain both the donkey and its colt (a young donkey), so they brought both, yet Jesus rode only upon the colt in fulfillment of prophecy (Matthew 21:5-7; Mark 11:7; Luke 19:35; John 12:14-15). It appears as if Matthew is the only Gospel that records the disciples bringing both animals, as the other accounts focus on the colt that Jesus rode.

The association of anointing a king of Israel with a procession involving the king passing over garments the people have placed in front, while he is also proclaimed king to the sound of trumpets, goes back to traditions performed in the time of David and Solomon, which continued to be repeated during the kingdom of Judah (1 Kings 1:33-34; 2 Kings 9:11-13).

The language used and actions depicted in the triumphal entry of Jesus also would bring to mind records of kings and conquerors being welcomed into cities during the Hellenistic and early Roman periods, including the Spartan general Brasidas, the Macedonian general Apelles, Alexander the Great, Antigonus I Monophthalmus, Antiochus III, Judas Maccabeus, Simon Maccabeus, Cicero, and Marcus Agrippa (Josephus, *Antiquities* and *Wars*; 1 Maccabees 4:19-25; 5:45-54; 13:51).

This developed into a set procession by the time of the Empire and the 1st century. In ancient Roman culture, a triumphant victor, known as *vir triumphalis* ("man of triumph") would enter the city in a celebration parade wearing the laurel wreath and a purple garment, which identified him with the royal and the divine, while riding in a chariot pulled by four horses, alluding to Sol the sun god. After entering the city, the victor would go to the temple of Jupiter and make a sacrifice in thanks to the gods. In Rome, this procession would begin at the Campus Martius, outside the boundary of the city at the western bank of the Tiber River. Then the victor would enter the city through a triumphal gate, continue through the Circus Flaminius near the Capitoline Hill, go along the triumphal way towards the Circus Maximus, onto the Via Sacrum, into the Forum, and then to the Temple of Jupiter on the Capitoline Hill where sacrifice was offered (Beard, *The Roman Triumph*).

By the time of the Roman Empire and the life of Jesus, the requirements and meaning of a triumphal entry had shifted slightly from its earlier roots associating it with a conquering hero, as it became even more significant and

A Roman triumphal entry of Titus, depicted on the 1st-century AD Arch of Titus

representative of kingship and divinity. According to the list of Triumphs on the Fasti Triumphales, which concludes with a triumph in 19 BC, by the time of Augustus the triumph had become part of the Imperial cult, and only the emperor could receive this honor and recognition as king and divine (Cassius Dio, *Roman History*; Suetonius; Pliny).

In a comparable fashion, Jesus began the triumphal entry outside the boundaries of Jerusalem in Bethphage on the Mount of Olives, rode on a donkey like the kings of ancient Israel, descended down the road into the Kidron Valley, entered the city through the Susa Gate, then went to the temple where he cleansed it of merchants and moneychangers. The similarities to the Roman Imperial triumph and the ancient Israelite kingship procession would have been obvious to the informed observer.

Therefore, the triumphal entry of Jesus had significance and implications for both the cultures of Israel and Rome, as Jesus carried out traditions associated with both an ancient king, conquering victor, and the divine all in one procession. While this could have been seen as subversive or as a claim to kingship by the Romans, apparently the procession either went unnoticed or largely ignored by the Roman authorities. This may have been due to the understated nature of the procession in which Jesus rode on a donkey, without a crown or purple clothing, and was primarily noticed by his followers and a few opposing religious leaders.

In fact, an alleged king riding on a donkey would have been comical for the Romans. This ridicule of Jesus associated with a donkey by Roman pagans is displayed on the Alexamenos Graffito, found etched into a wall of a building on the Palatine Hill in Rome.

The chief priests, scribes, and Pharisees certainly observed the acclamations of the people toward Jesus as the king, since they were astonished and told Jesus to rebuke his followers for these statements. Although Jesus entered Jerusalem as the King, God, and Messiah, he was not received as such by the majority of the religious, political, and academic leaders of the city. As a result of the rejection, Jesus prophesied the fate of Jerusalem (Luke 19:36-44). In AD 70, Jerusalem was destroyed by the Romans, and for this victory the general and future emperor Titus, along with his father, Emperor Vespasian, received a triumph celebration with praise and welcome from the entire city when they returned to Rome the next year.

THE GOLDEN GATE

The gate commonly called the Golden Gate was a prominent architectural feature on the eastern side of the ancient Jerusalem temple complex of the 1st century, and it was probably the gate through which Jesus entered Jerusalem and the temple during the triumphal entry (Matthew 21:10-12; Mark 11:11; Luke 19:37-46). According to the Mishna, there were five external gates around the temple complex, but only one on the east side, called the Eastern Gate, which had a picture of the city of Shushan/Susa and was used for access to and from the Mount of Olives (Middoth 1.3; cf. Nehemiah 3:29). This depiction of Susa on the gate is why it is often called the Shushan Gate rather than by its more ancient name of the Eastern Gate.

Since this gate was the only gate on the eastern side of the Jerusalem temple complex during the time of Jesus, and the prophet Ezekiel mentioned the Eastern Gate as the gate through which God enters the temple (Ezekiel 44:1-3), the geography and divine association seem to point to the Golden Gate as the entry point Jesus used.

The popular name Golden Gate goes back to a nickname that began to be used in the Byzantine Christian period. Because Latin *aurea* ("golden") and Greek *horaios* ("beautiful") sound similar, the Eastern Gate was often equated with the Beautiful Gate mentioned in Acts 3:2. But the Beautiful Gate was the Nicanor Gate, also called the Corinthian Gate, inside the actual temple complex according to Josephus and the Mishnah (Josephus, *Wars* 5.201-206; Middoth 1.4). This was a massive gate between the temple court and the Court of the Women or Court of the Nations rather than the Eastern Gate at the east side of the Temple Mount. Josephus described this Nicanor Gate as made of bronze, 75 feet high and 60 feet wide, which makes the description "beautiful" appropriate.

Although the Golden Gate can be seen today, this is not the same Golden Gate or Eastern Gate that Jesus went through in AD 33. The current gate was built in the 6th or 7th century AD. The gate seems to be shown on the Madaba Map, suggesting that it had been rebuilt in the Byzantine period, perhaps before the Persians took Jerusalem in AD 614 or soon after. The Byzantine emperor Heraclius supposedly entered Jerusalem through the Golden Gate, although he could have used Stephen's Gate instead, which is on the northeastern side of the city and would have provided more direct access to the Church of the Holy Sepulchre.

The Eastern Gate was still in ruins in the 6th century, and then seems to have been rebuilt later in the 6th or 7th century, so perhaps the emperor walked through the ruins of the gate (Pilgrim of Piacenza). It has been sealed multiple times from the destruction of Jerusalem in AD 70 to a rebuilding and sealing of the gate by Sultan Suleiman in 1541, and it remains in this state today.

The rebuilt Eastern Gate under which ruins of an earlier gate were discovered and identified as the possible 1st-century Golden Gate

According to brief archaeological investigation, the current Golden Gate is built directly over the ruins of the ancient Eastern Gate or Golden Gate. By accident, what appear to be ruins of the ancient Eastern Gate were discovered about eight feet below the base of the current Golden Gate and underneath what is now an Islamic cemetery. In particular, part of an arch from an earlier gate was uncovered and a 1st-century oil lamp discovered in front of the gate ruins, and it was suggested based on the discovery that there were probably two arches, a north and south, similar to the design of the currently visible gate structure. However, the original ground level of the Golden Gate was probably more than 30 feet below the current ground level, as evidenced by the discovery of a wall just east of the gate. A large wall, about 15 meters east of the Golden Gate, formed what was probably a wall for a road leading into the Golden Gate from the east, and may have been built in the 2nd or 1st century BC before the time of Herod the Great, although it could have been repaired during the Roman or Byzantine period.

Exactly what the Golden Gate looked like during the time of Jesus is primarily conjecture based upon limited architectural remains and parallels from other gates. The arched stones, which may have been above a horizontal lintel, appear to have been smooth, as was probably also the case with the 1st-century Double Gate on the southern side of the temple complex. Herod occasionally used smoothed stones in his construction projects, such as the mausoleum at the Herodium, as well as the commonly known bosse technique (margins or frame around the edge of the face of the stone). The 1st-century AD Herod Agrippa II gate at the northern wall of Jerusalem also utilizes a similar architectural structure and smoothed stones as those seen in photographs of the underground remains at the Golden Gate.

Inside the current Golden Gate, two massive stone gateposts may have originally been part of the Eastern Gate from the 1st century. While the exact form and size of the Eastern Gate from the time of Jesus is not known, the gate existed approximately where the current Golden Gate is today, and it served as the entry point into Jerusalem and the temple complex from the east, which Jesus would have used at the conclusion of the triumphal entry.

THE UPPER ROOM

The Upper Room mentioned in the Gospels is the typical name given to the location where the Last Supper of Jesus occurred (Mark 14:12-16; Luke

22:7-13). It is also known as the cenacle from the Latin word *cenaculm*, which means "upper room," and was adopted from the Latin Vulgate. In the Gospels, the word used to describe the room usually refers to an upper floor of a house, which generally would not leave behind discernable archaeological traces.

The traditional site of the cenacle or Upper Room is near the top of Mount Zion in the southwestern section of ancient Jerusalem. The structural evidence for the precise location is circumstantial, but it has been accepted since at least the 4th century AD when a church was built by Theodosius I adjacent to the original Church of the Apostles on Mount Zion. Earlier texts suggest the tradition of a church meeting at the building going all the way back to the 1st century, as writers mention a cenacle church on Mount Zion in existence during the time of Emperor Hadrian ca. AD 130 that supposedly originated from a house church of the 1st century—perhaps even the house that contained the Upper Room (Cyril of Jerusalem; Epiphanius, *Treatise on Weights and Measures*; *Itinerarium Egeriae*).

According to these ancient sources, the building apparently survived the destruction of AD 70 and continued to be used as a church in the Byzantine period, although it was probably abandoned for several years when the Christians temporarily left Jerusalem during the revolt (Eusebius, *Ecclesiastical History*). Even if the building identified in the 4th century is not the exact location of the Upper Room, it was probably in the immediate vicinity, and 1st-century architectural remains were found underneath the ruins of the later church that verify the presence of a building from the time of Jesus and the disciples. The orientation of the building points toward the Church of the Holy Sepulchre, and a church at that location is depicted on the 4th-century Pudenziana mosaic, the 5th-century Santa Maria Maggiore mosaic, and the 6th-century Madaba map, with the artwork appearing to show the ancient house church and former Upper Room adjacent to the Byzantine church.

For the earliest Christians, rooms inside houses became some of the first churches or gathering places due to the lack of any actual buildings designated for that purpose. Architectural layout allowed many people to gather in one large room, such as the house of Mary in Jerusalem, which was large enough for many people to gather (Acts 12:12-14). In 1st-century Judea, many houses had an upper floor that was used for living space, gathering places, or bedrooms and reached either by a staircase attached to a wall or by a ladder.

Large, decorative houses or manors with multiple stories, matching the description of the Upper Room, have been discovered in the area of southwest

Interior of the traditional Upper Room site with architecture from various periods

Jerusalem, where a wealthy neighborhood was located. The nearby Burnt House, which dates to before the AD 70 destruction of Jerusalem, is a wonderfully preserved mansion that included wall frescoes, colored mosaic floors, bathtubs, and ritual baths. Slightly to the northwest, in the Armenian Quarter, the "house of Caiaphas" on Mount Zion is another example of a 1st-century residence appearing to belong to a wealthy priestly family, although its identification with Caiaphas is speculative. Slightly to the south and just outside the present Old City walls, excavations have discovered remains of a third large mansion from the 1st century.

Based on the remains of similar buildings, the house containing the Upper Room would have been built primarily of limestone, with mosaic floors, plastered walls that may have been painted, high windows, and probably a bathroom and ritual bath. While we cannot see the actual ruins of the Upper Room, we can identify its probable location and have an idea of what it looked like based on architectural parallels.

THE GARDEN OF GETHSEMANE

Just across the Kidron Valley to the east of Jerusalem on the lower slope of the Mount of Olives was a place called Gethsemane that has been remembered in connection with Jesus for over 2000 years (Matthew 26:36; Mark 14:32; Luke 22:39-40; John 18:1). Matthew and Mark give the name Gethsemane, while John specifies that it was a garden or orchard. Luke recorded events that occurred at Gethsemane, but only mentioned that it was at the Mount of Olives.

The name Gethsemane is Aramaic, from *gat shemane* meaning "oil press," although the Hebrew version of the name is almost identical. This orchard apparently contained olive trees from which olives were harvested and then pressed into oil, and even today many ancient olive trees still stand in the general area. However, according to recent tests, the most ancient of these trees are about 1000 years old, with the possibility that they may have grown back from the roots of trees centuries older.

All of the trees in Gethsemane from the time of Jesus were probably cut down with the rest of the trees around Jerusalem for use during the Roman siege of the city in AD 70, while the trees that grew back after the 1st century were probably also cut or burned during later attacks on the city (Josephus, *Wars* 5.522-523).

The ancient Garden of Gethsemane was located on the lower northwestern slope of the Mount of Olives, although the exact location of the events in the Gospels cannot be ascertained from the 4th-century written sources (Eusebius, *Onomasticon*; Bordeaux Pilgrim, *Itinerarium Burdigalense*). The current building at the site, called the Church of All Nations, was built over the ruins of a 4th-century Byzantine church constructed to commemorate the events of the life of Jesus that took place in the Garden of Gethsemane. The rock now inside the church, mentioned by the Bordeaux Pilgrim in about AD 333, is supposedly the place where Jesus prayed, although this is conjecture. However, a Roman-period ritual bath was discovered in excavations underneath the modern church, indicating use of the area around the 1st century, while north of the church an ancient oil press was found in a cave.

In the solitude of Gethsemane at night, Jesus prayed to the Father that his cup might pass, but he was ready to carry out the plan of God no matter how difficult or painful it might be (Matthew 26:36-46; Mark 14:32-42; Luke 22:39-46). The events in this garden may be contrasted with Eden, where Adam gave in to temptation, while at Gethsemane Jesus Christ prevailed over temptation (Genesis 3:6; Romans 5:12-21; 1 Corinthians 15:20-22,45).

Garden and ancient ruins adjacent to the Church of All Nations at Gethsemane

Jesus kneeling down during this prayer in the garden may also have been the origin of the Christian practice of kneeling prayer, which was later emulated by Peter, Paul, and Luke (Matthew 26:39; Mark 14:35; Luke 22:41; Acts 9:40; 20:36; 21:5).

During this prayer, the Gospel of Luke relates that Jesus was so overwhelmed with anxiety that his sweat was "like drops of blood" (Luke 22:44). In modern medicine, this rare condition is called *hematidrosis*. It comes from two Greek words, *haimatos* meaning "blood" and *hidros* meaning "sweat." The phenomenon can occur in situations of extreme stress, such as knowledge of impending death, causing a reaction in which capillary blood vessels feeding the sweat glands rupture, mixing blood with sweat and creating a "blood sweat." Although an extremely rare occurrence, hematidrosis was known in ancient times at least as early as the time of Aristotle in the 4th century BC, and it was also mentioned by Apollonius of Rhodes, Theophrastus, and Lucan (Aristotle, *Historia Animalium* 3.19; Apollonius of Rhodes). Being a physician, it is understandable that Luke would be the only author to include this detail, and Luke also correctly specifies that while Jesus was praying, his sweat became "like" or "just as" blood and not that it was simply and only blood. This is an important distinction because according to medical studies, hematidrosis causes a mixture of blood and sweat, but it is not the sweating of pure blood. Although several ancient manuscripts omit the prayer and sweating of blood recorded in the Gospel of Luke, some of the earliest Gospel manuscripts also include the section, and analysis indicates that the section was purposely removed due to theological variances, probably by Marcionites.

Gethsemane was a real place outside of 1st-century AD Jerusalem that had a garden or orchard including olive trees, it was the site where Jesus prayed that the will of the Father would be done, and is where Jesus was arrested by the religious leaders. Thanks to descriptions in the Gospels, early church writings, and a Byzantine church preserving the memory of the location, the area can still be identified nearly two millennia after those events.

THE BETRAYAL BY JUDAS ISCARIOT

Judas Iscariot, the disciple famous for betraying Jesus, held the money box for the group and was remembered by John as a selfish thief who would steal from the treasury (John 12:4-6). This love of money and selfishness was further displayed when Judas accepted payment from the chief priests, surely including Annas and Caiaphas, in exchange for leading them to Jesus and identifying him so that they could arrest him (Matthew 26:14-16; Mark 14:10-11; Luke 22:4-6). The payment, 30 silver coins in an unspecified denomination, would have been equivalent to at least a month's wages, but perhaps significantly more. The type of coin referred to as the "30 pieces of silver" paid to Judas by the priests was most likely the Tyrian shekel, although various denominations of silver coins, such as the drachma and denarius, also circulated throughout the Eastern Mediterranean region in the 1st century (Luke 15:8). If these coins were Tyrian shekels, it was a substantial sum for a commoner, but certainly not a fortune.

On the night before the crucifixion, Judas led the chief priests, scribes, elders, and their guards to Jesus in the Garden of Gethsemane where they arrested him (Matthew 26:47-50; Mark 14:43-46; Luke 22:47-54; John 18:2-12). The next morning, after the Sanhedrin determined to execute Jesus and then delivered him to Pilate, Judas felt remorse for his betrayal and decided to return the 30 pieces of silver, acknowledging his sin and betrayal by throwing the silver into the interior of the temple (Matthew 27:1-3). The chief priests, remarking that it was against the Law to put his silver into the temple treasury because it was blood money, instead purchased the Potter's Field as a burial place for foreigners (Matthew 27:6-8).

This field, commonly known as Akeldama from *haqel dama* ("field of blood") in Aramaic, is located just to the south of ancient Jerusalem and also shown on the 6th-century Madaba Map (Acts 1:19). Archaeological excavations have demonstrated that the field did become a burial place for foreigners in the Roman period, in agreement with the statement in Matthew about that being the new use for the field beginning in the 1st century AD.

A an exquisitely decorated tomb identified as the possible Tomb of Annas located in Akeldama near the Tomb of the Shroud

In this area, at the intersection of the Kidron and Hinnom valleys, tombs were carved into the limestone bedrock. Archaeological analysis of these tombs, including radiocarbon tests, has shown that the place was not used for burials until around the middle of the 1st century AD. Investigations have also uncovered inscriptions in Greek and Aramaic that gave insight into the identity of the deceased, including "Ariston of Apamea" and a tomb of the "Eros" family from Syria, demonstrating that the field was indeed used for tombs and burials of people who had come from outside of Judea.

Another particularly significant tomb discovery at Akeldama uncovered not only the skeleton of a man who had suffered from both tuberculosis and leprosy (*mycobacterium leprae*), but also remains of his burial shroud. Due to this finding, the tomb has been designated the Tomb of the Shroud. Although lepers are mentioned in all three synoptic Gospels, this was the first archaeological evidence of the existence of leprosy in Jerusalem and Judea around the time of Jesus (Matthew 8:1-3; Mark 1:40-42; Luke 5:12-13).

SELECTED BIBLIOGRAPHY
(CHAPTER 6)

Arndt, W., F.W. Gingrich, F.W. Danker, and W. Bauer. *A Greek-English Lexicon of the New Testament and Other Early Christian Literature*. Chicago: University of Chicago Press, 1996.

Avni, Gideon, and Zvi Greenhut. *The Akeldama Tombs: Three Burial Caves in the Kidron Valley, Jerusalem*. Jerusalem: IAA, 1996.

Botha, Pieter. "Houses in the World of Jesus." *Neotestamentica* 32, no. 1 (1998).

Brown, Francis et al. *Enhanced Brown-Driver-Briggs Hebrew and English Lexicon*. Oak Harbor, WA: Logos, 2000.

Capper, Brian. "Essene Community Houses." *Jesus and Archaeology*, ed. James Charlesworth. Grand Rapids: Eerdmans, 2006.

Carney D. Matheson et al. *Molecular Exploration of the First-Century Tomb of the Shroud in Akeldama, Jerusalem*. *PLOS One*, 2009; 4 (12): e8319.

Chen, Doron. "On the Golden Gate in Jerusalem and the Baptistery at Emmaus-Nicopolis." *Zeitschrift des Deutschen Palästina-Vereins* 97 (1981).

Clermont-Ganneau, Charles. *Archaeological Researches in Palestine*. London: Palestine Exploration Fund, 1899.

Clivaz, Claire. "The Angel and the Sweat Like 'Drops of Blood' (Lk 22:43-44): P69 and f13." *Harvard Theological Review* 98 (2006).

Coakley, J.F. "Jesus' Messianic Entry into Jerusalem." *Journal of Theological Studies* 46, no. 2 (1995).

Debloois, Nancy. "Coins in the New Testament." *BYU Studies Quarterly* 36 (1996).

Duff, Paul. "The March of the Divine Warrior and the Advent of the Greco-Roman King." *Journal of Biblical Literature* 111 (1992).

Evans, Craig. *Jesus and the Manuscripts*. Peabody, MA: Hendrickson, 2020.

Felsenthal, B. "Additional Aramaic Words in the New Testament." *Hebraica* 1, no. 3 (1885).

Fleming, James. "The Undiscovered Gate Beneath Jerusalem's Golden Gate." *Biblical Archaeology Review* 9:1 (1983).

Hesemann, Michael. *Jesus of Nazareth: Archaeologists Retracing the Footsteps of Christ*. San Francisco: Ignatius, 2021.

Holoubek, J.E., and A.B. Holoubek. "Blood, Sweat and Fear: A Classification of Hematidrosis." *Journal of Medicine* 27 (1996).

Keresztes, Paul. "The Emperor Antoninus Pius and the Christians." *Journal of Ecclesiastical History* 22 (1971).

Kinman, Brent. "Parousia, Jesus' 'A-Triumphal' Entry, and the Fate of Jerusalem." *Journal of Biblical Literature* 118, no. 2 (1999).

Liddell et al. *A Greek-English Lexicon*. Oxford: Clarendon, 1996.

Magness, Jodi. "Ossuaries and the Burials of Jesus and James." *Journal of Biblical Literature* 124 (2005).

McRay, John. *Archaeology and the New Testament*. Grand Rapids: Baker Academic, 1991.

Meyers, Eric, and Mark Chancey. *Alexander to Constantine: Archaeology of the Land of the Bible, Volume 3*. New Haven, CT: Yale, 2012.

Murphey-O'Connor, Jerome. "The Cenacle and Community: The Background of Acts 2:44-45." Coogan et al. eds. *Scripture and Other Artifacts*. Louisville: Westminster John Knox, 1994.

Naveh, Joseph. "Nameless People." *Israel Exploration Journal* 40 (1990).

Negev, Avraham, and Shimon Gibson, eds. *Archaeological Encyclopedia of the Holy Land*. New York: Bloomsbury Academic, 2003.

Petersen, Joan. "House-Churches in Rome." *Vigiliae Christianae* 23, no. 4 (1969).

Pixner, Bargil. "The Church of the Apostles Found on Mount Zion." *Biblical Archaeology Review* 16:3 (1990).

————. "Mount Zion, Jesus, and Archaeology." *Jesus and Archaeology*, ed. James Charlesworth. Grand Rapids: Eerdmans, 2006.

Saller, Sylvester. *Excavations at Bethany (1949–1953)*. Jerusalem: Franciscan, 1957.

Saller, Sylvester, and Emmanuele Testa. *The Archaeological Setting of the Shrine of Bethphage*. Jerusalem: Franciscan, 1961.

Stripling, Scott. "Have We Walked in the Footsteps of Jesus?" *Bible and Spade* 27.4 (2014).

Tsafrir, Yoram. "The 'Massive Wall' East of the Golden Gate, Jerusalem." *Israel Exploration Journal* 40 (1990).

Welch, John. "Miracles, Maleficium, and Maiestas in the Trial of Jesus." *Jesus and Archaeology*, ed. James Charlesworth. Grand Rapids: Eerdmans, 2006.

CHAPTER 7

The Trial and Crucifixion of Jesus

In Nisan of AD 33, following the betrayal of Judas Iscariot and the arrest in the Garden of Gethsemane at night, Jesus was taken through a series of informal and formal trials in front of high priests, the Sanhedrin, and the Roman prefect of Judea, including the leaders Annas, Caiaphas, Herod Antipas, and Pontius Pilatus (Matthew 26:57-68; 27:11-26; Mark 14:53-65; 15:1-15; Luke 22:66–23:25; John 18:12–19:16).

THE TRIAL OF JESUS

This trial began when Jesus was brought before the religious leaders of Judaism, including the former high priest Annas, to answer various accusations that included his prediction of "this temple" being destroyed, sorcery or miracles, and blasphemy or apostasy. The Babylonian Talmud may also contain reference back to a contemporary document about Jesus and the reason for his trial. A section recorded an indictment against Yeshu the Nazarene that prescribed stoning for his practice of sorcery and enticing Israel into apostasy, requested that anyone with information on his location tell the Sanhedrin in Jerusalem, and stated that he was hanged on the eve of Passover (Tracate Sanhedrin 43a; cf. Deuteronomy 18:10-14 and Leviticus 19:26-31; 20:27). Similarly, Trypho the Jew recorded that Jesus was executed as an alleged sorcerer and seducer of the people according to the 2nd-century writings of Justin Martyr, a Roman polytheist who converted to Christianity (Justin Martyr, *Dialogue with Trypho* 69).

The first encounter was with Annas, a former high priest who still held considerable influence and was the father-in-law of Caiaphas, the acting high priest (John 18:12-24). This appearance before Annas at his priestly mansion may have been in the same palatial complex in which Caiaphas lived, shared by the family. After a brief questioning, Jesus was taken to Caiaphas (Matthew 26:57; Luke 22:66). According to the 1st-century sources, Joseph son of Caiaphas was the full name of this high priest (Josephus, *Antiquties* 18.34-35). While the location of the "House of Caiaphas," and possibly the house of Annas, has not been definitively pinpointed, there are remains of 1st-century priestly mansions in the southwest area of ancient Jerusalem that could have been the house of Caiaphas or at least serve as an example of how that residence looked. The sites, located on Mount Zion and near the former palace of Herod, include elaborate remains of priestly mansions from the 1st century AD, including ruins of a house on Mount Zion with ritual baths, preserved basement rooms, ritual artifacts such as stone purification jars and bowls, and even an inscribed ritual cup containing the name Yahweh and perhaps music and lyrics sung by the priests.

Additionally, excavations in the Jewish Quarter of Old City Jerusalem, also referred to as the Herodian Quarter, revealed an impressive priestly mansion from the 1st century AD with decorative mosaic floors, wall frescoes, ritual purification baths, ritual vessels, and even an Aramaic inscription "son of Kathros" found on a stone weight. Discoveries there attest to the presence of a large and ornate residence occupied by a priestly family. The "house of Kathros" was noted in the Talmud as being a high-priest family (Pesahim 57a).

This mansion is also referred to as the "Burnt House" because it was found destroyed by a fire. It may be significant that the palace of Annas the high priest was burnt together with the palace of Agrippa and Berenice (Josephus, *War* 2.426). The location, decor, ritual baths and vessels, association with a priestly family, and its burning in the 1st century suggest a possible identification with the house of Annas the high priest, which may have been the same house or housing complex as his son-in-law Caiaphas.

While it is not definitively known who lived in these priestly houses during the time of the trial of Jesus, it is within the realm of possibility that one of them was the house of Caiaphas or Annas. Archaeological discoveries such as the tomb of the Caiaphas family and three inscribed ossuaries, along with ancient records, also demonstrate that the high priest Joseph Caiaphas, who played a key role in sentencing Jesus to death by crucifixion, was a prominent person in 1st-century AD Jerusalem and the acting high priest of Judaism from AD 18–36 (Josephus, *Antiquities* 18.34-35; Matthew 26:3-4; Luke 3:2; John 18:24). The

A 1st-century AD priestly mansion in Jerusalem destroyed in AD 70, where an inscription of the high priestly Kathros family was found

mention of Annas in the records of Josephus, and the possible identification of the family tomb of Annas in the Akeldama area also coincides with information in the Gospels and expands our knowledge about the life and times of Jesus.

Once the interrogations by Annas and Caiaphas were finished, Jesus was led to the assembly of the Sanhedrin after sunrise. According to the Talmud, in AD 30 the meeting place of the Sanhedrin had moved to the Hall of Hewn Stones on the Temple Mount, which may have been located either on the north side or more likely inside the Royal Stoa on the south side of the temple complex, near the main entrance to the Temple Mount (Talmud Shabbat 15a; Babylonian Talmud Sanhedrin 88b). Although the exact location of this building is speculative, there are areas on the southern side that could have accommodated the meeting place, and reconstructions often place the building in this location.

At this meeting of the Sanhedrin, the religious leaders of Judaism may have been convinced that Jesus must be executed, but ultimately it was necessary for the Roman prefect of the province to make the final decision about capital punishment, since the Sanhedrin had lost authority to enforce death penalties when Rome took direct control of Judea in AD 6 (Josephus, *Antiquities* 18.2). The year after the crucifixion of Jesus, Stephen was illegally stoned by a raging mob (Acts 6:8–7:60), and decades later around AD 62 when James was stoned

Probable location of the Sanhedrin meeting place on the south side of the Jerusalem temple complex

by order of the high priest Ananus, the Roman procurator removed Ananus from office for exceeding his authority (Josephus, *Antiquities* 20.9). The only religious capital punishment that the Romans allowed in Judea was executing foreigners who had violated the sacred area of the temple (Josephus, *Wars* 6.2).

At the same time, early in the morning when the Sanhedrin was discussing amongst themselves the fate of Jesus, all four of the Gospels relate that Peter heard the "rooster crow" (Matthew 26:31-75; Mark 14:27-72; Luke 22:31-62; John 18:15-27). During excavations in Jerusalem at the southwestern corner of the retaining wall of the Temple Mount, a finely crafted limestone fragment with an inscription from the 1st century AD was discovered in the rubble that was a result of the AD 70 destruction of Jerusalem and the temple. The preserved artifact is about 84 cm long, and it was inscribed with an ancient Hebrew text. Although at least one additional word was probably present, the broken text can be translated as "for the place of trumpeting to declare…" (IAA 78-1439).

The Judean commander who became an official historian for the Roman Empire, Josephus, wrote that at a high point of the temple complex in Jerusalem one of the priests would blow a trumpet to announce the beginning and end of the Sabbath, and other important times (Josephus, *Wars* 4.9.12). This trumpeting occurred in the 1st century prior to the destruction of the temple in AD 70, at which point it ceased. All four Gospels state that Peter denied Jesus three times and then the "rooster" sounded early in the morning on the Sabbath. Although many English translations render this phrase as a rooster crowing, the Greek word *alektor* was also used metaphorically of a trumpeter in ancient times, and the Gospel writers were probably referring to a trumpeter and the sound of the trumpet from the southwest corner of the temple complex. It is also indicative that this "rooster crow" was the trumpet call heard throughout Jerusalem because Matthew, Peter, John, and eyewitnesses used by Luke all knew exactly when this trumpet blast occurred and recorded it happening early in the morning before Jesus was taken to Pilate.

Finally, Jesus was taken bound to the Roman prefect Pontius Pilatus, who wanted to avoid the consequences of angering the Judean religious leadership, which would endanger his political position and favor with Emperor Tiberias. When Pilate was made prefect of Judea Province, Tiberius was emperor, but Lucius Aelius Sejanus, commander of the Praetorian Guard, eventually accumulated so much power and influence that he effectively ruled the Empire while Tiberius lived on the island of Capri (Suetonius, *Life of Tiberius* 65). Because

The "place of trumpeting" inscription from the southwestern corner of the Temple Mount

this rise to power occurred just before Pilate was sent to Judea Province, Pilate may have been appointed prefect by Sejanus rather than Emperor Tiberius (Philo of Alexandria, *Embassy to Gaius* 159-160).

After a series of events that put Pilate at odds with many of the Judeans, matters were made even more complicated when Sejanus was accused of a plot in October of AD 31 and subsequently, followed by the arrest and execution of many of his associates, now making Pilate directly accountable to an emperor who was seeking to rid himself of enemies (Josephus, *Antiquities* 18.181-182; Juvenal, *Satire* 10.67-72; Dio, *Roman History* 58.9-11). Rare coins of Sejanus, issued in Augusta Bilbilis of Hispania in AD 31 demonstrate the extent of his power and his drastic fall, as many of the surviving coins have his name scratched out in accordance with the order of *damnatio memoriae* (condemnation of memory) by the Senate.

The trial of Jesus occurred about 18 months after this drastic change. Because Pilate had already angered the Judeans on multiple occasions and may have had an association with Sejanus, he was in a very delicate position that required him to stay in favor with the emperor, lest he be exiled or even executed. Thus, when the Judeans told Pilate that if he released Jesus he was no "friend of Caesar," Pilate clearly understood that to be a threat to destroy his political favor with Tiberius and endanger not only his career but his life (John 19:12-13). While Josephus and Philo depict Pilate as a cruel and strong leader, rather than somewhat weak and accommodating as portrayed in the trial narratives of the Gospels, this change in attitude is understandable when the situation is understood (cf. Luke 13:1).

Rather than pronounce a swift decision, Pilate sent Jesus to Herod Antipas, the local ruler of Galilee (Luke 23:6-12). Antipas, who would have been temporarily staying somewhere in Jerusalem for the festival of Passover, did not have jurisdiction over the Jerusalem area, but Pilate may have hoped to escape the responsibility of dealing with this explosive Jesus situation.

Herod Antipas the tetrarch, named as one of the rulers inheriting a portion of the kingdom after the death of Herod the Great, is known from coins, the writings of Josephus, and an allusion in the writings of Philo (Josephus, *Antiquities* 18.111-137; Philo of Alexandria, *Embassy to Gaius* 300; Luke 3:1). Jesus was taken to this particular ruler because Herod Antipas presided over Galilee, and Pilate had learned that Jesus was from Galilee. Like the other officials involved in the trial of Jesus, the tetrarch Herod Antipas is firmly attested as a local ruler of Galilee during the time of Jesus, and his short involvement in the trial of Jesus is perfectly logical. However, Antipas received no answers from Jesus and seemed completely uninterested in condemning him, merely mocking him before sending him back to Pilate, who would have to decide whether or not Jesus was deserving of death.

Pontius Pilatus, the Roman prefect of Judea Province from AD 26–36, is mentioned numerous times by ancient writers of the Roman period. He minted coins during his time in Judea and commissioned a monumental stone inscription for Emperor Tiberius that has survived the centuries at Caesarea. A ring bearing his name was even found in excavations at Herodium. Roman historians mentioned Pilate as the governor of Judea in the reign of Tiberias and recounted events such as the golden shields that he had placed in Jerusalem or his use of the temple treasury to build an aqueduct, which angered many of the Judeans (Tacitus, *Annals* 15.44; Josephus, *Antiquities* 18.55 and *Wars* 2.169; Philo of Alexandria, *Embassy to Gaius* 299).

The trial of Jesus before Pilate occurred at a place called the Praetorium, while Jesus was standing on the Stone Pavement and Pilate was situated at the bema or judgment seat (John 19:8-13). All of the Gospel narratives state that the trial occurred in Jerusalem, but John recorded additional specifics.

The Praetorium was the residence of the Roman governor, and in the case of Judea Province there was a Praetorium both in Caesarea (the Roman capital) and in Jerusalem due to the importance of maintaining a Roman presence at the center of worship for Judaism. The structure received its name from earlier Roman usage, referring to the place where a commander resided. According to Roman-period documentation, the place where Gesius Florus was residing

Remains of the Roman Praetorium of Jerusalem

before the war and Pontius Pilate lived while in Jerusalem—the governor's residence or Praetorium—was in the former palace of Herod the Great, located on the western edge of the current Old City Jerusalem walls (Philo of Alexandria, *Embassy to Gaius*; Josephus, *Wars* 2.14.8 and *Antiquities* 15.8.5).

Part of this area has been excavated, although much of the Roman-period remains were destroyed in subsequent periods. The Stone Pavement (Greek *lithostrotos*) was a place paved with flat blocks of stone, like a street or courtyard. According to the Gospel of John (19:13), the Aramaic designation for this Pavement was *Gabbatha*, which means "height, raised place, or ridge," and therefore gives an additional detail describing how this Stone Pavement was situated on a raised platform. Excavations revealed a large stone platform that seems to have been part of Herod's palace in Jerusalem, then reused by the Romans in the Praetorium. This raised stone platform with many paving stones still in existence seems to be the location of Gabbatha at the Praetorium (Mark 15:16). Although many are unaware of its existence or significance, a section of the Stone Pavement from the courtyard of the Praetorium in Jerusalem was uncovered during excavations after being covered by dirt and debris for centuries.

The judgment seat, or bema, is another architectural feature mentioned in the context of the Jerusalem Praetorium and the trial of Jesus. A bema was typically also a raised platform, and in its basic sense means "step," although it is often translated as "judgment seat." A more precise translation referring to its specific form and function is tribunal or judicial "bench." It originated in Greece and was used by both orators and law courts, but it was later adopted around the Roman world.

Gabbatha, the "stone pavement," and the bema at the Praetorium

The way the bema at the Jerusalem Praetorium is described indicates that it was located at the Stone Pavement or Gabbatha, but it was a distinct feature, suggesting that the bema itself was a smaller raised step or platform on the Gabbatha (John 19:13). Analysis of the architecture uncovered from excavations shows that the bema itself was also probably discovered amongst the remains of the Praetorium. Significantly, the bema at Gabbatha and in the Praetorium was where Pilate pronounced his decision that he would allow Jesus to be crucified, and the official Roman historians Josephus and Tacitus recorded that Jesus was condemned by Pilate to be crucified in Judea during the reign of Tiberias (Josephus, *Antiquities* 18:63-64; Tacitus, *Annals* 15:44).

Jesus, the central character in the trial narratives, is mentioned by several writers of the 1st and 2nd centuries, including Josephus, Tacitus, Celsus, Justin Martyr, Pliny the Younger, Suetonius, and Lucian. Additionally, Jesus may even be attested by an inscription on an ossuary in Jerusalem from only decades after the trial. A controversial but important 1st-century AD ossuary, or bone box, dating to before AD 70, contains an inscription mentioning a Jesus as the brother of the deceased James, son of Joseph. One of the long sides of this ossuary was inscribed in Aramaic, translating as "James, son of Joseph, brother of Jesus." From the late 1st century BC to AD 70 in Judea and Galilee, use of a carved stone box called an ossuary, in which the bones of the deceased were stored and then placed within a tomb, was popular. Approximately 25 percent of around 1000 ossuaries from this period and region have inscriptions. The James Ossuary is a carved limestone box acquired under mysterious circumstances with an incredible Aramaic inscription. Due to the location, date, and names, the inscription was proposed as referring to Jesus of Nazareth, whose father was Joseph and whose brother was the famous Jerusalem church leader and New Testament epistle author named James. The possible historical connections to James and Jesus in 1st-century AD Jerusalem made the artifact immediately famous.

This James Ossuary artifact was part of a larger forgery trial, and although several scholars had questioned its authenticity or questioned sections of the inscription, the subsequent examination and evidence acquired has demonstrated that not only was the box itself from 1st-century Jerusalem, but the entire inscription appears to have also been written in the 1st century before being placed in a tomb. Analysis showed that the ossuary (50.5 cm x 25 cm x 30.5 cm) was made of local Jerusalem limestone. The craftsmanship of the artifact and the style of the letters also indicate an origin in 1st-century AD Jerusalem.

Further inspection revealed that the patina (ancient residue) inside the letters demonstrated that the entire phrase had been inscribed in antiquity when the ossuary was placed in a tomb in the Kidron Valley of Jerusalem. Eventually, many scholars concluded that the box and its inscription are ancient and authentic. James, the brother of Jesus, is referenced multiple times in the New Testament, and the epistle of James is attributed to him (Matthew 13:55; Mark 6:3; Acts 12:17; 1 Corinthians 15:7; Galatians 1:19; James 1:1; Jude 1). The writings of Josephus record the martyrdom of James in Jerusalem about AD 62 and that he was the brother of Jesus (Josephus, *Antiquities* 20.200). Because this ossuary dates to before AD 70, comes from a tomb in Jerusalem, and specifies three names and their relationship, it could refer to James the apostle, Jesus Christ, and their father Joseph. Further, of all known inscribed ossuaries only one other mentions a brother, meaning that this brother "Jesus" was very significant. Historically, there is no other known James, son of Joseph, brother of Jesus from this period, and a statistical study determined that those three names in that particular familial relationship during the 1st century in Jerusalem would probably account for less than two possible people identified as James son of Joseph brother of Jesus, indicating that the inscription mentions Jesus of Nazareth rather than another unknown Jesus.

Therefore, the data suggests that the inscription was for James the leader of the Jerusalem church, identifying him with his father, Joseph, and his brother, Jesus Christ. If this ossuary inscription contains a 1st-century reference to Jesus of Nazareth, it could be the earliest material artifact mentioning Jesus. However, another artifact of Egyptian origin also appears to have 1st-century references to Jesus Christ. Even more recently, a "magician's cup" was discovered in the underwater ruins of Alexandria during excavation of the harbor. The cup itself was probably manufactured around the late 2nd century BC to the early 1st century AD, based on pottery typology, but the Greek inscription on the cup seems to have been added in the 1st century AD and could be translated as "through Christ the sorcerer," although it cannot be stated with certainty that this cup invokes Jesus Christ.

CAIAPHAS THE HIGH PRIEST

Joseph Caiaphas was the acting high priest of Judaism in Jerusalem from about AD 18 to 36 according to the Gospels, Acts, and Josephus (Matthew 26:3; Luke 3:2; John 11:49; Acts 4:6; Josephus, *Antiquities* 18.34-35, 95).

The James Ossuary, with an Aramaic inscription that reads "James son of Joseph brother of Jesus" © Paradiso. The James ossuary was on display at the Royal Ontario Museum from November 15, 2002 to January 5, 2003.

It is also likely that Caiaphas is briefly referred to in the Mishnah and the Babylonian Talmud. While the Gospels mention him with the official designation Caiaphas the high priest, the writings of Josephus provide additional information by recording that his first name was Joseph, but he was called Caiaphas, which explains why the Gospels and Acts merely use Caiaphas in referring to him.

Apparently the Roman prefect Valerius Gratus made Caiaphas high priest after Eleazar, then with the departure of Pilate and arrival of a new prefect, Marcellus, Caiaphas was deposed and replaced by Jonathan, son of Ananus. As a high priest descended from a long line of priests and related by marriage to another high priest, Caiaphas would have been a powerful and influential man in 1st-century Jerusalem.

Caiaphas is also known from an ossuary recovered from a tomb outside of 1st-century AD Jerusalem, accidently discovered during construction, then subsequently excavated and documented. Discovered in 1990 in a tomb in the "Jerusalem Peace Forest" about one mile south of the Old City of Jerusalem, the tomb contained four niches for twelve ossuaries, but six of the ossuaries had already been disturbed when archaeologists investigated the tomb. Of the six undisturbed ossuaries, two contained inscriptions in Aramaic, both mentioning the family name "Caiaphas." One particularly ornate ossuary had an Aramaic inscription reading *Yehosef bar Qayafa* ("Joseph, son of Caiaphas"), which fits the New Testament spelling of the family name Kaiafa perfectly.

Skeletal remains of six individuals were discovered inside the ossuary, including a man about 60 years old, which may have been the high priest. Highly decorative ossuaries typically indicate that the person was wealthy and prominent in society, although a plain ossuary does not necessarily indicate a person of lower social or financial status. The somewhat crude form of the inscription "Joseph, son of Caiaphas" suggests that it was carved with an iron nail found in the tomb after the ossuary had already been put on the shelf.

In addition to the name, location, and decorative quality of the ossuary, further evidence comes from the date of the burial. Ossuaries appeared in tombs of the Jerusalem area during the reign of King Herod the Great, but disappeared in about AD 70 when the city was destroyed by the Romans. The presence of a coin of King Herod Agrippa I that was found with the ossuaries, dated to AD 42/43, demonstrates that the tomb was in use by AD 43, not long after the end of the high priestly tenure of Caiaphas, but that use must have ceased about 70 AD. This coin was found in the skull inside an ossuary inscribed "Miriam, daughter of Simeon," having been originally placed in the mouth, following the ancient Greek tradition of payment for Charon the boatman to cross the River Styx in the underworld. This demonstrates the influence and adoption of certain Hellenistic and Roman practices even by a priestly family, and suggests identification with the Sadducees rather than less syncretized groups such as the Pharisees and Essenes.

Another ossuary from southwest Judah mentions that the Caiaphas family was of the priestly lineage of Ma'aziah, a priest from the tribe of Levi who was appointed during the time of David, and it seems that his descendants continued to serve in the priesthood for centuries (1 Chronicles 24:18; Nehemiah 10:8). The Miriam ossuary dates to the late 1st century AD, probably after AD

The ossuary of the high priest Joseph Caiaphas

70, which would correlate well with the lifespan of a daughter of Caiaphas the high priest.

Joseph Caiaphas was the son-in-law of Annas, another Roman-appointed high priest (John 18:13; Josephus, *Antiquities* 18.34). Luke mentions both Caiaphas and Annas as high priests in the fifteenth year of Emperor Tiberius (Luke 3:1-2). Caiaphas was the acting high priest at this time, but Annas is also mentioned because he had held the office earlier and was still living. The position of high priest for life had ceased by the Roman period, when the appointment and removal of various high priests by Roman officials was the practice (Josephus, *Antiquities* 18.34-35, 95; Luke 3:2; John 13:18; Acts 4:6).

Even before the time of Jesus, the position of high priest had developed into a special office that was appointed by the political leadership and held great power, rather than descending from Aaron. But in Hellenistic and Roman times the lineage was of little consequence compared to which families happened to be in power or had political influence (Josephus, *Antiquities* 15.22, 20.15-16; 2 Maccabees 4:7-29). This was in contrast to the Mosaic Law, which appointed a high priest for life, although there was ancient precedent of high priests being deposed for political reasons (Numbers 35:25-28; 1 Kings 2:27). The combination of high priestly tradition and Roman appointments explains why former high priests were still alive and functioning in a lesser role during the time of Jesus.

A member of the priesthood and part of the Sanhedrin, Caiaphas was also part of the sect of the Sadducees (Acts 4:1-6; 5:17). Generally, the Sadducees were connected to the priestly class, were friendly with the Romans, often adopted aspects of Hellenism, did not believe in resurrection or the immortality of the soul, and served in political and judicial roles. Pharisees, on the other hand, were tied to the synagogue, the Mosaic Law, and were very opposed to the Romans and to Hellenism. As members of the political elite, the Sadducees may have allied with the Romans in order to retain their power, influence, and wealth.

The house of the high priest Annas would have been situated in the upper city, and the house of Caiaphas was probably located nearby in the same neighborhood, or it may have even been the same housing complex or mansion where both were living (Josephus, *Wars* 2.426). Information from the Byzantine period suggests that the house of Caiaphas was located near the top of Mount Zion, also called the Western Hill. Excavations in this neighborhood have revealed houses from the 1st century AD matching what would be expected of the residence of a high priest, including intricate mosaic floors, colorful wall frescoes, ritual baths, and many stone vessels used for ritual purification. Yet, three different dwellings which could be described as high priestly mansions have been suggested as the house of Caiaphas, although none can be definitively identified with Caiaphas since no inscription connecting any of the houses to Caiaphas has yet been located. These buildings do, however, provide a glimpse of how the house of Caiaphas may have looked.

As the highest-ranking religious leader in opposition to Jesus and a major force behind attempting to implicate Jesus on charges of blasphemy or treason and seize him for execution, Caiaphas was seen as an enemy of Jesus and his followers (Matthew 26:3-5,65-66; Mark 14:55-65; Luke 20:19-26; John 11:47-53). Since he held the position of high priest until AD 36, Caiaphas was also one of the primary leaders behind the early persecution of Christians in Jerusalem (Acts 4:1-6; 7:1; 8:1).

THE CRUCIFIXION OF JESUS

Various forms of crucifixion had been used as punishment by ancient cultures prior to the Romans, such as the Assyrians, Persians, Carthaginians, and Greeks, but the Roman Republic and Empire made the practice a science and a powerful political tool. Due to the extreme pain and shame associated with crucifixion, it was typically not allowed for use in the execution of Roman citizens.

The words *cross* and *crucify* are derived from Latin *crux*, meaning cross, tree, or stake on which a person was impaled, hanged, or executed, although the verb *crucify* was originally used to refer more generally to torture or execution. In the Gospels, the equivalent Greek word for cross is *stauros*.

Neither of these words were restricted to a particular type of stake used for torture or execution, but in the time of the Roman Empire when death by crucifixion was employed on a massive scale, two major types of crosses came to be more common than a simple stake or tree. The Romans typically used a vertical pole with a beam across the top (*patibulum*), appearing like a Latin T, or a vertical pole with an intersecting crossbeam, which according to early iconography associated with Christianity seems to have been the type used in the crucifixion of Jesus. Regardless of the exact shape of the cross, the victim of execution, whether still living or already dead, was placed on the cross as a public spectacle (Josephus, *Wars*; Pseudo-Quintillian, *The Lesser Declamations*).

In the Republic and the Empire, punishment by crucifixion was usually

reserved for slaves, criminals of low social standing, and foreign rebels, while cru-
cifying a Roman citizen was almost unheard of (Josephus, *Wars*; Cicero, *Caius
Rabirius*). However, when one committed treason against the state, which was
considered among the highest of crimes by Romans, citizens and even leaders
were sometimes executed by crucifixion (Cicero, *Caius Rabirius*; Livy, *War with
Hannibal*). In Roman times, crucifixions were usually conducted outside of the
sacred border of a city or military camp and along the major roads so that all could
see and the maximum effect on the public could be reached (Pseudo-Quintillian,
The Lesser Declamations; Appian, *Civil Wars*; Josephus, *Wars*). In Rome the typical place for public executions was outside the Esquiline Gate (Tacitus, *Annals*).

Once the sentence had been approved, the convicted criminal would first
undergo flogging with a flagellum or rods, sometimes placed in a *furca* (a fork-
like yoke), and often other forms of torture that severely weakened the victim
and could even kill them before they were placed on the cross (Josephus, *Antiquities* and *Wars*; Dionysius of Halicarnassus, *Roman Antiquities*; Lucian, *Pisca-
tor*; Cicero, *Verres*). The convicted then were bound to and forced to carry their
crossbeam, weighing up to 100 pounds, to the place of execution, if possible
(Plutarch, *Coriolanus*; Platus, *Miles Gloriosus* and *Carbonaria*; Clodius, *History*).
After arriving where the crucifixion would occur, the convicted would be nailed
to the crossbeam and the stake, either being raised up to connect the crossbeam to the stake, or raising the entire apparatus after the pieces of wood were
attached (Diodorus Siculus, *Bibliotheca Historica*; Seneca, *Dialogue to Marcia
on Consolation*; Herodotus, *Histories*; Pseudo Manetho, *Apotelesmatica*).

However, alternative positions were also used when the executioners chose
(Josephus, *Wars*). The nailing could include feet in addition to arms (Platus,
Mostellaria). The Alexamenos Graffito and the Orpheos Bakkikos crucifixion
seal indicate that in some cases a small crossbeam may have been used for the
feet to be nailed to. Nails, rather than ropes, were the standard means of attach-
ment for crucifixion known from ancient records, including sources referring to
people who believed that crucifixion nails had magical powers (Apuleius, *Meta-
morphoses*; Pliny, *Natural History*).

Those fastened and raised on a cross were probably not very far from the
ground, as ancient sources suggest that animals could reach the legs of the corpse
(Philo, *Against Flaccus*; Pseudo Manetho, *Apotelesmatica*; Horace, *Epistles*). The
convicted was stripped either naked or down to minimal clothing (Dionysius of
Halicarnasus, *Roman Antiquities*; Melito of Sardis, *Passion*; Artemidorus, *Onei-
rokritikon*; Alexamenos graffito).

Death by crucifixion was normally slow and agonizing unless severe punishment or torture prior to being placed on the cross sped up the process (Seneca, *Letters*). However, the severe trauma of the preliminary beatings and then nailing to the cross was so great, very few could survive even if rescued.

In the 1st century, although three associates of Josephus were removed from their crosses and given immediate medical care, only one of them lived (Josephus, *Life* 420-421). Ultimately, death was a result of hypovolemic shock (blood or fluid loss), heart failure, dehydration, asphyxiation, or stabbing by the attending soldiers. The soldiers might also break the legs of the crucified person (*crurifragium*) if a speedier death was desired.

Skeletal remains of two individuals have been recovered that show conclusive signs of the use of nails in crucifixion during the 1st century AD in Judea Province. The remains of Yehohanan (or Jehohanan) indicate that he had been attached to the cross by placing nails in his wrists between the radius and ulna bones, and a 11.5 cm iron nail still present in the heel bone with remnants of wood demonstrated that the feet were nailed to the cross. Subsequent examinations have both agreed and disagreed with the conclusions of the primary study, but no conclusive evidence was shown to refute the original reconstruction. On the contrary, skeletal remains of another recently discovered crucified man

A heel bone of the Judean crucifixion victim Yehohanan, with an iron nail still lodged in the bone, found in a 1st-century burial site in Jerusalem

from Roman-period Judea demonstrate the use of nails driven into the wrists, as the nail was still lodged between the bones when discovered. Thus, skeletal remains indicate that nails were driven into the wrists near the hands and into the foot through the heel. Further, the skeletal analysis indicates that the legs of Yehohonan were broken, presumably to lead to a quick death.

Most crucifixion victims in Roman-period Jerusalem were probably buried in pit or trench graves, not rock-cut tombs with ossuaries, and the nails were almost always pulled out of the body when removing it from the cross or before burial. Additionally, the vast majority of Roman-period burials around Jerusalem were disturbed before archaeologists were able to excavate or analyze them. Therefore, while the discovery and analysis of only two definitive crucifixion victims with nails lodged in their bones might seem meager, they are exceptional findings.

After it was confirmed by the Roman soldiers that the crucified person had died, the corpse could be removed from the cross and buried. Roman law in rule and in practice allowed the bodies of those crucified to be given to relatives for burial or other funeral rites, although the body also may end up in a mass grave with other criminals (Ulpian, *Digest*; Philo, *Against Flaccus*). Survival was not an option for the crucified, but an excruciatingly painful and humiliating death sentence that one hoped would be swift.

According to the Gospels, Jesus was sentenced to and endured death by crucifixion, experiencing the same punishments, protocols, and sequences known from antiquity and especially the Romans. After the trial of Jesus concluded, he was handed over for execution alongside two convicted criminals (Matthew 27:22-26; Mark 15:15; Luke 23:33). Jesus was not a Roman citizen and therefore, even though he was not deemed to be guilty of treason, he could be executed by crucifixion rather than by a swift and clean beheading.

The preliminary torture that Jesus endured included flogging, beating, and a crown of thorns, which except for the crown of thorns was common methodology preceding a crucifixion in the Roman Empire (Matthew 27:26-28; Mark 15:17-18; John 19:1-2). After administering to Jesus a severe beating that many others would not even survive, the Romans tried to force him to carry his wooden crossbeam to the place of execution (John 19:16-17). However, Simon of Cyrene ended up carrying the crossbeam at least part of the way, probably because Jesus was too weak at that point to do it himself (Matthew 27:31-32; Mark 15:20-22; Luke 23:26).

This Simon of Cyrene, father of Alexander and Rufus, is possibly attested by ossuary inscriptions discovered in a tomb in the Kidron Valley during a 1941 survey. The relevant ossuaries might have belonged to two of his children, both specifying that their father was named Simon, but one ossuary includes a name of his son as Alexander and the possible designation "Cyrenean." Specifically, ossuary 9 contains a Greek inscription translated as "Alexander, son of Simon" and an Aramaic inscription reading "Alexander QRNYT [Cyrenean?]." Ossuary 5 has a Greek inscription mentioning "Sara, daughter of Simon, of Ptolemais," which may provide another possible connection since Sara was a common name in Cyrene and Ptolemais was the name of one of the five major cities (Pentapolis) in Cyrene.

Once the procession reached Golgotha, the place of the execution, Jesus was nailed to the cross and crucified (Matthew 27:33-35; Mark 15:22-24; Luke 23:33; John 19:17-18). The piercing of the wrists and feet by nails in the crucifixion of Jesus is specified by two of the Gospel writers (Luke 24:39-40; John 20:20-27). Although it is usually thought to be the hands of Jesus that were nailed, the Greek words used for "hand" in those passages (*xeir*) can also refer to the wrist or arm, which would be a more logical placement of nails for holding a body on a cross than through the palms of the hands, and in agreement with what is known from other ancient texts and archaeological discoveries.

Near the top of the cross, above his head, an inscribed *titulus* (caption, title, or inscription) from Pontius Pilate stated the accusation against Jesus, identifying him as Jesus the Nazarene, the king of the Judeans, in Aramaic, Greek, and Latin (Matthew 27:37; Mark 15:26; Luke 23:38; John 19:19-20). The exact contents of the inscription may have varied from language to language.

This aspect of the crucifixion accounts in the Gospels may have been rare in Roman executions, but it is known from a few instances from the 1st century BC through the 2nd century AD, including an inscription stating the reason that a condemned man would be crucified in Rome, and inscriptions with the accusations of others condemned to death (Cassius Dio, *Roman History*; Suetonius, *Caligula and Domitian*; Eusebius, *Ecclesiastical History*).

The titulus was probably inscribed on a wooden board and whitened, perhaps with gypsum, and the letters may have been painted in black or red to be easily visible, as was a known practice for inscriptions during the period. Of historical and archaeological interest is an alleged wooden titulus mentioned in antiquity that was inscribed in Aramaic, Greek, and Latin. That text read "Jesus the Nazarene, king of the Judeans" and was supposedly found at the site of Golgotha in the 4th century AD after the dismantling of the Roman temple (Egeria,

Itinerarium Egeriae; Macarius of Jerusalem; Ambrose, *Death of Theodosius*; Rufinus, *Church History*; John Chrysostom, *Commentary on John*).

A wooden artifact of unknown date and origin, supposedly this same titulus, has been housed at the Church of Santa Croce in Gerusalemme since at least 1145. Recently, examination of the inscription and the wood was conducted. The fragmentary plaque is made of walnut wood that appears to have been painted white, measuring 25 cm by 14 cm and 2.6 cm thick, with letters about 1.3 cm high. It is inscribed on one side with what might be Aramaic, Greek in reversed script, and Latin in reversed script, although many of the letters are no longer visible. Several epigraphers analyzed the inscription and placed the form of the letters from the 1st century to the 4th century AD. However, radiocarbon tests conducted on the wood dated it to about the 10th century AD. As a result, it has been identified as either a medieval forgery or a medieval copy of the original, or possibly a Byzantine- or Roman-period artifact that shows later radiocarbon dates due to contamination from the medieval period.

Just as crucifixions were conducted outside of the city walls of Jerusalem, it was typical Roman practice to hold executions outside the sacred border of a city or military camp. It is obvious that execution for the Romans was used not only as a harsh punishment for the offender, but as a public demonstration and deterrent to all observers, exemplified by practices such as conducting crucifixions on the most frequented roads (Pseudo-Quintillian, *The Lesser Declamations*).

Citizens, and in particular the elite, were generally given more lenient punishments than noncitizens and slaves (Justinian, *Digest*). However, even the elite suffered the death penalty for treason and certain murders. In fact, the most brutally punished capital offenses in ancient Rome were treason and parricide (murder of a family member), which reflects the Roman cultural belief in the primacy of the state and the family. While the method of execution typically differed for citizens and was less extreme, in cases of treason a Roman might be crucified, lashed to death, or burned alive. In the case of parricide, a special type of capital punishment called *poena cullei* (punishment of the sack) was employed in which the offender was placed in a leather sack with a rooster, a dog, a snake, and a monkey, then thrown into the sea, lake, or river.

Other methods of execution included beheading, strangling, being cast from a great height, being buried alive, drowning, and death by beast. Rather than face impending execution and public dishonor, suicide was often chosen as what Romans considered a more honorable option. However, the elite senatorial and equestrian classes, being in control of politics and the courts, typically received less harsh punishments unless enforced by the emperor or another very powerful Roman. Instead, exile was often used, which ranged from temporary to permanent. As an alternative to execution for slaves or the lower classes, being sent to the mines or to the gladiatorial games likely but not always resulted in death.

During the time of Jesus, local magistrates such as legates, prefects, and procurators had the power of life and death in their hands in the various provinces. Roman leaders recognized that at times people were executed unjustly, but as in the case of Jesus this was usually intentional and politically expedient. In the Roman Empire, capital punishment was a brutal and feared sentence meant to deter treason, rebellion, and various crimes, but from time to time even the innocent faced death for what was seen as the common good.

In addition to the detailed portrayal of Roman crucifixion in the Gospel accounts, the crucifixion of Jesus is also briefly described by a few Roman-period writers and depicted on a wall in Rome. In the late 1st century AD, while writing as an official Roman historian, Josephus recorded that Pilate had condemned Jesus to be crucified (Josephus, *Antiquities*). Lucian, a Roman living in the 2nd century AD who enjoyed mocking Christians, thought it was humorous how Christians worshipped a man who had been crucified (Lucian, *Death of Peregrinus*). Celsus, another 2nd-century AD Roman who criticized Christianity, affirmed that Jesus was nailed to a cross (Celsus in Origen, *Contra Celsus*). Around the same time, Justin, a pagan turned Christian, wrote to Emperor Antoninus Pius in defense of Christianity, mentioning the crucifixion of Jesus and how the events in the Gospels can be confirmed by checking the Roman records such as the Acts of Pilate (Justin Martyr, *Apology*).

An early Jewish source recounted in the Talmud claims that "on the eve of the Passover Yeshu [the Nazarene] was hanged. For forty days before the execution took place, a herald went forth and cried, 'He is going forth to be stoned because he has practiced sorcery and enticed Israel to apostasy. Anyone who can say anything in his favor let him come forward and plead on his behalf.' But since nothing was brought forward in his favor he was hanged on the eve of Passover" (Sanhedrin 43a).

The darkness at the time of the crucifixion of Jesus was allegedly mentioned in *Histories* by Thallus, who explained it as an eclipse, writing in approximately AD 50. This passage was then cited and discussed by Julius Sextus Africanus around AD 220 in the context of the darkness and earthquake mentioned in the Gospels (*Greek Papyri* 10.89; cf. Matthew 27:45; Mark 15:33; Luke 23:44).

The torn veil of the temple at the time of the crucifixion of Jesus might also be alluded to in a pseudepigraphal book called *Lives of the Prophets (Habakkuk)*, probably composed during the 1st century AD, which mentions the tearing of the veil between the Holy Place and the Holy of Holies (cf. Matthew 27:51; Mark 15:38; Luke 23:45). A cryptic passage in the Jerusalem Talmud that claimed that about 40 years before the destruction of Jerusalem (meaning around AD 30), the temple doors that had been closed at night would be found wide open in the morning has also been suggested as being connected

The Alexamenos Graffito from Rome, depicting a crucified Jesus

to this event of the tearing of the veil at the time of the crucifixion, although the wording makes this association difficult (Tractate Yoma 6:3). The Toledot Yeshu, probably a medieval composition that discusses Jesus and his miracles and crucifixion, is a substantially later compilation that seems to be based on older sources such as Celsus, the Mishnah, the Infancy Gospel of Thomas, and the four Gospels of Matthew, Mark, Luke, and John.

The earliest known pictorial representation of the crucifixion of Jesus comes from Rome, found inscribed into a wall of the Paedagogium on the Palatine Hill, probably by servants. Known as the Alexamenos Graffito, the drawing shows Jesus on the cross with the head of a donkey and a man looking up to the cross, while the accompanying Greek inscription reads "Alexamenos worships (his) god." Because the building it was found in association with was originally constructed ca. AD 90, then modified and partly buried ca. AD 200, it dates to somewhere within this period.

Therefore, not only are the accounts of the crucifixion of Jesus in the Gospels perfectly consistent with what is known about Roman-period crucifixion from various ancient sources and archaeological discoveries, but the event of Jesus being crucified in Jerusalem is confirmed by multiple sources from the 1st and 2nd centuries AD and even illustrated by ancient artwork.

AD 33 AND JESUS

The question of the year of the trial, crucifixion, burial, and resurrection of Jesus has been explored and debated for centuries. Over time, new archaeological discoveries and ancient manuscript analyses have brought us closer and closer to answering this question, and with the currently available information, a very probable date can be ascertained based on multiple lines of evidence from numerous 1st century sources.

Crucial in this investigation is that the Gospel narratives name political and religious officials in power during the final days of Jesus, allowing only a specific range of years in which the events could have occurred. Data from ancient manuscripts, inscriptions, and coins demonstrates that when the crucifixion of Jesus occurred, Tiberius was the Emperor of Rome (AD 14–37), Pontius Pilatus was the prefect of Judea Province (AD 26–36), Joseph Caiaphas was the acting high priest in Jerusalem (AD 18–36), Herod Antipas was ruler of Galilee (4 BC–AD 39), and the high priest Annas (AD 6–15) was also alive but not in power, while Jonathan son of Annas (AD 36–37) might also be mentioned as an important bystander soon after the time of Jesus (Josephus, *Antiquities* and *Wars*; Tacitus, *Annals*; Philo of Alexandria, *Embassy to Gaius*; Matthew 27:2; Mark 15:1; Luke 3:1-2; John 18:13; Acts 4:6).

Archaeological discoveries directly and indirectly attesting these aforementioned people include statues, coins, and inscriptions of Tiberius from all over the Roman Empire, a Latin inscription of Pilate found at Caesarea and a ring bearing the name of Pilate in Greek found at Herodium, the inscribed ossuary of Joseph Caiaphas and the ossuary of the granddaughter of Caiaphas the priest, coins and various official inscriptions of Herod Antipas, and possibly the tomb of Annas south of Jerusalem. Joseph Caiaphas and Annas are both mentioned as high priests in the context of the ministry of Jesus because Caiaphas was the acting high priest at this time, while his father-in-law Annas had held the office earlier and was still living (Luke 3:1-2; John 18:24).

Alone, the naming of these individuals and their particular positions limits the parameters of the events at the end of the life of Jesus to the period of AD 26–36 , but the specification of the fifteenth year of Tiberius and that the temple had been under reconstruction for 46 years at the beginning of the ministry of Jesus narrows the year to the range within AD 28–36 (Luke 3:1; John 2:20). Because Jesus was crucified on the eve of Passover, Nisan 14 and a Friday, astronomical calculations demonstrate that this could only have been in the years AD 30, 33, or 36. When the additional factor of the Gospel of John recording Jesus observing at least three or even four Passovers in Jerusalem is accounted for, this seems to further restrict the time period to the years AD 31–36 and disqualifies AD 30 as a possibility (John 2:23; 5:1; 6:4; 13:1).

A trial and crucifixion after AD 30 also better explains the behavior of Pontius Pilatus at the trial of Jesus due to the recent assassination of Lucius Aelius Sejanus in AD 31. Because Pilate was appointed in AD 26 as prefect of Judea to replace Valerius Gratus, and this is the same year in which Tiberius withdrew to Capri and Sejanus began controlling much of the Empire, it is plausible and even likely that Pilate and Sejanus were connected politically. Regardless, after AD 31 and the execution of Sejanus and his political allies, Pilate would have been increasingly wary of displeasing Tiberius and giving him reason to remove him from power, exile him, or even execute him. Pilate wanted to be regarded as a "friend of Caesar," meaning a Roman politician who was favored by the emperor (John 19:12). This potential accusation of being regarded as no friend of Caesar was a direct threat to Pilate.

Josephus and Philo typically record Pilate as cruel and strong, rather than the portrayal of weak and forgiving seen at the trial of Jesus (Josephus, *Antiq-uities* 18.3.1; *Wars* 2.9.2-4; Philo of Alexandria, *Embassy to Gaius* 301-302). For this reason, the trial narrative has often been criticized as incorrectly portraying Pilate being fearful and submitting to the demands of the Jews, even though earlier in his career the Gospels depict Pilate as an uncompromising and harsh Roman governor (Luke 13:1; John 19:12-13). Yet, this change in attitude coin-cides with events in Roman politics and escalating problems in Judea Province. Pilate, earlier in his time as governor, had already encountered complaints and riots by displaying in Jerusalem standards with the image of the emperor, using funds from the sacred treasury to build an aqueduct, the mysterious episode of the blood of Galileans being mixed with their sacrifices, and the inscribed votive shields for the emperor in the Jerusalem Praetorium. While the incident of the shields and the resulting petition to Tiberius by the sons of Herod led to Pilate resolving the problem and being on better terms with Antipas by about AD 32–33, many of the people in Judea would have had an especially negative and even hostile attitude towards Pilate by the time of the trial of Jesus (Hoehner, *Herod Antipas*; Luke 23:12).

The votive shield may have been an attempt by Pilate at gaining favor with Tiberius following the execution of Sejanus, but this action simply caused more anger and friction with the Jews, prompting an official complaint sent to the emperor, and ultimately Tiberias chastised Pilate (Philo of Alexandria, *Embassy to Gaius* 299-305).

By AD 33, Pilate may have been only one incident away from being removed from office, as evidenced by the next documented grievance in AD 36, when his handling of a Samaritan rebellion and subsequent official complaint resulted in him being recalled to Rome.

Following political disasters and now embroiled in a potentially explosive situation, Pilate found himself in a precarious position at the trial of Jesus. Although the Gospels record that Pilate thought Jesus was innocent and even attempted to release him, in order to save himself, Pilate made the choice to please the Jews and avoid further angering Tiberias, which probably would have resulted in his exile or execution. Considering Pilate's past actions, the rebuke by Tiberius, and the recent Sejanus affair, any additional unrest and complaints was too much of a risk for Pilate, and this historical and political context explains the change in his demeanor while also indicating that the trial of Jesus occurred after the AD 31 execution of Sejanus.

Therefore, both the observed Passovers recorded in the Gospel of John and the Roman political context appear to disqualify AD 30 as a potential date for the trial and crucifixion of Jesus. A trial and crucifixion in AD 36 seems unlikely because it would require an approximately eight-year ministry of Jesus, it would be the same year in which both Pilate and Caiaphas were removed from office and Marcellus and Jonathan were installed, it might conflict with the possible mention of Jonathan son of Annas in Acts as an observer rather than high priest in the months or year following the resurrection, and it seems incompatible with the dates for the conversion and ministry of the apostle Paul, which are established based on chronological markers in Acts, the Epistles, and the tenure of Junnius Gallio as governor of Achaia.

After taking into account all of these variables, the remaining option for the trial, crucifixion, and resurrection date is AD 33. Therefore, it can be stated with a high degree of confidence that the crucifixion of Jesus probably occurred on Friday, Nisan 14 of AD 33, just prior to the Sabbath of Passover.

THE LOCATION OF GOLGOTHA

After the trial and scourging of Jesus, the execution was to be carried out by means of crucifixion, administered by the Roman soldiers. Carrying his own crossbeam, Jesus walked to the site where he was nailed to the cross and died. Although a traditional location for Golgotha has been placed near the tomb of Jesus in the Church of the Holy Sepulchre since antiquity, the identification is tentative and has been challenged due to lack of clarity in the archaeological and historical sources. As a result, alternative sites have been proposed and confusion about Golgotha abounds.

However, an analysis of the ancient sources and available evidence can clarify details about Golgotha and point to a probable location. This place of crucifixion, called Golgotha or Calvary, was a hill near the city but outside the walls, near a gate, near a road, and was visible from far away because of its elevation and unobscured location (Matthew 27:33-39; Mark 15:21-40; Luke 23:33; John 19:17-20; Hebrews 13:12). Although the hill typically identified as Golgotha is inside the walls of Old City Jerusalem, these walls were built in the 16th century by the Ottomans. At the time of the crucifixion of Jesus in AD 33, this site of Golgotha would have been north and west of the "second wall" of ancient Jerusalem, built during the time of Herod the Great, while the "third wall" built by Agrippa I around AD 44 stretched the walled part of the city north and encompassed far beyond the area of Golgotha (Josephus, *Wars* 5.140-155).

Golgotha means "place of a skull" in Aramaic, related to very similar Hebrew words referring to a wheel, round shape, and a skull, while *Calvary* is the equivalent Latin word (Matthew 27:33; Mark 15:22; John 19:17). The place was identified in ancient writings as a hill resembling the top of a skull rather than the face of a skull, which agrees with the round shape conveyed by the equivalent Hebrew words. Additionally, all four Gospels refer to the hill using the Greek word *kranion*, meaning cranium or the rounded upper part of the skull. Therefore, it was merely a rounded hill and not the face of a skull.

The mistaken understanding of the description has led to misidentifications for the location of Golgotha. In about AD 383, Egeria mentioned Golgotha as an area, which is congruent with the description in the Gospels of Golgotha being a place outside the city that was a cranium-shaped hill rather than just a particular point on a hill (*Iteneraria Egeriae*).

In modern times, however, alternative identifications have been suggested. The 19th century brought many explorers seeking to identify ancient sites, and another Golgotha location was proposed north of Damascus Gate because of a small rocky cliff face that slightly resembles the face of a skull, with holes interpreted as eyes and a mouth. Proposed in 1842 by German scholar Otto Thenius and then promoted by General Charles Gordon in 1882, the site came to be known as Gordon's Calvary. Unfortunately for this theory, not only was the original Golgotha a cranium-shaped, rounded hill, but the cliff face may have come to loosely resemble a skull only in much later times due to quarrying activities during the Ottoman period.

The Gennath (Garden) Gate mentioned by Josephus as part of the "first wall" and beginning of the extension of the "second wall" is currently the only known gate located nearby the traditional location of the crucifixion of Jesus (Josephus, *Wars* 5.146). Of course, roads led in and out of city gates, so the road passing near the hill and going into this gate would be a logical choice for a place where people would be able to see the hill of the crucifixion while walking on the road.

Writing around AD 160 when the Roman temple had been built for only about 30 years, Melito stated that Jesus was crucified in the midst of Jerusalem and in a wide area (*plateia*) or plaza (Melito of Sardis, *Peri Pascha*). In 2nd-century AD Aelia Capitolina (Jerusalem) this would have been the area of the forum, flanked by the major streets the Cardo and the Decumanus, which was also where the temple of Venus was located.

The Golgotha site was still known near the end of the 3rd century AD when

Eusebius learned of it and eventually mentioned its general location in Jerusalem "on, at, or near" the north slope of Mount Zion, which would be the Mount Zion in the Roman and Byzantine periods located in southwestern Jerusalem (Eusebius, *Onomasticon*; Josephus, *Antiquities*). This geographical information is somewhat ambiguous, although it agrees with the site being in the vicinity of the Church of the Holy Sepulchre rather than much farther to the north beyond the "third wall" of the city.

Cyril, a Christian bishop and resident of Jerusalem in the 4th century, also located the hill of Golgotha near the tomb of Jesus and inside the city at that time (Cyril of Jerusalem, *Catechetical Lectures*). Jerome wrote that a statue to Venus had been placed on the top of the hill during the reign of Hadrian, which would have sat atop the place of the crucifixion, remaining there until the time of Constantine (Jerome, *Letter to Paulinus*). This served as a helpful marker on the hill for the identification of Golgotha during the time of Constantine. The location where the crucifixion was thought to have occurred was then more clearly marked after Helena of Constantinople came to Jerusalem, ordered the Roman temple dismantled with the result that the hill was no longer obscured.

About this time, in AD 333, the Bordeaux Pilgrim stated that the small hill of Golgotha was to the south and about a stone's throw from the tomb of Jesus (Bordeaux Pilgrim, *Itinerarium Burdigalense*). In about AD 335, the Martyrium Basilica was completed as a commemorative church in honor of the cross and crucifixion of Jesus, memorializing what had been identified as the location of the hill of Golgotha. In the early 5th century, after the sites had been clearly marked, Eucherius wrote that Golgotha was very near the tomb in the church that Constantine had built, and that the rock on which the cross had stood was still visible (Eucherius of Lyon, *Letter to Faustus*).

The current Church of the Holy Sepulchre now encompasses both the area of the tomb and this traditional site of Golgotha. Inside the church complex are the remains of a stone hill, now visibly only about 16 feet (5 meters) high due to the raising of the floor level, although the actual height is approximately 30 feet (9 meters) above the level of the original Byzantine church, and part of this rock hill was probably cut away due to the construction of Aelia Capitolina.

Although the traditional location fulfils the requirements of the ancient textual references and the archaeological findings, depending on the exact location of the major streets of the late Roman period, it is also possible that the site of the crucifixion of Jesus was located either slightly east or slightly south of the traditional site, but still in close proximity.

An alternative theory places the crucifixion site about 200 meters south of the traditional hill of Golgotha based on a hypothetical reconstruction of streets and the Gennath Gate, but the archaeological and historical evidence does not necessitate a movement of the site. Another recent study suggests that Golgotha was near the traditional place of the cross, but essentially on the same rock hill. Archaeological excavations also revealed that the traditional Golgotha site was outside the city walls during the time of Jesus, as multiple tombs from around the 1st century BC and 1st century AD were discovered in the area with no evidence of dwellings until the 2nd century AD. However, by about AD 44, the walls of Jerusalem had expanded north and included this area within the city walls, eventually leading to building in an area that had once been used for tombs and a garden.

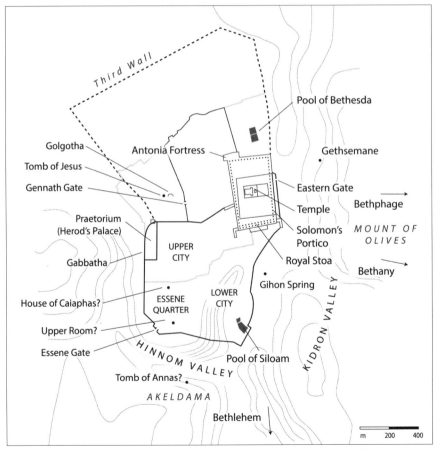

Locations in Jerusalem during the arrest, trial, crucifixion, and burial of Jesus

The Gospel of John describes both the tomb of Jesus and the place of the crucifixion in the same garden area, indicating close proximity (John 19:41). Archaeological analysis has demonstrated that the area around the tomb of Jesus in the Holy Sepulchre and other 1st-century tombs was the former site of a quarry that had been filled with soil by the 1st century, suggesting the possibility of the garden location.

Additionally, the Garden Gate in this area was eventually uncovered through excavation, linking the archaeological findings of a gate, a garden, and 1st-century tombs to the description of the crucifixion location and showing that the nearby rock hill regarded from ancient tradition as the crucifixion site is plausible (Josephus, *Wars* 5.141-146; Hebrews 13:12). Therefore, the site marked as Golgotha in the 4th century AD is the most probable location of the crucifixion of Jesus, at least approximately, due to its agreement with the ancient historical sources and archaeological analysis.

Although the two criminals crucified next to Jesus had their legs broken to ensure a quick death, the soldiers saw that Jesus appeared already dead, confirming this by piercing his side with a spear to see the separated blood and water pour out. Then the body was removed from the cross and allowed to be taken for burial (Mark 15:43-45; John 19:33-38).

Various medical theories have been suggested about the blood and water flowing out after Jesus's side was pierced, but the exact cause seems undecided, with possibilities such as a buildup of fluid around the lungs and a ruptured heart. Removal from the cross and subsequent burial was especially important in the observation of the Mosaic Law (John 19:31; Deuteronomy 21:22-23; Josephus, *Wars*). Following his death, Jesus's body was taken down from the cross and buried in a new tomb, which is now located inside the edicule (a small structure or shrine used to protect an important religious object) at the Church of the Holy Sepulchre.

SELECTED BIBLIOGRAPHY
(CHAPTER 7)

Avigad, Nahman. *Discovering Jerusalem*. Jerusalem: Shikmona, 1980.

Bahat, Dan. "Does the Holy Sepulchre Church Mark the Burial of Jesus?" *Biblical Archaeology Review* 12:3 (1986).

Bahat, Dan, and Magen Broshi. "Excavations in the Armenian Garden." Yadin (ed.), *Jerusalem Revealed. Archaeology in the Holy City 1968-1974*. Jerusalem: Israel Exploration Society, 1976.

Ball, David. "The Crucifixion and Death of a Man Called Jesus." *Journal of Mississippi State Medical Association* 30 (1989).

Barbet, Pierre. *A Doctor at Calvary*. New York: Image, 1963.

Bella, Francesco, and Carlo Azzi. "14C Dating of the Titulus Crucis." *Radiocarbon* 44, issue 3 (2002).

Blomberg, Craig. *Jesus and the Gospels*. Nashville: Broadman and Holman Academic, 2009.

Broshi, Magen, and Gabriel Barkay. "Excavations in the Chapel of St. Vartan in the Holy Sepulchre." *Israel Exploration Journal* 35 (1985).

Brown, Francis et al. *Enhanced Brown-Driver-Briggs Hebrew and English Lexicon*. Oak Harbor, WA: Logos, 2000.

Chancey, Mark and Adam Porter. "The Archaeology of Roman Palestine." *Near Eastern Archaeology* 64.4 (2001).

Cook, John. "Envisioning Crucifixion: Light from Several Inscriptions and the Palatine Graffito." *Novum Testamentum* 50, fasc. 3 (2008).

Corbo, Virgilio. *Il Santo Sepolcro Di Gerusalemme: Aspetti Achaeologici Dalle Origini Al Periodo Crociato*. Jerusalem: Franciscan, 1981.

Crossan, John Dominic, and Jonathan Reed. *Excavating Jesus: Beneath the Stones, Behind the Texts*. New York: HarperCollins, 2001.

Curran, John. "'The Long Hesitation': Some reflections on the Romans in Judaea." *Greece and Rome*, second series, vol. 52, no. 1 (2005).

Edwards, William, Wesley Gabel, and Floyd Hosmer. "On the Physical Death of Jesus Christ." *Journal of the American Medical Association* 255 (1986).

Egmond, Florike. "The Cock, the Dog, the Serpent, and the Monkey. Reception and Transmission of a Roman Punishment, or Historiography as History." *International Journal of the Classical Tradition* 2, no. 2 (1995).

Evans, Craig. "Excavating Caiaphas, Pilate, and Simon of Cyrene: Assessing the Literary and Archaeological Evidence." *Jesus and Archaeology*, ed. James Charlesworth. Grand Rapids: Eerdmans, 2006.

———. *Jesus and the Manuscripts*. Peabody: Hendrickson, 2020.

Geva, Hillel. *Jewish Quarter Excavations in the Old City of Jerusalem, vol 1: Architecture and Stratigraphy*. Jerusalem: Israel Exploration Society, 2000.

Gibson, Shimon. *The Final Days of Jesus: The Archaeological Evidence*. New York: Harper-Collins, 2009.

———. "New Excavations on Mount Zion in Jerusalem and an Inscribed Stone Cup/Mug from the Second Temple Period." Amit et al. eds. *New Studies in the Archaeology of Jerusalem and Its Region: Collected Papers*, volume IV. Jerusalem: IAA, Hebrew University, Moriah, 2010.

———. "The Trial of Jesus at the Jerusalem Praetorium: New Archaeological Evidence." Evans ed. *The World of Jesus and the Early Church*. Peabody, MA: Hendrickson, 2011.

Gibson, Shimon, and Joan Taylor. *Beneath the Church of the Holy Sepulchre*. London: Palestine Exploration Fund, 1994.

Goren, Yuval, and Boaz Zissu. "The Ossuary of Miriam Daughter of Yeshua Son of Caiaphas, Priests Ma'aziah from Beth 'Imri." *Israel Exploration Journal* 61, no. 1 (2011).

Green, William. "An Ancient Debate on Capital Punishment." *Classical Journal* 24.4 (1929).

Greenhut, Zvi. "Burial Cave of the Caiaphas Family," *Biblical Archaeology Review* 18:5 (1992).

———. "The 'Caiaphas' Tomb in North Talpiyot. Jerusalem," *'Atiqot* 21 (1992).

Harden, John. *Dictionary of the Vulgate New Testament*. New York: Macmillan, 1921.

Haas, Nico. "Anthropological Observations on the Skeletal Remains from Giv'at ha-Mivtar," *Israel Exploration Journal* 20 (1970).

Hengel, Martin. *Crucifixion in the Ancient World and the Folly of the Message of the Cross*. Philadelphia: Fortress, 1977.

Hoehner, Harold. *Chronological Aspects of the Life of Christ*. Grand Rapids: Zondervan, 1978.

————. *Herod Antipas: A Contemporary of Jesus Christ*. Grand Rapids: Zondervan, 1980.

Kanael, Baruch. "Ancient Jewish Coins and Their Historical Importance." *Biblical Archaeologist* 26, no. 2 (1963).

Kennedy, Titus. "The Trial of Jesus in Archaeology and History." *Bible and Spade* 25:4 (2012).

Kenyon, Kathleen. *Digging Up Jerusalem*. London: Ernest Benn, 1974.

Koskenniemi, Erkki et al. "Wine Mixed with Myrrh (Mark 15,23) and Crurifragium (John 19,31-32): Two Details of the Passion Narratives." *Journal for the Study of the New Testament* 27 (2005).

Lemaire, Andre. "Burial Box of James the Brother of Jesus." *Biblical Archaeology Review* 28:6 (2002).

Liddell et al. *A Greek-English Lexicon*. Oxford: Clarendon. 1996.

Maier, Paul. "The Inscription on the Cross of Jesus of Nazareth." *Hermes* 124 (1996).

————. "Sejanus, Pilate, and the Date of the Crucifixion." *Church History* 37, no. 1 (1968).

Magness, Jodi. "Ossuaries and the Burials of Jesus and James." *Journal of Biblical Literature* 124 (2005).

Maslen, Matthew, and Piers Mitchell. "Medical Theories on the Cause of Death in Crucifixion." *Journal of the Royal Society of Medicine* 99 (2006).

McRay, John. *Archaeology and the New Testament*. Grand Rapids: Baker Academic, 1991.

Nazenie de Vartavan, Garibian. *La Jerusalem Nouvelle et les premiers sanctuaires chrétiens de l'Arménie. Méthode pour l'étude de l'église comme temple de Dieu*. London: Isis Pharia, 2008.

Peleg, Yifat. "Gender and Ossuaries: Ideology and Meaning." *Bulletin of the American Schools of Oriental Research* 325 (2002).

Reich, Ronny. "Caiaphas' Name Inscribed on Bone Boxes." *Biblical Archaeology Review* 18:5 (1992).

Retief, F.P., and L. Cilliers. "Medical History: The History and Pathology of Crucifixion." *South African Medical Journal* 93 (2003).

Rosenfeld, Amnon, Howard Feldman, and Wolfgang Krumbein. "The Authenticity of the James Ossuary." *Open Journal of Geology* 4 (2014).

Rüpke, Jörg. "You Shall Not Kill: Hierarchies of Norms in Ancient Rome." *Numen* 39 (1992).

Taylor, Joan. "Golgotha: A Reconsideration of the Evidence for the Sites of Jesus' Crucifixion and Burial." *New Testament Studies* 44 , issue 2 (1998).

Thenius, Otto. "Golgatha et Sanctum Sepulchrum." *Zeitschrift für die Historische Theologie* (1842).

Vaananen, Veikko, ed. *Graffiti Del Palatino I. Paedagogium.* Helsinki: Institutum Romanum Finlandiae, 1966.

Vardaman, Jerry. "A New Inscription which Mentions Pilate as 'Prefect'." *Journal of Biblical Literature* 81 (1962).

Wolff, Samuel. "Archaeology in Israel." *American Journal of Archaeology* 100, no. 4 (1996).

Yadin, Yigael. "Epigraphy and Crucifixion." *Israel Exploration Journal* 23 (1973).

Zias, Joe, and E. Sekeles. "The Crucified Man from Giv'at ha-Mivtar: A Reappraisal." *Israel Exploration Journal* 35 (1985).

CHAPTER 8

The Burial, Tomb, and Resurrection of Jesus

After the crucifixion of Jesus, the body was placed in a tomb according to typical practices and rituals of Judea in the 1st century AD. The burial traditions common in Judea during the Roman period followed the basic commands of the Mosaic Law, combined with the use of local stone tombs and secondary burial, while certain people had even adopted a few Hellenistic and Roman customs. After death, a corpse would be prepared for burial by washing and anointing with oils, then wrapped in a linen shroud before being placed in the tomb as soon as possible (Matthew 26:12; 27:59-60; Mark 15:46; Luke 23:53-56; John 11:44; 19:38-40; Acts 5:6; 9:36-37). In some cases, the corpse may have also been placed in a coffin as wooden coffins seem to have been used just before the time of Herod in the Hasmonean period, although the prevalence of this practice is unknown (Luke 7:12-15).

Discoveries of 1st-century BC to AD 70 tombs in the Jerusalem area indicate that typical practices included artificially hewn rock tombs carved into the bedrock, tombs outside the walls of the city, tombs used by families over generations and not just one individual, bodies initially wrapped in a burial shroud and placed in the tomb individually, and that only wealthier people had rock-carved tombs while those of less financial means used pit and trench graves.

Crucifixion victims in 1st-century Judea were allowed proper burial at least occasionally, as evidenced by the discovery of the tomb of Yehohanan and his ossuary, although most bodies of the crucified, generally being criminals or rebels, were probably buried in pit or trench graves rather than expensive rock-hewn tombs. According to the Mosaic Law, it would have been protocol for Jesus to be buried on the same day that he was crucified, and it needed to be done before Passover started on Friday evening (Deuteronomy 21:22-23).

1st-century stone cut, rolling stone tomb of the Herodian family outside the walls of Jerusalem, similar to the tomb in which Jesus was buried

Because easily cut limestone was available throughout the region, the people utilized tombs carved into a rocky hillside or a shaft into the ground, cut with chisels. Most of these tombs had an entryway that could be closed and opened by moving the rolling stone or blocking stone, a central chamber, multiple extension chambers or burial benches, ossuaries, and various types of pottery (Matthew 27:60; Mark 15:46; 16:5; Luke 23:53–24:2; John 11:38-39; 19:41–20:1).

The ritual of placing grave goods does not seem to be attested in all tombs, and in many cases probably only had sentimental significance rather than a reflection about views of the afterlife. The outside of a tomb usually had no markers or decorations, and burials were traditionally supposed to be simple, except in the case of either the wealthy or those emulating Hellenistic and Roman practices, which usually included priestly families (Josephus, *Antiquities* and *Wars*).

The main chamber of a tomb was normally flanked on three sides with raised benches carved out of the stone, while extensions for additional burials would be carved out from this main chamber. Tombs with burial niches extending out from the main chamber are often referred to as loculi tombs, and these were the most common during the period. A family could continue to add more burial niches as more members of the family were buried in the tomb.

The outsides of tombs were occasionally decorated, while the insides may have contained pottery and rarely inscriptions on the walls. In a few instances, coins have been found in association with skulls, reflecting the adoption of the Hellenistic practice of placing a coin in the mouth to pay the boatman Charon for passage across the River Styx into the underworld.

The less elaborate and less expensive burials consisted of a simple shaft or trench dug into the ground in which only one person would be interred. Many of these have been found from the Roman period in Judea, but only a small percentage of them are cut deep into the rock, which of course required much more work.

Skeletal analysis has demonstrated that tombs in 1st-century Judea were primarily used for family groups, that the interred could be of any age group or gender, and that over time, ossuaries or burial niches came to be used in secondary burial for several individuals, probably due to space constraints. The tradition of ancestral tombs goes all the way back to at least the time of the patriarchs and is embodied in the phrases "gathered to his people" or "gathered to his father" (Genesis 25:8; 49:29-33; Judges 2:10; 2 Kings 22:20; 2 Chronicles 34:28). The tomb of Jesus, however, was a new tomb no one had been interred in and no one used afterward.

Typically, after the flesh had decayed in the tomb, the skeletal remains were placed in ossuaries for secondary burial. An ossuary is a box, usually carved out of stone, that was used to hold the bones of the deceased. Ossuaries in Judea were usually around 2.5 feet by 1 foot by 1 foot, designed to hold only a collection of bones. The emergence and use of ossuaries in Judea and Galilee seems to have been part of the adoption of Roman and Hellenistic practices, and in particular the use of cinerary urns and stone boxes to hold the remains of the deceased.

Even though the use of a container box was probably adopted, the Roman practice of cremation was not. Instead, the bones of the deceased were preserved in order to accommodate ancient burial practices and beliefs of Judaism, including resurrection. Ossuaries first appear during the time of Herod the Great, who was appointed king by the Romans, and the use of ossuaries nearly ceased following the AD 70 destruction of Jerusalem by the Romans.

Hundreds of inscriptions on ossuaries are known, although most ossuaries are uninscribed. Usually, the inscription mentions the name of the deceased and perhaps his or her father, although in rare instances geographical locations, curses, mothers, grandfathers, grandmothers, and even brothers appear. Ossuary inscriptions vary from rudimentary to highly artistic, including blue or red pigment in the lettering. Decorations are most often geometric, but rosettes and palm trees were also quite common.

In Judea, ossuaries were mainly used from around 20 BC until the destruction of Jerusalem in AD 70, while in the wider region their use persisted into the 3rd century AD. According to a few studies, even early Christians in the Jerusalem area used ossuaries in the 1st century, such as those found at the Dominus Flevit tombs. The controversial James Ossuary appears to also attest to this practice.

THE SHROUD

When Jesus was buried, his body was wrapped in a shroud and placed on the stone burial bench inside the rock carved tomb, which was then sealed with a massive stone (Matthew 27:59; Mark 15:46; Luke 23:53; 24:12; John 19:40; 20:3-7). The "tomb of the shroud" in the Akeldama area just south of ancient Jerusalem provided archaeological evidence of this burial-shroud practice in Roman-period Judea when an adult male entombed with a burial shroud in the 1st century AD was discovered. The cloth remains found in this tomb include a burial cloth and a separate face cloth. The weave was a simple two-way method.

In contrast, the famous and yet mysterious Shroud of Turin has an unknown provenance, as it was not recovered in an archaeological excavation, the separate face cloth is missing, and its weave is more complex. It is an artifact, or perhaps a relic, whose age of origin, image method, and relevance to history is still debated after extensive testing, analysis, and historical research. This shroud measures 4.4 meters by 1.1 meters, and it was woven from linen in a 3:1 broken-twill pattern.

Analysis of the images on the shroud, particularly of photographic negatives, show that it appears to depict a bearded man bearing wounds consistent with the process of Roman crucifixion and the crucifixion of Jesus as recorded in the Gospels. The image consists of yellowish fibers located only on the tops of threads that seem to show no evidence of paints, dyes, stains, or applied coloring material. The radiocarbon tests in 1988 dated the shroud to AD 1260–1390, but subsequently several scientists argued that contamination could have flawed the test results, such as testing a section repaired during the Middle Ages or the fire in 1532 that damaged the shroud and might have contaminated the results.

Other evidence might indicate a 1st-century origin, such as this weave type being known from cloth discovered at Masada, dating to Roman-period Judea. Pollen samples from the shroud also suggest a point of origin in the Middle East and the Mediterranean, including garland chrysanthemum that is found in the area of Judea. Analysis of dirt particles found travertine aragonite limestone that matched chemical signatures from Jerusalem tombs.

One historical reconstruction traces the shroud back to Constantinople, Edessa, and finally Jerusalem, identifying it as an object known from ancient sources as early as the 2nd century and usually referred to as the Image of Edessa or Mandylion. One of the tested substances on the shroud was blood, and probably human blood, although the results were not definitive.

Because of the ancient historical tradition, the image of what appears to be a crucified man, and the presence of blood on a centuries-old linen cloth, one hypothesis claims that the Shroud of Turin was the burial shroud (*sindon*) of Jesus. Objections have been raised that even if it originated in 1st-century Judea, this could not possibly be the

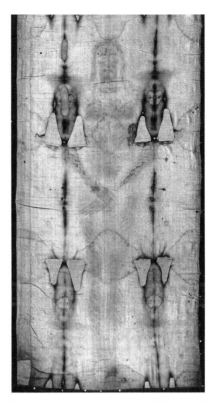

The enigmatic and debated Shroud of Turin

burial shroud of Jesus because John mentioned a separate face cloth, although perhaps a linen sheet could have been placed over the entire head in addition to a face cloth.

However, chemists and physicists have not yet been able to clearly explain how the image was formed, no consensus has been reached, and the mystery and debate about the shroud will likely continue until new data is brought to light. Regardless of who the Shroud of Turin belonged to or where it originated, other archaeological discoveries have demonstrated the use of burial shrouds and a separate face cloth for entombed individuals in 1st-century Jerusalem.

THE TOMB OF JESUS

According to the Gospels, the tomb of Jesus, which would have been quite costly, was financed by a wealthy man named Joseph of Arimathea, who was a member of the Sanhedrin. The tomb was described as a new tomb just outside the city, hewn out of the rock, single chambered, having a bench or trough on which to place the body, and sealed with a large stone (Matthew 27:57-60; Mark 15:42-46; 16:5; Luke 23:50-53; John 19:38-41; 20:11-12). Rock-hewn and stone-sealed tombs with a bench are of a type known from Judea and the Jerusalem area during the Roman period, and several examples have been discovered nearly intact. Details about the tomb recorded in the Gospels allow specific criteria to be applied to evaluation of ancient tombs, in addition to any historical sources from antiquity and ancient traditions for the location.

Once the body of Jesus had been put in the tomb, the tomb was sealed with a stone and guards were posted outside the entrance to deter the disciples of Jesus from taking the body. As a province ruled by a Roman prefect, it is logical that the law enforcement would be Roman. The temple guard would have had no true jurisdiction outside of the temple, which is why the high priests and other religious leaders asked Pontius Pilate "to give orders," but they did not ask him for permission to use their temple guards. Matthew used the Greek word *stratiotes* meaning "soldier, professional soldier, officer in the imperial service" for these guards, but when the temple officers or guards are mentioned in the Gospels, this word is not used. Philo, the Mishnah, and the Talmud describe the duties of the temple guards as primarily in the temple precinct guarding or acting as gatekeepers to make sure the wrong people did not enter where they were not allowed (Matthew 28:12; Philo, *The Special Laws*).

When the soldiers failed their mission to guard the tomb, the religious leaders promised to keep them out of trouble—which might have included execution—if the Roman prefect happened to hear about the body of Jesus going missing during their watch (Matthew 28:14). Therefore, the Gospel sources indicate that the tomb would have been guarded by Roman soldiers, and that knowledge of the location of the tomb in the 1st century was widespread, including among the disciples of Jesus, the Sanhedrin, and the Romans.

The Christian community has revered this location for the tomb of Jesus since antiquity, remembering the event and location and passing this information down from generation to generation. The tradition for the location of the tomb of Jesus likely traces all the way back to AD 33, since a substantial Christian community remained in Jerusalem from the time of Jesus through the Byzantine period except for a brief departure from about AD 66–73, during the First Judean Revolt against Rome, when many Christians moved to Pella and other nearby areas not involved in the revolt.

Marble slab covering the original limestone-carved burial bench inside the tomb at the Church of the Holy Sepulchre

Multiple historical sources from antiquity mention the tomb of Jesus and buildings that were placed over it in the Roman and Byzantine periods, showing that the location was not forgotten even when it was obscured. Eusebius, a Roman historian and Christian bishop of Caesarea who lived in the 3rd and 4th centuries AD, recorded that the rock-cut tomb of Jesus had been covered by a temple to Venus (also known by the Greek name for the goddess Aphrodite) by Emperor Hadrian around AD 135 (Eusebius, *Life of Constantine*). Jerome, a 4th- and 5th-century church father who lived much of his life in Bethlehem, also affirms that a Roman temple had occupied the location of the tomb of Jesus, although Jerome mentions Jupiter rather than Venus (Jerome, *Letter to Paulinus*). These two scholars lived in the area and were very familiar with the city of Jerusalem, Roman history, and church history, in addition to obtaining information from locals and church leaders and sources we no longer have access to.

Even before the church was built and possibly before the Roman temple was built, Christian pilgrims from far away may have been visiting the site and leaving their mark. Excavations in the Chapel of St. Vartan at the Church of the Holy Sepulchre discovered an interesting but enigmatic drawing of a ship with an accompanying Latin inscription *domine ivimus*, possibly meaning "Lord, we went," referring to a pilgrimage and perhaps from the 2nd century AD (cf.

Psalm 122:1). However, the date of the ship and the exact meaning of its accompanying inscription are contested.

The seemingly problematic reference to both Venus and Jupiter may be explained by the possibility of a double temple to Jupiter and Venus at the site. This double-temple concept built on an east-west axis, especially involving Venus, has precedent in other building projects of Hadrian, such as the famous double temple of Venus and Roma dedicated in AD 135, situated between the Forum and the Colosseum at Rome. The temple to Venus and Jupiter in Jerusalem erected by Hadrian was also next to the Roman Forum in Jerusalem, which conforms to typical Roman practice and is also in agreement with the location of the Church of the Holy Sepulchre.

Eusebius was obviously aware of the tradition of the tomb of Jesus as early as the 3rd century AD, but if the information that he conveys is correct, then Emperor Hadrian also knew the location of the tomb of Jesus, or at least where Christians in the early 2nd century AD considered the tomb to be located. It is not only likely but nearly certain that Christians would have passed down a continuous memory of the location of the tomb from the time of the burial in about AD 33 in light of the tomb being the location of the most important event in Christianity—the resurrection of Jesus.

Remnants of the double temple of Venus and Roma in Rome

This covering of sites associated with Jesus was part of a concerted effort by Hadrian to suppress and eliminate Christianity by building pagan temples and shrines at locations important to Christians, which also occurred at Bethlehem, the Pool of Bethesda, and probably the Pool of Siloam. Excavations underneath the Church of the Holy Sepulchre revealed that a Roman temple, to Venus and apparently also Jupiter, had been built over a 1st-century tomb in the time of Emperor Hadrian during the reconstruction of Jerusalem as Aelia Capitolina around AD 135.

Although a few scholars have suggested that there may have been another temple in the city dedicated to Jupiter Capitolinus, whom the city was partially named after, the presence of a second Roman temple located elsewhere in the city from the time of Hadrian has not been confirmed by written or archaeological sources. While Hadrian may have intended to build another Roman temple on the Temple Mount, this seems to have been thwarted by the Bar Kokhba Revolt and construction was never completed. There is no evidence of any Roman temple on the Temple Mount, but only statues of the emperors Hadrian and Antoninus Pius placed on the remaining platform.

A coin issued by order of Emperor Hadrian in Jerusalem reads "COL(onia) AEL(ia) KAP(itolina)" and shows a temple with three figures inside. These figures are typically identified as the deities Jupiter, Juno, and Minerva who composed the Capitoline Triad. As the temple that was over the tomb of Jesus may have been a double temple to Venus and Jupiter, common in the Roman period and especially during the reign of Hadrian, who believed his family had a connection to Venus, the coin may even be depicting part of the temple that was placed over the tomb of Jesus. One of these coins was even found in excavations under the church, which also revealed remnants of the Roman temple.

Not long after the time of Jesus, Christianity was already causing problems in the Roman Empire due to its radically different worldview and culture, which did not mesh with traditional Roman beliefs and practices. In about AD 116, the Roman historian Tacitus wrote that in an effort to suppress the rumor of Jesus and the resurrection, which had originated in Judea and spread to Rome, Emperor Nero falsely charged Christians and punished them with torture and death at least as early as AD 64 (Tacitus, *Annals* 15.44).

According to another noteworthy Roman historian, Emperor Claudius had earlier expelled Jews from Rome because they made "disturbances" about Christ (Suetonius, *The Twelve Caesars*; Acts 18:2). The people involved were probably Christians, who in the early years of Christianity the Romans mistakenly identified as practicing Judaism until the distinction became clearer to them, and Jews who were opposed to Jesus and Christianity. The Romans were also familiar with the peculiar claims of Jesus rising from the dead and leaving the tomb, as is demonstrated by the records of Josephus in the late 1st century AD remarking that people had reported about the resurrection of Jesus.

Further, an edict issued by one of the emperors, probably Claudius, that appears to acknowledge the empty tomb, imposed the death penalty for anyone who would attempt to steal a body from this type of tomb. The "Nazareth Inscription," as the stone inscription of this edict is usually called, focuses on perpetrators who have taken away a corpse from a tomb for "wicked intent," and in particular a type of rock-cut tomb that is sealed with a stone, which was only used in Judea Province until about AD 70. The policies of many of the emperors continued to attempt to rid the Empire of Christianity through law, propaganda, persecution, and the building program of Hadrian, including his Roman temple over the site of the tomb of Jesus.

The adorned entrance to the tomb of Jesus in the Church of the Holy Sepulchre

Christianity in the Roman Empire not only persisted, but it grew to such an extent that it was legalized in AD 313 by the Edict of Milan during the reign of Emperor Constantine. Soon after, construction of the Church of the Holy Sepulchre began under the architect Zenobius in about AD 326. Archaeological and historical evidence seems to point to the tomb of Jesus as being located inside this church.

While no other site has an ancient tradition as the tomb of Jesus, not all agree that the Church of the Holy Sepulchre marks the location of that tomb. Due to misunderstandings about the location of the walls of Jerusalem in antiquity, several scholars in the past mistakenly thought the Church of the Holy Sepulchre was located inside Jerusalem during the time of Jesus. In reality, during the life of Jesus, the walls of Jerusalem did not extend as far west as the area of the Church of the Holy Sepulchre until construction began on the "third wall" around AD 41–44 by Herod Agrippa I, and may not have been completed until just before the First Jewish Revolt (Josephus, *Wars* 5.148-155). Yet, because of mistaken understandings, alternative options were sought.

The Garden Tomb, which is located outside the Old City walls and far from the walls or gates of Jerusalem dating to the time of Jesus, was investigated and advanced in the late 19th century by German scholar Conrad Schick after Charles Gordon in 1883 proposed the nearby Gordon's Calvary as an alternative location for the crucifixion site. However, archaeological analysis of the Garden Tomb has demonstrated that it was originally constructed, or carved out, in the Iron Age II around the 7th or 8th century BC, and therefore it is hundreds of years too early to be the tomb of Jesus. Over a thousand years later, this tomb was reused by Christians as a burial place in the Byzantine period in about the 5th or 6th century as evidenced by the human skeletal remains found within.

Additionally, the Garden Tomb had two chambers rather than one, and the construction is not of the type that would allow for a rolling stone to seal the tomb—for example, Iron Age II tomb ceilings such as the "Garden Tomb" were flat rather than vaulted, unlike the arcosolium type tomb of the 1st century

The exterior of the Garden Tomb in Jerusalem

in which Jesus was buried. Thus, the Garden Tomb does not match ancient descriptions of the tomb of Jesus in date, design, or location. Instead, the Garden Tomb area may serve as a general visual example of what the garden area around the tomb of Jesus would have been like in the 1st century AD.

Recently, another alternative location for the tomb of Jesus was proposed at a place referred to as the Talpiot tomb, although this site has received little acceptance in either the Christian or scholarly communities. The names found carved on six of the ten Talpiot ossuaries are of interest, although they are common names during the Roman period in Jerusalem and the surrounding area. The names inscribed on the ossuaries include a "[…?] son of Joseph," which has been proposed as "Jesus son of Joseph," but several scholars prefer "Hanun son of Joseph" or that the first part of the inscription is mostly indecipherable. The names by themselves suggest nothing other than that the tomb was used by Judeans during the Roman period.

There are also no Christian markings on the Talpiot tomb, and no ancient tradition or record associating the Talpiot tomb with Jesus or early Christianity. The data demonstrates that neither the Garden Tomb nor the Talpiot tomb were the tomb of Jesus, nor were they ever regarded as such until modern times.

Before constructing the Church of the Holy Sepulchre, Constantine had the temple to Venus dismantled, and once removed, what was identified as the tomb of Jesus underneath was visible again. This chamber tomb of particular interest, cut into the limestone, dates back prior to the building of the Roman temple, and it was clearly regarded as the tomb of Jesus in both the 2nd century AD and 4th century AD by the Roman government and Christian community as evidenced by the building of the temple and church above and around the tomb.

According to excavations, this tomb had a single, short hallway passage from the entrance into a single square-shaped room where the body would lay. The architecture of the entrance suggests that a large circular stone had sealed the tomb, although similar tombs do exist that have square sealing stones rather than round. The description of the tomb in the Gospels makes it clear that it was a single-chamber. rock-cut tomb, and that a round circular sealing stone was used, which would agree with archaeological findings (Matthew 27:59-60; Mark 15:46; Luke 24:2).

The Church of the Holy Sepulchre was erected around the site of the tomb rather than above it, but during construction it seems the builders cut away much of the rock hill around the tomb so that it could be more easily integrated into the church. The church was dedicated in September of AD 335 by Bishop Macarius of Jerusalem. Due to destruction of the church and tomb by the Islamic caliph known as Hakim the Mad in 1009, what remains today requires much more imagination than what was obvious during the Byzantine period.

The traditional rock of Calvary or Golgotha, which is inside the far end of the present church, was also not in the original building. Ancient sources have much less to say about this location, although the rock hill, which is at least nine meters higher than the floor of the 4th-century church, and its proximity to the tomb make it a plausible candidate for the cranium-shaped hill of the crucifixion (John 19:17,41).

Archaeological investigations in Jerusalem have also shown that the Church of the Holy Sepulchre lies outside and west of the walls of Jerusalem from the time of Jesus, so burials would have been allowed in the area. In fact, excavations uncovered the existence of several ancient tombs cut into the hillside, which may have been called "Gareb" (Jeremiah 31:39). One of these tombs, approximately 20 meters west of the tomb of Jesus and called the Tomb of Joseph of Arimathea, appears to have been cut between the 1st century BC and AD 44. This was a multi-chamber tomb that had nine oval-shaped recesses along the walls.

Another 1st-century tomb near the tomb of Jesus in the Church of the Holy Sepulchre

The other rock-cut tombs in the immediate area primarily date to the 1st century BC and 1st century AD. A few other ancient tombs in the vicinity of the church appear to have been of the more common loculi type, which utilizes slots in the walls in which to place bodies or ossuaries, and often have multiple hallways and chambers. By AD 44, however, Herod Agrippa I had expanded the walls of Jerusalem to the north and west, encompassing the area around the tomb. The Church of the Holy Sepulchre was also constructed in an area that had been a quarry until the 1st century BC, when it was filled with soil and converted into a garden.

It seems that Joseph of Arimathea had a tomb cut into a rocky hill in this garden area, and Jesus was placed into this tomb after the crucifixion. Evidence from archaeology, ancient historical sources, geography, and Christian tradition all point to the Church of the Holy Sepulchre as housing the remains of the tomb of Jesus, which can still be visited today.

The resurrection was recorded in detail in all four Gospels and mentioned in Acts and multiple Epistles, meaning at least seven different authors wrote about the resurrection around three decades or less from the event. According to Matthew, Mark, Luke, and John, early in the morning on the third day of being in the tomb, Jesus arose from the dead, left the stone-sealed tomb, and began appearing to many of his followers (Matthew 27:59–28:17; Mark 15:46–16:14; Luke 23:52–24:43; John 19:41–20:20). The physical resurrection of Jesus is also attested to in Acts, and both Paul and Peter affirm Jesus's resurrection and appearances to his followers (Acts 1:3; 17:2-3; Romans 1:1-4; 1 Corinthians 15:3-20; 1 Thessalonians 1:8-10; 1 Peter 1:3).

The preserved historical record for the event is quite early, comes from eyewitness testimony, was widely circulated, which would allow critical analysis, and it is attested by multiple written sources. Two notable Roman historians who lived in the 1st century, Josephus and Tacitus, also indicate knowledge of the resurrection of Jesus in their writings. Another text of importance is a 1st-century Roman inscription that may also connect to the story of the empty tomb and the resurrection of Jesus. This artifact is referred to as the Nazareth Inscription.

THE NAZARETH INSCRIPTION

In the 19th century, a marble slab approximately 23.7 inches tall, 14.8 inches wide, and 2.4 inches thick (60 cm by 37.5 cm by 6 cm) with 22 lines of Greek inscribed on one side was purchased and by 1878 ended up in Paris in the possession of an antiquities collector named Wilhelm Froehner. According to a note found in his collection, the inscription was sent from Nazareth. Since Froehner's death in 1925, it has been in possession of the Bibliothèque Nationale in Paris.

Although its exact location of original discovery or excavation is unknown, since it was most likely looted, it has been affirmed as authentic and the majority of scholars have proposed that it was probably issued in Judea, Galilee, or the Decapolis area. Based on epigraphy, the inscription would date between the 1st century BC and the 1st century AD. Spelling, grammar, and word usage, however, narrow the date considerably.

Multiple studies have been done on the inscription over the past 90 years, with scholars generally dating the inscription to the reigns of Augustus, Tiberius, Claudius, Caligula, or Nero, spanning approximately the first 68 years of the 1st century AD (Tsalampouni, "The Nazareth Inscription"). The periods of Tiberius and Claudius are the most agreed upon by scholars for the composition of the edict, although a few have suggested later reigns such as Hadrian or even Septimius Severus.

According to Roman parallels, the Nazareth Inscription may have been a translation of the original Latin order sent by letter from the emperor to the governor (or King Agrippa I). It shares similarities to replies of Emperor Trajan to Pliny, governor of Bithynia. However, it is even more similar to a letter of Claudius in AD 41 written to Alexandria, forbidding Jews of Alexandria to bring or invite other Jews from Syria Province, and it is classified as a "rescript" like the Nazareth Inscription.

If the rescript was sent to the area of Galilee where it surfaced, a date early in the reign of Claudius is particularly likely because of the expansion of the realm of Herod Agrippa to include both Judea and Galilee in AD 41 and the urgency to address problems that had developed in the Empire after the disastrous and neglectful reign of Caligula. Thus, the composition date was probably around AD 41 or so when Claudius took power as emperor and began taking action, or perhaps in AD 44 when the area transferred back to direct Roman control under a procurator. Claudius is known to have taken extreme measures concerning Christianity, including the expulsion of Judeans from Rome due to constant disturbances involving Christ (Suetonius, *Divus Claudius*; cf. Acts 18:1-2).

The content of the inscription, however, is by far its most interesting aspect. The edict focuses on anyone who has taken away a corpse from a tomb for "wicked intent," specifically a type of rock tomb that is sealed with a stone. Previously, corpse robbing had not been an important issue, and the penalty was typically settled by paying a fine. However, this edict drastically elevated the status of a particular type of corpse stealing, commanding the ultimate punishment of death for committing the crime.

As a result of the location, time period, and content of the inscription, several scholars have argued that this edict was issued by the Romans in reaction to the story of the resurrection of Jesus. Rather than state that Jesus of Nazareth did not rise from the dead, the edict instead reads as if the story that the Roman soldiers were paid by the priests and elders of Judaism to spread about the disciples of Jesus supposedly stealing his body from the tomb while the soldiers were asleep was the accepted explanation in the Imperial administration (Matthew 28:11-15). The edict reads as follows:

> Edict of Caesar: This is my decision [concerning] burial tombs. Whoever has made them for the religious observances of parents, or children, or household members, that these remain undisturbed forever. But if anyone legally charges that another person has destroyed, or has in any manner extracted those who have been buried, or has moved with wicked intent those who have been buried to other places, committing a crime against them, or has moved sepulcher sealing stones, against such a person, I order that a judicial tribunal be created, just as [is done] concerning the gods in human religious observances. Even more so will it be obligatory to treat with honor those who have been entombed. You are absolutely not to allow anyone to move [those who have been entombed]. But if [someone does], I want that [violator] to suffer capital punishment under the title of "tomb breaker."

The edict on the Nazareth Inscription records specifics that suggest a link to the resurrection of Jesus: the stealing of a corpse from a rock tomb, particularly a stone-sealed tomb, and an unprecedented extreme reaction to the crime as a deterrent against similar possible problems in the future. Roman knowledge of the resurrection claims correlates perfectly with the concern of the edict about people stealing a corpse from a tomb with "wicked intent," rather than looting the tomb for valuable items, which was the normal practice of tomb robbers. The wicked intent phrase implies that there was a specific agenda behind removing the corpse from the tomb, and that this agenda was at odds with Roman beliefs and culture.

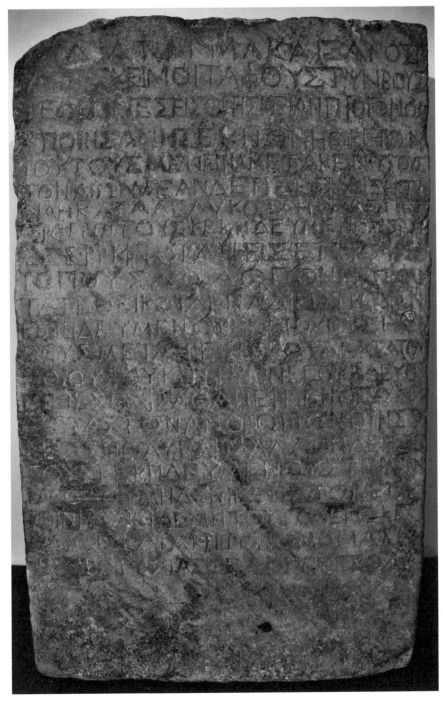

The imperial rescript known as the Nazareth Inscription

The second matching detail is that the type of tomb mentioned is a stone-sealed tomb, demonstrating that the edict referred to a tomb with a sepulcher sealing stone, which was commonly used for rock-cut tombs in Judea Province only until the First Judean Revolt in about AD 66–73. This type of rock-cut, stone-sealed arcosolium tomb was exactly the type of tomb Jesus of Nazareth had been buried in (Mathew 27:59-60).

The third notable detail is the extreme reaction to the crime of stealing a corpse from a tomb. Normally, tomb robbers were after valuable grave goods that were buried with people, such as jewelry, coins, pottery, and glassware. However, if a body was stolen and the perpetrator caught, the punishment was usually a fine paid to the offended family. Yet, the edict commands a new punishment that is the severest punishment possible for any crime.

Combining indicators from epigraphic analysis, content, and context suggest a time of issue in the 1st century AD, and more specifically perhaps around AD 41–44 when Claudius came into power as emperor and the whole area of Judea, Samaria, and Galilee was under one jurisdiction—first ruled by Herod Agrippa I beginning in AD 41, then transferred to Roman control under a procurator in AD 44 (Acts 11:28).

It is noteworthy that Herod Agrippa I spent much of his life in Rome among the Julio-Claudian family and future emperors Caligula and Claudius who befriended him, and he even had an important role in the rise of Claudius becoming the next emperor of Rome (Cassius Dio, *Roman History*; Josephus, *Antiquities* and *Wars*). A relevant and significant coin depicts Herod of Chalcis and Herod Agrippa I crowning Roman Emperor Claudius. Herod Agrippa I was also a zealot for Judaism and violently opposed to Christianity, with examples such as the arrest and abuse of Christians, the imprisonment of Peter, and the execution of James the son of Zebedee because of their preaching about Jesus (Philo of Alexandria, *Embassy to Gaius*; Josephus, *Antiquities*; Acts 12:1-4).

This background information makes it probable that Herod Agrippa I would have had conversations with Claudius about Jesus and the Christians, and that he would have requested the emperor to support him in his attempt to suppress Christianity. Claudius, who is also known to have dealt with tensions in the Roman Empire due to Christianity, such as expelling Jews from Rome related to a dispute about Christ in AD 48, is therefore an obvious candidate contextually for the Caesar who ordered the new law (Suetonius, *Claudius*; Acts 18:2).

If the text of the Nazareth Inscription was specifically addressing the problem of Christianity and the issue of the resurrection of Jesus, then its presence in Nazareth would be logical since the early Christians were known to be called the "sect of the Nazarenes" and Jesus was often referred to as being from Nazareth (Acts 24:5).

The "Edict of Caesar" on the Nazareth Inscription, probably sent as a letter from Rome and then inscribed onto the stone, addressed a serious problem and specifically prohibited the moving or stealing of bodies from stone-sealed tombs with "wicked intent." It stated that its purpose was concerned with anyone who has "extracted those who have been buried, or has moved with wicked intent those who have been buried to other places...or has moved sepulcher-sealing stones...You are absolutely not to allow anyone to move those who have been entombed." Consequently, the edict describes the same type of tomb Jesus was buried in according to Judean custom—a rock-cut tomb sealed with a large stone. There is also no reference to a coffin, a sarcophagus, or a cemetery.

Romans, on the other hand, were typically cremated, used sarcophagi, and cemeteries were the common location of burials. This crime was connected to the religious sphere and said to be an offense against the gods, and the severity of it apparently caused the government to proscribe a new and extreme penalty of death in the edict. The robbing of grave goods had been a problem since the earliest civilizations, and desecration of a corpse was a serious violation in Roman culture, but this intentional moving of a body from a specific type of tomb appears to be another issue entirely. It is an important distinction that the Nazareth Inscription seems to be far more concerned about moving bodies from specific types of graves or tombs rather than looting or desecration of burials.

According to Matthew, the false story that the disciples stole the body of Jesus was spread by the religious leaders of Judaism via the Roman soldiers, and this rumor perhaps reached the ears of the emperor. "You are to say, 'His disciples came at night and stole Him while we were asleep.'...And they took the money and did as they had been instructed; and this story was widely spread among the Jews and is to this day" (Matthew 28:11-15).

By the time of Claudius, knowledge of Christianity and the story of the resurrection of Jesus had spread throughout many areas of the Roman Empire, beginning to cause problems in the realms of religion, politics, and society. Unlikely a coincidence, the Nazareth Inscription was probably a reaction to rumors about the resurrection of Jesus of Nazareth, and in particular the version the Roman soldiers guarding the tomb were paid to tell. After hearing the story of Jesus and how widespread it had become, Emperor Claudius seems to have attempted to prevent any future claims of the resurrection of the dead that would spark religious revolution and departure from standard Roman beliefs. Therefore, the edict recorded on the Nazareth Inscription appears to be the Roman response to the story of the resurrection of Jesus Christ.

A new hypothesis concerning the Nazareth Inscription claims that the stone was inscribed on the island of Kos as part of an edict issued by Emperor Augustus in response to the desecration of the tomb of Nikias of Kos around 30 BC. Nikias, the local ruler of Kos, was described as a tyrant ruler of the island (Strabo, *Geography*). After his death, the angry residents of the island broke into his tomb, dragged his body out into the open, and desecrated it as their way of exacting justice, since they were unable to while he was alive and in power.

Chemical analysis conducted on a small sample removed from the marble slab of the Nazareth Inscription had a close match to the composition of marble at a quarry on Kos, an island immediately off the western coast of Turkey and only a few miles from the town of Akyarlar, Turkey, just west of the famous Mausoleum at Halicarnassus. The analysis tells us that the origin of the marble slab used for the Nazareth Inscription might be from Kos, since the chemical signature "closely matched" through enrichment of carbon 13 and depletion of oxygen 18. Although, it is also possible it could have come from elsewhere that has a very similar chemical signature. Yet, even if the marble was sourced from a quarry on Kos, this does not demonstrate that the Nazareth Inscription originated in Kos or applied to a situation in Kos.

Further, during the Roman period in Judea, Galilee, and the surrounding area, marble was imported, and much of it was from the area of nearby Turkey. In fact, Herod the Great is known to have imported marble specifically from Kos. If this same logic were applied to all Roman-period marble inscriptions and artwork, one would have to suggest that all sorts of artifacts originated from places where they were not actually made or sent, simply because the marble was sourced elsewhere.

Since the emergence of the Nazareth Inscription was in Galilee, it more than likely was discovered in the Galilee or Judea areas, or possibly nearby Samaria or the Decapolis. At the time of its rediscovery and appearance in 1878, Nazareth was a tiny and insignificant village in the Ottoman Empire, known for nothing except its connection with Jesus, and certainly not a hub of the antiquities market.

Because Nikias was probably allied with Mark Antony, the enemy of Augustus, it is unlikely that Augustus would have issued a drastic edict in response to the desecration of the tomb and corpse of Nikias. If Nikias died around 30 BC, this scenario is nearly impossible since Augustus was not even declared emperor until 27 BC and would probably not bother making a new law connected to the desecration of the corpse of one of his minor enemies that had occurred some years before. Even if Nikias died closer to 20 BC, it is still extremely unlikely that Augustus would send a special edict to Kos in response to this act, which had no effect on the current political situation.

As for the possibility of the Nazareth Inscription being an edict related to Nikias of Kos based upon the content of the decree, there are further problems. The language used in the inscription does not match how Roman or Greek tombs were typically constructed, nor does it match the tomb of Nikias specifically, nor does it closely match the narrative about the desecration of Nikias known from historical sources. Consider how Krinagoras of Mytilene described the event in an epigram: "Look at the fate of Nikias of Kos. He had gone to rest in Hades, and now his dead body has come again into the light of day. For his fellow citizens, forcing the bolts of his tomb, dragged out the poor hard dying wretch to punishment."

If this is compared to the language and circumstances of the Nazareth Inscription, stark differences can be easily noticed: "…the religious observances of parents, or children, or household members—that these remain undisturbed forever…moved with wicked intent those who have been buried to other places…moved sepulcher-sealing stones…You are absolutely not to allow anyone to move…"

The Nazareth Inscription revolves around moving a body and taking it elsewhere with "wicked intent," perhaps hiding it, mentions sepulcher-sealing stones, and is a general populace address. None of those apply to Nikias, whose tomb was different and his body was dragged out into the light of day so his corpse could be publicly defiled and seen, not secretly moved elsewhere with "nefarious" motives causing uproar in the Empire.

This new information that the marble used for the Nazareth Inscription may have been sourced from a quarry on Kos does nothing to discredit the theory that the edict was issued in response to the stories spread by Roman soldiers and others about the empty tomb and missing body of Jesus of Nazareth.

THE RESURRECTION OF JESUS

Various alternative explanations have been proposed by scholars seeking to interpret the history of the resurrection from a materialistic viewpoint. The suggestion that Jesus was not really dead, and on the third day in the tomb he woke up and walked out is a common explanation, but it is historically indefensible. According to this suggestion, Jesus did not die when he was executed by crucifixion, and therefore the resurrection of Jesus was not a resurrection but simply waking up after being placed in the tomb.

However, not only is this an explanation that does not appear in the ancient accounts of Jesus, but it is historically and scientifically implausible. Due to the severity of punishment, many people died before they even made it to the cross, and the Romans always made sure those crucified were dead before leaving them to hang or removing them from the cross. People did not survive crucifixion except in rare cases when they were pardoned, or immediately removed from the cross and given immediate medical care—but even then many still died, as can be seen from history when two out of three friends of Josephus did not survive even in those circumstances (Josephus, *Life*).

A pardoning was not the case with Jesus. Roman practice was to kill or confirm death of each of the crucified, then to eventually give the corpse to the family for burial, throw it in a mass grave, or display it as a warning (Ulpian, *Digest*; Philo, *Against Flaccus*). Further, that Jesus was crucified and actually died is stated by multiple Roman sources that range from skeptical to sarcastic to hostile towards Christianity.

In the late 1st century AD, while writing as an official Roman historian, Josephus recorded that Pilate had condemned Jesus to be crucified (Josephus, *Antiquities*). Lucian, a Roman living in the 2nd century AD who enjoyed mocking Christians, thought it was humorous how Christians worshipped a man who had been crucified (Lucian, *Death of Peregrinus*). Celsus, another 2nd-century AD Roman who was deeply opposed to and critical of Christianity, affirmed that Jesus was nailed to a cross (Celsus in Origen, *Contra Celsus*). About AD 73, the Syrian Stoic philosopher Serapion wrote to his son and mentioned the execution of the "wise King" of the Judeans and the eventual destruction of Jerusalem and dispersion of the Judeans as a result (Serapion, *Letter to His Son*). The famous Roman historian Cornelius Tacitus wrote around AD 116 that Jesus Christ was put to death by Pontius Pilate (Tacitus, *Annals* 15.44). Decades later, Justin, a Roman and a pagan turned Christian, wrote to the Emperor Antoninus Pius about Christianity, mentioning the crucifixion of Jesus and how those events in the Gospels can be confirmed by checking the Roman records such as the Acts of Pilate (Justin Martyr, *Apology*).

Therefore, it is clear that even according to Roman historical sources and the writings of those opposed to Christianity in the 1st and 2nd centuries AD, the crucifixion of Jesus resulted in death, nullifying the hypothesis that Jesus did not die and merely woke up in the tomb.

Other explanations of the resurrection claim the disciples experienced psychologically induced hallucinations that they explained as resurrection appearances, or that the entire story was falsified as a myth to support the founding of Christianity, or that the resurrection of Jesus was meant to be totally symbolic and not historical. These alternative interpretations have been circulating since antiquity.

As early as the 2nd century AD, the Roman philosopher Celsus was aware of the resurrection of Jesus story but suggested ideas such as the followers of Jesus were not of sound mind or perhaps they saw a specter that they thought was Jesus (Celsus in Origen, *Contra Celsum*). The falsification hypothesis often suggests that the resurrection story was adopted from pagan myths that predated Jesus. However, these cite alleged resurrection myths that are actually apotheosis or reincarnation or rebirth or appearance in a dream, which are all quite different from the physical resurrection of Jesus recorded in the Gospels. Many claims of appearances of presumably resurrected people following their deaths date to centuries after the Gospels were written, and have no more than a single source with few details for evaluation. These have no historical corroboration and may even be influenced by the story of the resurrection of Jesus.

Reference to the bodily resurrection of Jesus is also found in Roman sources written only decades after the crucifixion of Jesus. In a monumental historical work written by Josephus over many years and finished about AD 93, he recorded how disciples had reported that Jesus appeared to them alive three days after the crucifixion (Josephus, *Antiquities*). Although a version of this text appears to have been slightly modified by Christians and sounds as if Josephus became a Christian, a more recently discovered Arabic copy seems to reflect the original tone, noting that a resurrection of Jesus was what people reported without endorsing a belief in Jesus as the Messiah.

The Roman historian Tacitus also made reference to the claim of the resurrection of Jesus in about AD 116, writing that the "mischievous superstition" about Jesus and his resurrection had caused problems throughout the Empire, even after attempts had been made to repress Christianity and the claims about the resurrection of Jesus (Tacitus, *Annals* 15.44).

Although neither Josephus nor Tacitus stated their belief in a physical resurrection of Jesus, their writings make it clear that people reported this event, believed it, and knowledge of it spread rapidly throughout the Roman Empire. This suggests that not only were the resurrection claims known, but that the claims had not been refuted in the several decades after Jesus.

Part of the failure by the Romans and the Judean religious leaders to refute the resurrection of Jesus seems to have been a result of the missing body. The modern proposal that the corpse of Jesus was still in the tomb many days after his death is in conflict with the historical sources and logic. No ancient writing, even those highly critical of Christianity, claimed that the body of Jesus was still in the tomb days after his death. To make a resurrection claim when the Roman authorities could parade the body or refute the claims, or the curious could open the tomb and look inside, would have resulted in a swift refutation of the resurrection idea in Judea Province and beyond. Rather, as both the Gospel of Matthew and a 1st-century AD Roman edict suggest, the body of Jesus was absent from the tomb and a rumor circulated that disciples of Jesus had stolen the body and hidden it.

The Nazareth Inscription indicates that whatever had happened in Judea Province in association with the stealing of a corpse prior to the reign of Claudius had caused a significant enough problem that the Roman government intervened and enacted a new law that would attempt to prevent any repeat of this type of event. An imperial rescript issued in the regions of Judea and Galilee, and perhaps specifically set up in Nazareth, only several years after the resurrection of Jesus suggests there was widespread knowledge of the event.

The Roman government seems to have reacted to the rapidly spreading story of the resurrection of Jesus in the hopes that the disciples and the message could be thwarted, and no future incidents of this nature would happen. Worship of the emperor and total obedience to Rome were in the best interest of Imperial Rome, and the belief in and worship of Jesus of Nazareth as God were seen as a threat.

Of course, the Romans were unsuccessful at stopping the spread of the message of Jesus using new laws and even harsh persecutions. This Roman edict, along with the records of Josephus and Tacitus, demonstrate that throughout the Empire it was known that the corpse of Jesus had mysteriously gone missing from the tomb. Only two explanations were offered in ancient times—either the disciples somehow stole the body of Jesus while sealed in a tomb guarded by Roman soldiers, or Jesus miraculously rose from the dead and left the tomb.

The story circulated by those Roman soldiers that the disciples successfully carried out a plot to steal the body of Jesus from the tomb in order to make it look like Jesus had been resurrected and walked out himself is problematic in light of the proficiency of Roman soldiers, and especially the willingness of so many eyewitness followers of Jesus to die for their belief that he had actually been raised from the dead.

According to sources of the 1st and 2nd century AD, eyewitnesses to the life of Jesus such as Peter, Stephen, James the son of Zebedee, and even James the Just and Paul of Tarsus who converted after the resurrection, all believed so positively in the deity and resurrection of Jesus that they were prepared to die, and in fact were executed as a result of their belief and unwillingness to deny it (Josephus, *Antiquities*; Ignatius, *Letter to the Ephesians*; Tertullian, *Prescription Against Heretics*; Acts 7:58-60; 12:1-2). Slightly later sources record the martyrdom of additional disciples who were also eyewitnesses (Eusebius, *Ecclesiastical History*).

The total commitment to belief in the resurrection of Jesus by those who personally knew him, even to the point of death for many of them, does not necessarily prove that Jesus did rise from the dead, but it does demonstrate that followers of Jesus truly believed in the resurrection story and that it was not a fictitious conspiracy story that they had created.

Numerous scholars have analyzed the arguments for and against the resurrection of Jesus as a historical event, and while many skeptics of varying degrees will continue to remain, there are others who suggest that the bodily resurrection of Jesus as recorded in the Gospels is the best explanation based on ancient sources, historical context, medicine, psychology, and logic. They typically focus on key aspects such as the death of Jesus by crucifixion, the empty tomb, the claims of the disciples and apostles, the conversions of James and Paul, and the willingness of eyewitnesses to die for their belief in the resurrection of Jesus.

A logical analysis of the historical possibilities of the empty tomb and resurrection of Jesus combined with the available historical evidence demonstrate that the only plausible scenarios are: 1) the body of Jesus was stolen from the tomb and a claim was made that he resurrected and appeared to many people through a vast and unlikely conspiracy involving Roman soldiers, many followers of Jesus, and adherents of Judaism in Jerusalem who opposed or were skeptical towards the claims of Jesus; 2) somehow Jesus revived from death after days due to a scientific anomaly that is medically unattested; 3) Jesus was resurrected by supernatural or miraculous means that defy a materialistic worldview.

If one denies the possibility of the supernatural, then only a naturalistic cause such as a vast conspiracy or an anomalous, unattested resuscitation can be accepted, however unlikely or improbable those explanations may be. Yet, if God exists and therefore miracles are possible, then the physical resurrection of Jesus as recorded in the Gospels, the epistles, mentioned by early historians and philosophers, alluded to by a Roman edict, and testified to by the martyrdom of many eyewitness followers of Jesus is more logical, plausible, and consistent with evidence.

THE ROAD TO EMMAUS

The road to Emmaus was the location of an event recorded in detail by Luke and also mentioned by Mark in which two disciples traveling away from Jerusalem on the day of the resurrection unknowingly encounter Jesus (Luke 24:13-35; Mark 16:12-13). Cleopas (cf. John 19:25) and an unnamed disciple were on the road leading to the village of Emmaus, where they had initially intended to stop for the night (Luke 24:18). By this time, it seems that most of the followers of Jesus were on their way home after hearing about or seeing the empty tomb (John 20:9-10). Although a message to go north to Galilee was relayed to the 11 disciples, these other two followers of Jesus may have been going back to their homes elsewhere in the region (Matthew 28:10; Mark 16:7).

Emmaus, meaning "warm spring" in Aramaic, is mentioned by name only once in the Gospels, but the geographical information from this passage specifies that it was 60 stadia from Jerusalem (Luke 24:13). Yet, the identification of this location is made more complicated because multiple towns during the Roman period had the name Emmaus. However, the historian and native of Judea, Josephus, seems to record this same town called Emmaus or Ammaus in Judea, that the Romans camped there after the destruction of Jerusalem in AD 70, and that it was 60 stadia from Jerusalem—except for Latin manuscripts that record the distance incorrectly as 30 stadia (Josephus, *Wars*).

By AD 300 or so, knowledge of the location of Emmaus may already have been lost. In the 4th century, Eusebius recorded what he thought was the location of Emmaus mentioned in the Gospel of Luke, placing it at the Byzantine town of Nicopolis about 160 stadia from Jerusalem (Eusebius, *Onomasticon*). This error seems to have been the result of a textual variant in a few ancient manuscripts of Luke that have 160 stadia instead of 60 stadia, and apparently Eusebius had consulted a manuscript with that misprint for the distance from Jerusalem and therefore miscalculated the location of Emmaus. Also according to Eusebius and Jerome, Kiriath-jearim (Abu Ghosh or Deir

The possible location of ancient Emmaus at Qubeiba

el-Azar), preservation in Arabic of the memory of Eleazar, who was steward of the ark of the covenant when it arrived at Kiriath-jearim (cf. 1 Samuel 7:1-2), was 9 Roman miles (about 9.3 miles or 15 km) from Jerusalem on the way to Diospolis, which does fit the Roman-road walking distance from ancient Jerusalem to Abu Ghosh.

The length of the unit of measurement called a stadion could vary slightly in ancient times, but the statement by Herodotus of a stadion being equivalent to 600 Greek feet is most often used in modern calculations. A study that compared stadia in ancient writings to calculated distance arrived at 157.7 meters or 517.4 feet as an average stadion. That calculation would place Emmaus about 5.9 miles from the walls of ancient Jerusalem. However, it is also possible that the 185-meter stadion was used in Judea Province, meaning Emmaus could have been up to about 6.9 miles from Jerusalem. Therefore, any site identified as Emmaus should be located about 60 stadia or approximately 5.9 to 6.9 miles from Jerusalem and have the 1st-century AD remains of a town.

Many candidates for the ancient site of Emmaus have been proposed, but most are either too far or too close to Jerusalem. Excavations at Abu Ghosh, the probable location of Kiriath-jearim, have demonstrated that the ancient site was a town during the Israelite period, and later had massive walls up to three meters thick built in the 2nd century BC, possibly by the Seleucid Empire who ruled over the area before the Maccabean revolt in 167–160 BC brought about the Hasmonean dynasty. These walls were then reused by the Romans for a military outpost in the 1st century AD, as evidenced by finds such as a Latin inscription mentioning a detachment of Legio X (the 10th Legion) of the Roman army at the fortress.

Yet, the location of Abu Ghosh in ancient times was around 90 stadia from Jerusalem, not 60 stadia. Emmaus was also a town the two disciples of Jesus were returning to, while the recent discoveries demonstrate that the site was used as a military outpost for the Romans, not a Judean town. However, two other sites, Qubeiba and Artas, are both approximately 60 stadia from Jerusalem, with Qubeiba located to the northwest and Artas located to the south. At Artas, no known remains from the Roman period have been discovered. The site of Qubeiba was considered the Emmaus of the Gospels during the Crusader periods (Castellum Emmaus), and although Byzantine remains have been found in the area, earlier traditions are unknown. However, there is a Roman road running through Qubeiba, and finds from the Roman period were discovered adjacent to the modern village, indicating that this site meets the requirements of distance and a 1st-century AD town. Therefore, near Qubeiba seems to be the most plausible candidate for Emmaus, while Abu Ghosh is the likely location of ancient Kiriath-jearim and a later Roman fortress.

THE GREAT COMMISSION, MOUNT ARBEL, AND ASCENSION

One of the final messages of Jesus was an instruction for the remaining 11 disciples to meet him at a designated mountain in Galilee. There, Jesus told his closest followers to take his message to all the nations, make more disciples, baptize, and teach them to follow his commandments (Matthew 28:16-20; Mark 16:14-18; Luke 24:46-49; cf. Acts 1:7-8). The location of this Great Commission was not specified beyond a mountain in Galilee, so proposed identifications are tentative. As the highest peak in the region, the distant but massive Mount Hermon has been one suggestion. However, the top of Mount Arbel overlooking

Mount Hermon and Galilee

the west side of the Sea of Galilee seems to be a likely possibility, and it has been a landmark for millennia.

In the late 1st century, Josephus noted the many caves on the side of this mountain and the village of Arbela near the Sea of Galilee (Josephus, *Life* and *Antiquities* and *Wars*). Mount Arbel is the most obvious mountain around the Sea of Galilee and also the tallest mountain adjacent to the lake, with a prominence of about 1250 feet (380 meters). It is also in close proximity to places such as Capernaum and the western side of the sea where Jesus and the disciples spent most of their time during his ministry in Galilee.

After the Great Commission on a mountain in Galilee, the disciples proceeded back to the Jerusalem area where Jesus led them to the village of Bethany on the Mount of Olives as the location of the ascension (Mark 16:19; Luke 24:50-51; Acts 1:3-12; cf. John 6:62). While pagans in the Roman Empire might have made an initial connection of the ascension of Jesus to heaven as *apotheosis* (making divine) of a mortal, after reading the Gospels it would be clearly seen that Jesus was presented as divine from the beginning rather than a human made into a god or a ruler deified after death, distinguishing him from proclamations of the Imperial Senate or popular mythological stories (Polybius, *Histories*; Plutarch, *Numa*).

The writings of Luke describe the location of the ascension of Jesus as around the area of Bethany on the Mount of Olives (Luke 24:50; Acts 1:12). Even prior to the building of commemorative churches by Constantine in the 4th century AD, Christians had designated a place on the Mount of Olives near Bethany as the site of the ascension.

After Helena was shown the various sites associated with Jesus around the Jerusalem area, the Basilica of Eleona was built on the Mount of Olives over a cave at the location where Christians had passed down the memory of Jesus teaching his disciples just before the ascension (Anonymous, *Itinerarium Burdigalense*; Eusebius, *Life of Constantine*). This location was also noted on the Mount of Olives by the Christian pilgrim Egeria after her 4th-century visit (Egeria, *Itinerarium Egeriae*).

Today, the modern Church of the Pater Noster is built adjacent to the ruins of the 4th-century Byzantine basilica. Sometime after AD 370, another nearby church was financed by Poimenia to commemorate the ascension. Following destructions and rebuilds, only a small octagonal edicule remains called the Chapel of the Ascension. Although pinpointing the place referred to by Luke is speculative, the Basilica of Eleona has the more ancient tradition, suggesting that to be the more likely approximate location.

SELECTED BIBLIOGRAPHY
(CHAPTER 8)

Baruch, Yuval, Danit Levi, and Ronny Reich. "The Tomb and Ossuary of Alexa Son of Shalom." *Israel Exploration Journal* 61 (2011).

Berlin, Andrea. "Jewish Life Before the Revolt: The Archaeological Evidence." *Journal for the Study of Judaism in the Persian, Hellenistic, and Roman Period* 36, no. 4 (2005).

Billington, Clyde. "The Nazareth Inscription: Proof of the Resurrection of Christ?" *Artifax* (2020).

Clermont-Ganneau, Charles. *Archaeological Researches in Palestine*. London: Palestine Exploration Fund, 1899.

Cook, John. "Envisioning Crucifixion: Light from Several Inscriptions and the Palatine Graffito." *Novum Testamentum* 50, fasc. 3 (2008).

Cumont, Franz. "Un rescrit imperial sur la violation de sepulture." *Revue Historique* 163 (1930).

Davies, J.G. "The Peregrinatio Egeriae and the Ascension." *Vigiliae Christianae* 8, no. 1/2 (1954).

Ehrlich, M. "The Identification of Emmaus with Abu Gos in the Crusader Period Reconsidered." *Zeitschrift des Deutschen Palästina-Vereins* 112 (1996).

Engels, Donald. "The Length of Eratosthenes' Stade." *American Journal of Philology* 106, no. 3 (1985).

Fischer, Moshe, and Itamar Taxel. "Yavne, Survey Map." *Hadashot Arkheologiyot: Excavations and Surveys in Israel* 118 (2006).

Gibson, Shimon. *The Final Days of Jesus: The Archaeological Evidence*. New York: HarperCollins, 2009.

Grzybek, E., and Sordi, M. "L'Edit de Nazareth et la politique de Néron à l'égard des Chrétiens." *Zeitschrift für Papyrologie und Epigraphik* 120 (1998)

Habermas, Gary. "Resurrection Claims in Non-Christian Religions." *Religious Studies* 25 (1989).

Habermas, Gary, and Michael Licona. *The Case for the Resurrection of Jesus*. Grand Rapids: Kregel, 2004.

Hachlili, Rachel. "A Second Temple Period Jewish Necropolis in Jericho." *Biblical Archaeologist* 43 (1980).

———. *Jewish Funerary Customs, Practices and Rites in the Second Temple Period.* Leiden: Brill, 2005.

Harper, Kyle, Michael McCormick, Matthew Hamilton, Peiffert Chantal, Michels Raymond, and Michael Engel. "Establishing the Provenance of the Nazareth Inscription: Using stable isotopes to resolve a historic controversy and trace ancient marble production." *Journal of Archaeological Science: Reports* 30 (2020).

Licona, Michael. *The Resurrection of Jesus: A New Historiographical Approach.* Downers Grove, IL: InterVarsity Press, 2010.

Liddell et al. *A Greek-English Lexicon.* Oxford: Clarendon, 1996.

Loke, Andrew. "The Resurrection of the Son of God: A Reduction of the Naturalistic Alternatives." *Journal of Theological Studies* 60, no. 2 (2009).

Luedemann, Gerd. *The Resurrection of Jesus: History, Experience, Theology.* Minneapolis: Fortress Press, 1995.

Magness, Jodi. "Ossuaries and the Burials of Jesus and James." *Journal of Biblical Literature* 124 (2005).

———. *Stone and Dung, Oil and Spit: Jewish Daily Life in the Time of Jesus.* Grand Rapids: Eerdmans, 2011.

Metzger, Bruce. *A Textual Commentary on the Greek New Testament.* New York: United Bible Societies, 1994.

Meyers, Eric, and Mark Chancey. *Alexander to Constantine: Archaeology of the Land of the Bible,* vol. 3. New Haven, CT: Yale, 2012.

Nagar, Yossi, and Hagit Torgee. "Biological Characteristics of Jewish Burial in the Hellenistic and Early Roman Periods." *Israel Exploration Journal* 53 (2003).

Price, Robert, and Jeffery Lowder, eds. *The Empty Tomb: Jesus Beyond the Grave.* Amherst, NY: Prometheus Books, 2005.

Rahmani, Levi. "Ancient Jerusalem's Funerary Customs and Tombs." *Biblical Archaeologist* 44 (1981).

Sanders, E.P. *The Historical Figure of Jesus.* New York: Penguin, 1996.

Sukenik, E.L. "The Earliest Records of Christianity." *American Journal of Archaeology* 51 (1947).

Tsalampouni, Ekaterini. "The Nazareth Inscription. A Controversial Piece of Palestinian Epigraphy (1920–1999)." TEKMHPIA 6 (2001).

Vermes, Geza. *The Resurrection: History and Myth*. New York: Doubleday, 2008.

Wright, N.T. "Jesus' Resurrection and Christian Origins." *Gregorianum* 83, no. 4 (2002).

———. *The Resurrection of the Son of God*. Minneapolis: Fortress, 2003.

Zissu, Boaz, and Eitan Klein. "A Rock-Cut Burial Cave from the Roman Period at Beit Nattif, Judaean Foothills." *Israel Exploration Journal* 61 (2011).

Zissu, Boaz. "'Qumran Type' Graves in Jerusalem: Archaeological Evidence of an Essene Community?" *Dead Sea Discoveries* 5, no. 2 (1998).

Conclusion

Following the brief ministry of Jesus, Christianity began to spread rapidly throughout the Roman Empire. At first, only those around Judea and Galilee were familiar with Jesus and Christianity, but within a matter of years this gospel was brought to many provinces of the Empire. Rather than a message invented by the church almost a century after Jesus, the Roman knowledge of Christianity demonstrates that this information was widely known within decades of the time of Jesus, and seemingly due to the dedication of the apostles and various disciples to bring the gospel to the nations, even in a time when communication and travel were relatively limited.

Slightly over a decade after Jesus, during the reign of Claudius in the late 40s, it is clear that Christianity had already spread as far as Rome. According to Suetonius, the message about Christ was causing disturbances in Rome, apparently in conflict with Judaism. As a result, those practicing Judaism, and possibly even Christians misidentified as a sect of Judaism, were expelled from Rome (Suetonius, *Divus Claudius*; Acts 18:2).

The Nazareth Inscription also suggests that by the 40s, Christianity was already causing problems for the Empire and so an edict was issued to prevent similar occurrences in the future. Christian symbols such as the anchor, boat, and cross also began to appear in various parts of the Empire by the late 1st century and early 2nd century.

Josephus, who lived in Judea Province before moving to Rome as a historian for the Empire, not only knew of Christians long before about AD 93, but he commented that they had not disappeared near the end of the 1st century AD, even though Jesus had been crucified 60 years prior and persecution of Christianity had been ongoing for decades (Josephus, *Antiquities*).

During the reign of Nero in AD 64, a great fire that he probably had intentionally started destroyed much of Rome (Cassius Dio, *Roman History*; Suetonius, *Nero*). Tacitus chronicled that Nero blamed this fire on the Christians, starting the major early persecution against Christianity in Rome (Tacitus, *Annals*). At the time, the pagan Romans generally hated Christians and considered their beliefs and practices an affront to the gods, the emperor, and the Roman religious system.

Decades later, the situation had not changed, and not only were people in Rome and the outlying provinces familiar with Christianity, but the government was seeking new ways to eliminate it. Pliny the Younger, while legate of Bithynia et Pontus, wrote a letter to Emperor Trajan in about AD 112 that communicated extensive knowledge of Christianity due to his trials of accused Christians. This included familiarity with practices such as meeting on Sunday, singing hymns, worshipping Christ as God, and their moral code, which was incompatible with Roman culture (Pliny the Younger, *Letter to Trajan*).

Just after this time, about AD 124, the emperor Hadrian thought Christianity had become so prolific in the Empire that he had to take immediate action to eliminate it, although his predecessors had been unsuccessful. Since violent persecutions had not been effective, Hadrian thought he could destroy Christianity through philosophy and adopting Christ into the pantheon, first debating with the Christian scholars Quadratus and Aristides in Athens (Aristides, *Apology*; Eusebius, *Ecclesiastical History*).

However, the initial stage of this strategy failed, so a few years later Hadrian tried to remove the memory of Christianity and replace it with paganism by building temples and shrines over significant locations related to Jesus. Still, Christianity persisted, and later in the 2nd century AD, Lucian mocked Christians for worshipping a crucified man and denying the pagan gods (Lucian, *Passing of Peregrinus*). For those who followed Hellenistic and Roman beliefs, the crucifixion of Jesus was foolishness, and denial of the gods was considered blasphemous atheism (1 Corinthians 1:23).

Although it may have taken several decades for Christianity to reach the edges of the Empire and beyond, within 30 years after Jesus it had already spread as far west as Rome and had such a wide following that even the emperor sought to destroy Christians. Instead of a relatively small group centered in one part of the Empire, only flourishing after Constantine legalized and endorsed Christianity, Roman sources demonstrate that the gospel of Jesus Christ had expanded so fast and far that the Imperial powers of Rome tried to destroy Christianity by any means necessary.

Ultimately, Christianity prevailed, adopted by Armenia in AD 301, legalized by Emperor Constantine in 313, and decreed the official religion of Rome by Theodosius I in 380, and eventually outlasting the Empire and spreading throughout the entire world.

The discoveries of archaeology and the preserved ancient writings, thoroughly researched and analyzed, have given an exceptionally clear window into the world and life of Jesus of Nazareth, the root of this unprecedented Christian movement. Although the Gospel accounts about Jesus are frequently referred to by skeptics and critics as mythical, embellished, historically unreliable theological writings, or even propaganda in the form of a biography, archaeology, and ancient texts of the Roman period have demonstrated the accuracy and historical reliability of the Gospels.

Myth, which comes from the Greek word *muthos* meaning "story," had a wide range of meaning and no specific implication about historical truth in ancient times. However, in modern usage a myth refers to a legendary story that usually contains deities and has fictitious elements. Therefore, to refer to the Gospels as mythical suggests that they are severely limited in their historical accuracy and value.

Yet, the Gospels record events that took place in real locations with real historical figures, not in mythical lands with characters unknown from any historical records or physical evidence. Prior to the development of archaeology and the widespread integration of archaeological discoveries and ancient manuscripts in evaluating the New Testament, many critical scholars and writers promoted a view of the Gospels as virtually devoid of history, with the most radical even denying the existence of an historical Jesus. Yet, due to archaeological and manuscript discoveries over the last century, there has been reevaluation and adjustment of many scholarly perspectives on Jesus and the Gospels.

An examination of people and places in the Gospels demonstrates that the narratives record events set in known locations, with historical people, and in a particular time. At least 16 people mentioned in the Gospels have been confirmed as historical figures through ancient artifacts and manuscript sources unassociated with Christianity in the approximately four-decade time window of the Gospels, including every major political and religious figure mentioned.

Additionally, groups of people such as the disciples of Jesus, Herodians, Judeans, Pharisees, Romans, Sadducees, Samaritans, Sanhedrin, and Zealots are all known from external historical sources. If ancient Christian sources were counted, and if tentative identifications were included, the number of historical figures attested would increase significantly.

Nearly every city, town, village, and region, and even many structures mentioned in the Gospels have been confirmed as historical locations in existence during this time by archaeological and ancient historical sources of the Roman period. These places include major cities such as Jerusalem and Caesarea Philippi, towns such as Bethlehem, Capernaum, and Nazareth, structures such as Jacob's Well, the Pool of Siloam, and the Temple Complex, and geographical features such as the Mount of Olives, the Jordan River, and the Sea of Galilee.

The writers of the Gospels, although focused on only one person from the fringe of the Empire who was not a political, military, or religious leader, and primarily only a select few years of his life, purposely included specific names and positions of people and names and descriptions of locations to demonstrate the historical nature of the writings, which allows historical analysis to confirm the precision and accuracy of the story.

The result of the demonstrated accuracy of locations, people, and general historical setting strongly suggests not only the intentions of the authors to record history, but the reliability of those accounts. A thorough examination and comparison with archaeological and historical material of the events recorded in the Gospels and the cultural, economic, religious, and political setting reveals that the books do not qualify as myth or merely theological treatises, but as accurate historical narrative set in 1st-century Judea and Galilee.

Despite the constant new discoveries connected to Jesus and the Gospels, specific narratives about Jesus are often accepted as historical only where external evidence clearly demonstrates the accuracy of a particular section of the text. Although this view acknowledges a degree of historicity present in the Gospels, many still classify the books as mythical or unreliable. Disregarding the discoveries of archaeology and history, the extreme claim that no evidence for Jesus exists outside of the New Testament continues to be repeated in certain circles. And yet investigation clearly demonstrates that the existence of Jesus and key information about his life have even been confirmed in Roman-period writings of the 1st and 2nd centuries by historians, pagans, philosophers, theologians, and polemicists. Occasionally uninformed skeptics claim that there is no historical evidence for the life of Jesus of Nazareth outside of the Gospels or the New Testament. Yet, focusing only on Jesus and key events of his life recorded in the Gospels, it is possible to reconstruct major information about Jesus using only ancient Roman sources and archaeological artifacts.

At the beginning of the life of Jesus, the Gospels make reference to him being born in Bethlehem, a small village in Judea. Further, the Gospels record that Jesus was born of a virgin who lived in a rural area, Nazareth, and was married to a carpenter or craftsman, Joseph (Matthew 1:20–2:1; 13:55; Luke 2:3-7; John 7:42). According to an outspoken Roman philosopher and critic of Christianity living in Alexandria in about AD 177, this was widely known and accepted information. Although Celsus disputed the virgin birth claim and said that Jesus "invented" that story, Celsus acknowledged the existence of Jesus and his birth in a Judean village to a woman from a rural area of Judea Province who was married to a carpenter (Celsus, *The True Word*).

After King Herod ordered that this baby and future king be found and executed, the family fled to Egypt to keep Jesus safe until Herod died (Matthew 2:13-23). Celsus also acknowledged that Jesus had lived in Egypt as a child before returning home (Celsus, *The True Word*). Early in the ministry of Jesus, when he was relatively unknown and had a small following, people were astonished at what he was saying and doing, since they only knew of him as the son of Joseph and Mary, and the brother of James, Joses, Simon, and Judas (Matthew 13:55; Mark 6:3).

According to the 1st-century writings of Josephus, Jesus of Nazareth was indeed the brother of this James who became a leader of the church in Jerusalem (Josephus, *Antiquities*). Further, an ossuary from before AD 70 in Jerusalem, scrutinized in regard to its authenticity but shown to be genuine, names James as the son of Joseph and the brother of Jesus.

Once Jesus began to travel around the region, teaching and performing miracles, his fame spread. Rather than deny or ignore the claims about the wisdom of Jesus and the miracles he performed, four sources from the Roman world in the 1st and 2nd centuries acknowledge that Jesus was a wise teacher and a miracle worker who had many disciples (Serapion, *A Letter of Mara*; Josephus, *Antiquities*; *Acts of Pontius Pilate* in Justin Martyr, *Letter to Antoninus Pius*; Celsus, *The True Word*). Due to his teachings and miracles, the religious leadership of Judaism saw Jesus as a threat and a blasphemer, and sought to arrest and eliminate him (John 11:57).

According to the Mishnah, which may possibly only relate reactions to Jesus after the spread of Christianity rather than 1st-century records, the religious leaders claimed that Jesus practiced sorcery and led the people into apostasy, and therefore should be arrested and executed by stoning (Sanhedrin 43a).

Eventually, Jesus was arrested and taken to trial before Pontius Pilatus, the Roman prefect of Judea Province, who consented to the request for Jesus to be crucified. The trial before Pilate and the death of Jesus by crucifixion is all corroborated by several Roman sources of the 1st and 2nd centuries (Josephus, *Antiquities*; Serapion, *A Letter of Mara*; Tacitus, *Annals*; Lucian, *Passing of Peregrinus*; Justin Martyr, *Letter to Antoninus Pius*). Additionally, artwork found in Rome that may date to as early as the end of the 1st century depicts Jesus on the cross with a man looking up to him, being mocked for worshiping a god who was crucified (Alexamenos Graffito).

After the crucifixion and burial of Jesus, claims of resurrection and removing the body from the tomb emerged (Matthew 28:11-15). The Romans seem to have responded to this with an edict that commanded the death penalty for stealing a body from a stone-sealed tomb (The Nazareth Inscription). However, the story of the resurrection of Jesus continued to spread, and it was reported by two Roman historians (Josephus, *Antiquities*; Tacitus, *Annals*).

Christianity continued to grow, adding new disciples, establishing the church, and becoming known to the Roman authorities, who never denied the existence of Jesus or major events of his life (Pliny the Younger, *Letter to Trajan*). Many of the locations associated with Jesus were also marked by the locals, built over with pagan shrines in a suppression attempt, but eventually becoming the site of commemorative churches.

Therefore, from only Roman writings and archaeological inscriptions, it can be established that Jesus was born in a village of Judea (Bethlehem) to a woman (Mary) from a rural area (Nazareth) that claimed to be a virgin at the time of birth, that Jesus and his family briefly lived in Egypt while he was young, that he had a brother named James who became a leader in the church, that Jesus was a great and wise teacher, that he performed miracles, that many disciples followed him, that Pontius Pilatus conducted a trial of Jesus and allowed him to be crucified, that the body of Jesus disappeared from the tomb and many claimed he had resurrected, and that the disciples of Jesus worshiped him as God and continued to spread the message throughout the Roman Empire.

Rather than a mythical character, Jesus of Nazareth is actually one of the most widely attested personalities in antiquity, and the narratives in the Gospels have been confirmed as historically reliable accounts by ever-increasing archaeological discoveries. Although Jesus only walked those paths until AD 33, and was unjustly executed in a tiny province on the fringes of the Empire, knowledge of his life and teaching rapidly spread across the vast Roman world and beyond. Centuries later, the ancient ruins, artifacts, and manuscripts continue to tell the incredible story.

APPENDIX ONE:

1st- and 2nd-Century Historians and Philosophers Mentioning Jesus Christ

FLAVIUS JOSEPHUS
(ca. AD 37–100)

"At this time there was a wise man called Jesus, and his conduct was good, and he was known to be virtuous. Many people among the Jews and the other nations became his disciples. Pilate condemned him to be crucified and to die. But those who had become his disciples did not abandon his discipleship. They reported that he had appeared to them three days after his crucifixion, and that he was alive. Accordingly, he was perhaps the Messiah, concerning whom the prophets have reported wonders. And the tribe of the Christians, so named after him, has not disappeared to this day" (*Antiquities* 18.63-64, ca. AD 93 Agapian version).

"Festus was now dead, and Albinus was but upon the road; so he assembled the Sanhedrin of judges, and brought before them the brother of Jesus, who was called Christ, whose name was James" (Josephus, *Antiquities* 20.200, ca. AD 93).

TACITUS
(ca. AD 56–117)

"Hence to suppress the rumor, he falsely charged with the guilt, and punished with the most exquisite tortures, the persons commonly called Christians, who were hated for their enormities. Christus, the founder of the name, was put to death by Pontius Pilate, procurator of Judea in the reign of Tiberius; but the pernicious superstition, repressed for a time, broke out again, not only through Judea, where the mischief originated, but through the city of Rome also" (Tacitus, *Annals* 15.44, ca. AD 116).

SUETONIUS
(ca. AD 69–130)

"Since the Jews constantly made disturbances at the instigation of Chrestus, he expelled them from Rome" (Suetonius, *Divus Claudius* 25, ca. AD 121).

PLINY THE YOUNGER
(ca. AD 61–113)

"[T]hey were in the habit of meeting on a certain fixed day before it was light, when they sang in alternate verse a hymn to Christ as to a god…" (*Letter to Emperor Trajan*, ca. AD 112).

LUCIAN OF SAMOSATA
(ca. AD 125–180)

"He learned the wondrous lore of the Christians, by associating with their priests and scribes in Palestina…they still worship, the man who was crucified in Palestina because he introduced this new cult into the world…denying the Greek gods and by worshipping that crucified sophist himself and living under his laws" (Lucian, *Passing of Peregrinus* 11-13, ca. AD 166).

CELSUS
(ca. AD 120-190)

"For he represents him disputing with Jesus, and confuting him, as he thinks, on many points; and in the first place, he accuses him of having 'invented his birth from a virgin,' and upbraids him with being 'born in a certain Jewish village, of a poor woman of the country, who gained her subsistence by spinning, and who was turned out of doors by her husband, a carpenter by trade, because she was convicted of adultery; that after being driven away by her husband, and wandering about for a time, she disgracefully gave birth to Jesus, an illegitimate child, who having hired himself out as a servant in Egypt on account of his poverty, and having there acquired some miraculous powers, on which the Egyptians greatly pride themselves, returned to his own country, highly elated on account of them, and by means of these proclaimed himself a god'" (Origen quoting Celsus, *The True Word* ca. AD 176, in *Contra Celsus* 1.28).

THALLUS
(ca. AD 50)

"[O]n the whole world there pressed a fearful darkness, and the rocks were rent by an earthquake, and many places in Judea and other districts were thrown down. Thallus calls this darkness an eclipse of the sun in the third book of histories, without reason it seems to me. For the Hebrews celebrate the Passover on the 14th day according to the moon, and the passion of our Saviour falls on the day before the Passover; but an eclipse of the sun takes place only when the moon comes under the sun" (Thallus, recorded in Julius Sextus Africanus ca. AD 220).

MARA BAR SERAPION
(1ST CENTURY AD)

"What advantage did the Jews gain from executing their wise King? It was just after that that their kingdom was abolished...God justly avenged these three wise men...the Jews, ruined and driven from their land, live in complete dispersion…Nor did the wise King die for good; he lived on in the teaching which he had given" (Serapion, *Letter to His Son* ca. AD 73).

JUSTIN MARTYR
(ca. AD 100–165)

"[S]o much is written for the sake of proving that Jesus the Christ is the Son of God and His Apostle, being of old the Word, and appearing sometimes in the form of fire, and sometimes in the likeness of angels; but now, by the will of God, having become man for the human race, He endured all the sufferings which the devils instigated the Jews to inflict upon Him…" (Justin, *First Apology* 63).

"'They pierced my hands and my feet,' a description of the nails that were fixed in His hands and His feet on the cross; and after He was crucified, those who crucified Him cast lots for His garments, and divided them among themselves; and that these things were so, you may learn from the 'Acts' which were recorded under Pontius Pilate. That he performed these miracles you may easily be satisfied from the 'Acts' of Pontius Pilate" (Justin, *Letter to Emperor Antoninus Pius*, ca. AD 150).

GALEN OF PERGAMON
(ca. AD 129–200)

"One might more easily teach novelties to the followers of Moses and Christ than to the physicians and philosophers who cling fast to their schools" (Galen, *De Differentiis Pulsuum* 3.3, ca. AD 180).

MISHNAH
(REDACTED ca. AD 200)

"Indictment against: Jesus the Nazarene. He shall be stoned because he has practiced sorcery and lured Israel into apostasy. Anyone who can say anything in his favor, let him come forward and plead on his behalf. Anyone who knows where he is, let him declare it to the Great Sanhedrin in Jerusalem" (The Mishnah tractate, Sanhedrin 43a).

APPENDIX 2:

Earliest Gospel Manuscripts About Jesus

MATTHEW

P103 (Oxy 4403) AD 100–200
P104 (Oxy 4404) AD 100–200
P64+67 (Magdalen Greek 17+ Barc. Inv. 1) AD 150–200
P77 (Oxy 2683 and 4405) AD 150–200
P1 (Oxy 2) AD 200–250
P45 (P. Chester Beatty I) AD 200–250
P37 (Michigan #1570) AD 250

MARK

P137 (Oxy 5345) AD 100–200
P45 (Chester Beatty I) AD 200–250

LUKE

P4 (Suppl. Gr. 1120) AD 150–200
P75 (Bodmer XIV–XV) AD 175–225
P45 (Chester Beatty I) AD 200–250
P111 (Oxy 4495) AD 200–250

JOHN

P52 (Rylands Greek 457) AD 90–175
P66 (Bodmer II) AD 100–200
P90 (Oxy 3523) AD 100–200
P75 (Bodmer XIV-XV) AD 175–225
P5 (Oxy 208 + 1781) AD 200–250
P22 (Oxy 1228) AD 200–250
P45 (Chester Beatty I) AD 200–250
P119 (Oxy 4803) AD 200–250

Gospel of Matthew manuscript Papyrus 37 verso

Timeline

63 BC Pompey the Great conquers Jerusalem for the Roman Republic

40 BC Herod the Great proclaimed king by the Senate

37 BC Herod the Great captures Jerusalem (Matthew 2:1)

27 BC Octavian becomes emperor (Luke 2:1)

19 BC Jerusalem temple reconstruction begins (John 2:18-21)

8 BC Census of Caesar Augustus (Luke 2:1-3)

7 BC John the Baptizer born six months before Jesus (Luke 1:36-66)

7 BC Jesus born in Bethlehem (Luke 2:4-21)

5 BC Magi, flight to Egypt, Herod kills babies of Bethlehem (Matthew 2:1-16)

4 BC Death of Herod, Joseph and family return from Egypt (Matthew 2:19-23)

AD 6 Archelaus exiled and Judea becomes a Roman province

AD 12 Tiberius receives equal powers

AD 14 Augustus dies and Tiberius becomes sole emperor (Luke 3:1)

AD 15 Annas removed as high priest by Valerius Gratus

AD 18 Caiaphas appointed high priest (Luke 3:2)

AD 23 Capital of Galilee moved to Tiberias (John 6:23)

AD 26 Pontius Pilatus appointed prefect of Judea (Luke 3:1)

AD 28 Baptism of Jesus at Bethany beyond the Jordan (John 1:24-34)

AD 28 Water into wine at Cana (John 2:1-12)

AD 29 The Sermon on the Mount (Matthew 5:1–8:1)

AD 31 John the Baptizer beheaded (Matthew 14:1-12)

AD 31 Sejanus executed in Rome

AD 33 Jesus of Nazareth crucifixion and burial (Luke 23:1–24:12)

AD 34 Stephen martyred in Jerusalem (Acts 7:54-60)

AD 39 Antipas exiled to Spain

AD 41 Reigns of Claudius and Agrippa I, Nazareth Inscription issued
(Acts 11:28)

AD 44 James Zebedee executed, death of Herod Agrippa I (Acts 12:1-23)

AD 62 James son of Joseph martyred in Jerusalem, James Ossuary
(Matthew 13:55)

AD 64 Great fire of Rome and Peter crucified (John 21:15-19)

AD 66 Revolt beings in Judea

AD 70 Jerusalem and the temple destroyed (Luke 19:41-44)

AD 93 Josephus completes his book *Antiquities of the Jews*

Also by Titus Kennedy

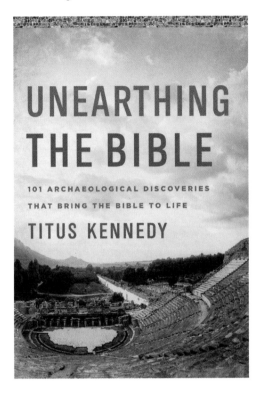

UNEARTHING THE BIBLE

In *Unearthing the Bible*, Dr. Titus M. Kennedy presents 101 objects that provide compelling evidence for the historical reliability of Scripture from the dawn of civilization through the early church. Gathered from more than 50 museums, private collections, and archaeological sites, these pieces not only reinforce the reliability of the biblical narratives, but also provide rich cultural insights into the ancient world.

Using this visual guide, you can find context for your faith as you make your way through the Bible. Dr. Kennedy's photographs and detailed descriptions enable you to examine each piece of fascinating evidence for yourself.

From the earliest tablets of creation to artifacts connected with the life and resurrection of Jesus, *Unearthing the Bible* shows you can be confident there is an abundance of archaeological support for the history told in the Scriptures.

To learn more about Harvest House books and
to read sample chapters, visit our website:

www.harvesthousepublishers.com

HARVEST HOUSE PUBLISHERS
EUGENE, OREGON